P9-DEO-000

The Ethics of Persuasive Preaching

The Ethics of Persuasive Preaching

Raymond W. McLaughlin

BAKER BOOK HOUSE
Grand Rapids, Michigan

ISBN: 0-8010-6051-6
Library of Congress Catalog Card Number 78-059311

To Drs.
Charles W. Koller
Faris D. Whitesell
and
Lloyd M. Perry
under whose teaching
I learned how to preach
the gospel

Contents

Preface

A theological student was supplying a church pulpit. When he stood up to preach he saw a little framed card affixed to the pulpit with the brief but pointed question: "What are you trying to do to these people?"[1]

This question should be asked of every preacher in America. Not only have I asked that question about the hundreds of student and pastoral sermons I have heard, but in recent years I have been asking that question of myself prior to every sermon I am about to preach.

The question, of course, relates virtually to every aspect of the sermon—its content, organization, delivery, and spirit-filled power. And these factors need to be and will be handled in a later work.

However, the question, What are you trying to do to these people? *ethically* from the pulpit has been plaguing me for some time. I became interested in the ethics of persuasion after extended reading and research. I was disappointed to find so little written on the subject in homiletical literature. This book is my effort to acquaint preachers, evangelists, missionaries, seminary and Bible school students, anyone involved in Christian persuasion, with the ethical problems we face in our task. I have also offered some practical suggestions on how to handle these problems.

Every writer draws from many sources. I have tried carefully to document my sources in footnotes and bibliography.[2]

---

1. Halford E. Luccock, *In the Minister's Worshop* (New York: Abingdon-Cokesbury Press, 1944), p. 52.

2. Some of the material appeared under the title of "The Ethics of Persuasive Preaching," *Journal of the Evangelical Theological Society* 15 (Spring 1972): 93-106, and is used by permission. Other material in chapter 7 of this work appeared

Several friends have read the manuscript and have made valuable criticisms, suggestions, and additions. These include the Reverends David MacDonald, Charles Gifford, David Strand, and Daniel Gross—pastors in the Denver area. Dr. Gordon Lewis, professor of systematic theology and Christian philosophy at the Conservative Baptist Theological Seminary of Denver, carefully read the manuscript and made helpful suggestions.

All of these observations I have deeply appreciated and have worked most of them into the book. Obviously, scholars and critics from whom I have drawn are not responsible for my views.

I thank the faculty, administration, and the board of trustees of the Conservative Baptist Theological Seminary of Denver for granting me a sabbatical leave to work on the book. I give special thanks to the faculty and administration of the Princeton Theological Seminary for granting me the use of their facilities as a visiting Fellow. I deeply appreciate the work my daughter Nancy did on the style of the manuscript. I am indebted to the Reverends Daniel Gross and James Dupree for developing the indexes of the book. I extend my sincere gratitude to my wife Alice, who tirelessly typed several editions of the manuscript. As usual, my family put up with my long study and writing hours, my weariness and preoccupation. I love them for their patience.

Great preaching, like great art, is not on trial. We are. What we do with both shows the maturity of our judgment. The gospel of Jesus Christ has not lost its power. But often we have lost our power as preachers. Our ability and credibility are on the line. In a time when many listeners are forsaking the rhetoric of words for the rhetoric of violence, preaching's last line of defense may well be how credible it sounds to this incredulous generation. That is why we ask Christian communicators "What are you trying to do to these people?"

---

in "Well, Are You Listening?" *The Pastor's Manual* (Summer 1976): 9-14, and is used by permission.

RAYMOND W. McLAUGHLIN
Denver, Colorado

Introduction

A reviewer of one of my earlier books wrote:

> Anyone who has not thought about it, knows that communication is nothing more than common sense. Common sense is that innate wisdom which tells us that the world is flat.[1]

Inasmuch as words are seldom read or heard as they are written or spoken, every effort should be made to correct such "common sense." One of these efforts of clarification or correction is defining one's terms.

Words like *ethics, communication, rhetoric, persuasion, proselytizing, manipulation,* and *coercion* are highly abstract and lend themselves to varied interpretations. Consequently, to start out on the right foot, brief definitions of these terms as I will be using them are offered below.

ETHICS

In a general sense, Dr. Thomas R. Nilsen writes,

> Ethics is that branch of the humanities studying values which relate to human behavior. Students of ethics concern themselves with the rightness and wrongness of human behavior and also with the goodness and badness of the results of behavior.[2]

Such a definition is broad enough to apply virtually to every act of mankind. Although it underlies all that is said in this book, this definition needs to be focused more sharply, such as Robert T.

---

1. Haddon W. Robinson, Review of *Communication for the Church* by Raymond W. McLaughlin in *Bibliotheca Sacra,* 126 (January-March 1969): 88-89.

2. Thomas R. Nilsen, *Ethics of Speech Communication,* 2d. ed. (Indianapolis: Bobbs-Merrill Co., 1974), p. v.

Oliver does when he writes: "Ethics are of vital concern in all our activities—including persuasive speaking. The ethical problems of persuasion may be isolated only in part from the broader questions of morality in general."[3]

Professor Nilsen sounds a similar note, stating,

> Presumably whenever and wherever human behavior affects the lives of others certain "rules" of conduct and moral obligation become significant. Communication, as a primary instrument of human behavior, pervasively touches and affects the lives of others. Therefore, as the argument goes, communication, if it is to contribute to the growth of society, must be associated with and governed by ethics. If such is not the case, the power of communication will be used by self-seeking and self-serving individuals and groups for essentially destructive ends.[4]

With slight changes in a few of Nilsen's words, his definition could be useful to preachers. "Preaching" simply would be substituted for "communication." The " 'rules' of conduct" he alludes to could be considered as the Bible and Christian theology revealed therein. Ethics for preachers, then, is concerned with human values—the good and the bad, rightness and wrongness in the preaching, and the reception of the Christian gospel as measured against the Bible and its doctrine.

COMMUNICATION

The terms *communication, rhetoric,* and *persuasion* are only slightly separated in meaning. They are frequently used interchangeably, depending on the purposes of the user.

Communication has been defined in terms of source or speaker orientation, message orientation, channel orientation, and receiver orientation. This work deals mainly with the source or speaker orientation. Communication may be defined in terms of metalinguistic, mathematical, rhetorical, psychological, semantic, and sociological models.[5] My approach is from the rhetorical point of view. Starting from a general definition the idea of communication will be narrowed to a view that best fits the preaching task.

---

3. Robert T. Oliver, *The Psychology of Persuasive Speech,* 2d. ed. (New York: Longmans, Green and Co., 1957), p. 23.

4. Nilsen, *Ethics of Speech,* p. v.

5. See Joseph A. DeVito, *The Psychology of Speech and Language: An Introduction to Psycholinguistics* (New York: Random House, 1970), chap. 4, "Communication Theory."

Although most definitions are adequate for preaching purposes, one must be sought that fits the ethics of persuasive preaching. Thus the definition of John R. Wenburg and William W. Wilmot, who define communication simply as "an attempt to get meaning,"[6] is acceptable. Howard H. Martin and C. William Colburn feel that communication should be more focused. They view communication transactionally, "as an effort by the speaker to influence his listeners."[7] Questioning the validity of communication as merely sharing information in a self-interested way, Martin and Colburn write, "But our observation of human communication has persuaded us that men do not speak to others unless they expect to achieve some private goal."[8] And Raymond S. Ross, writing in a similar vein says:

> We may thus operationally define intentional communication as a transactional process involving a cognitive sorting, selecting, and sharing of symbols in such a way as to help another elicit from his own experiences a meaning or response similar to that intended by the source.[9]

It is in these latter senses that I use the term communication in this book. Communication is a process, a transaction between preacher and listeners involving intent and purpose. Therefore Christian communication can be defined as "the sharing of information for the purpose of affecting receivers in some predetermined way consistent with the Christian Gospel and ethic."[10]

RHETORIC

Thus far, communication has been defined in very general terms. Rhetoric is usually thought of as a specialized form of communication concerned with persuasion. Aristotle (384-322 B.C.) defined rhetoric as "the faculty of discovering in the particular case

---

6. John R. Wenburg and William W. Wilmot, *The Personal Communication Process* (New York: John Wiley and Sons, 1973), p. 7.

7. Howard H. Martin and C. William Colburn, *Communication and Consensus: An Introduction to Rhetorical Discourse* (New York: Harcourt Brace Jovanovich, 1972), p. 29.

8. Ibid.

9. Raymond S. Ross, *Persuasion: Communication and Interpersonal Relations* (Englewood Cliffs, N.J.: Prentice-Hall, 1974), p. 57.

10. See Raymond W. McLaughlin, *Communication for the Church* (Grand Rapids, Mich.: Zondervan Publishing House, 1968), p. 17.

what are the available means of persuasion."[11] In modern times this emphasis has changed very little. Martin and Colburn write, "Rhetoric can be defined as communication intended to influence hearers."[12]

Rhetoric and persuasion, therefore, differ very little, and the two terms can be used interchangeably. There is little need to sharpen differences between the two disciplines, and they are used in the above defined ways throughout this book.

PERSUASION

Persuasion differs from the broader concept of communication mainly in purpose. Erwin P. Bettinghaus says, "There is general agreement that the variable of *intent* is what distinguishes the persuasive communication from other communication situations."[13] Therefore, he defines persuasion as "a conscious attempt by one individual to change the attitudes, beliefs, or the behavior of another individual or group of individuals through the transmission of some message."[14] Charles U. Larson enlarges slightly on such a view.

> A persuasive transaction as an instance of human behavior, inherently contains potential ethical issues because persuasion (1) involves a persuader attempting to influence other persons by altering their beliefs, attitudes, values, and overt actions, (2) involves conscious choices by the persuader among ends sought and rhetorical means used to achieve the end, and (3) necessarily involves a potential judge (any or all of the receivers, the persuader, or an independent observer).[15]

Inasmuch as persuasion and preaching can be viewed as virtually synonymous (see chapter 1), their goals are quite, though not wholly, similar. For example, preaching is viewed as having two main elements—evangelism and instruction or edification (see chapter 1). Both of these elements are persuasive. These elements are also part of secular persuasion, though voiced in slightly dif-

---

11. Lane Cooper, trans., *The Rhetoric of Aristotle* (New York: Appleton-Century-Crofts, 1932), p. 7.

12. Martin and Colburn, *Communication and Consensus*, p. 136.

13. Erwin P. Bettinghaus, *Persuasive Communication*, 2d. ed. (New York: Holt, Rinehart and Winston, 1973), p. 10.

14. Ibid.

15. Charles U. Larson, *Persuasion, Reception and Responsibility* (Belmont, Calif.: Wadsworth Publishing Co., 1973), p. 213.

ferent terminology. Winston L. Brembeck and William S. Howell write:

> In those persuasive messages where attitude change is the chief objective, the change may be a change in position on an acceptance-rejection scale or a change in intensity, that is, the firmness with which the position is held. Thus the persuader who is primarily interested in attitude change or formation has three purposes available: (1) the intensification of an established attitude without modifying its position on the belief or attitude scale, (2) the actual changing of the attitude or belief position, such as a change from moderate acceptance to total acceptance, from total rejection to neutrality, from total rejection through neutrality to acceptance, and (3) the creation of a new attitude, rather than the modification of an existing one.[16]

Herbert W. Simons maintains that there are three general goals of persuasion, namely, hostility reduction, conversion, and intensification.[17] These general goals he breaks down into subgoals such as:

> Reduce overt opposition; Reduce private opposition; Secure discontinuance of opposition and create genuine indecision; Convert disbelievers; Convert the uninformed and apathetic; Convert the conflicted [fence straddlers]; Reinforce favorable attitudes; Activate favorable attitudes; Increase behavioral commitments; and Maintain high levels of attitudinal and behavioral commitment.[18]

In the context of preaching the Word of God, the above definition and goals of persuasion are also the definitions and goals of preaching. Both disciplines become much more complex and detailed as they are developed. Both preaching and persuasion have similarities and differences. These similarities and differences will become more apparent throughout the book, but the above described nature and goals of persuasion are also those of preaching.

PROSELYTIZING

Oftentimes evangelism is confused with proselytism. Though both are forms of persuasion and thus use some similar approaches, crucial differences separate them. One of the best

---

16. Winston L. Brembeck and William S. Howell, *Persuasion: A Means of Social Influence,* 2d. ed. (Englewood Cliffs, N.J.: Prentice-Hall, 1976), p. 13.

17. Herbert W. Simons, *Persuasion: Understanding, Practice and Analysis* (Reading, Mass.: Addison-Wesley Publishing Co., 1976), p. 100.

18. Ibid., p. 99.

distinctions between these two activities, and therefore definitions of them, was written by John R.W. Stott.

> Evangelism and proselytism aren't the same thing. To proselytize is to win converts to one's particular sect, society or faction. To evangelize is to win converts to Jesus Christ.[19]

Maurice Boillat concurs in this description.

> What is the motive behind evangelism? What is the motive behind proselytism? Basically the proselytizer works for "the party," for the group, for the movement, even for the church in some instances. The evangelist works for God: better, he works with God; "Ye are God's husbandry, ye are God's building" (I Cor. 3:9). In proselytism the basic interest is in making converts for the group; in evangelism, the only concern is in making converts for God.[20]

Boillat affirms that although evangelism and proselytism have certain similarities (such as zeal, converts, strong convictions, and sometimes lack of tolerance), the differences between the two activities are the most significant.[21] The differences he suggests are that "evangelism is grounded in the scriptures"; the basic motives for proselyting are to benefit the group, organization, even church whereas those of the evangelist are to win converts to God; almost anyone can proselytize whereas only believers in Christ can evangelize; evangelism's main concern is for the individual, not for the mass; evangelism's concern is an expression of love whereas proselytism does not require love; and evangelism is oriented to theology whereas proselytism is not [implied].[22]

MANIPULATION

It should be obvious that all of us are manipulators to some degree and for various motives. Our manipulations are not always "bad," but the popular view of manipulation is generally negative. According to Dunnam, Herbertson, and Shostrom, "This is what a manipulator is: 'One who exploits, uses, and/or controls himself and others as things or objects.' "[23] By contrast, "actualizors" are

19. John R. W. Stott, "Evangelism in the Student World," *His* 21 (December 1960): 1 ff.

20. Maurice Boillat, "Evangelism and Proselytism," *Christian Heritage* 27 (January 1966): 13 ff.

21. Ibid., p. 13.

22. Ibid., pp. 13, 32.

23. Adapted from *The Manipulator and the Church* by Maxie Dunnam, Gary Herbertson, and Everett L. Shostrom. Copyright © 1968 by Abingdon Press. Used by permission.

those who do not intend to exploit listeners, but, instead, maintain a genuine interest in people and in fulfilling their needs.

Everett L. Shostrom contrasts the characteristics of manipulators with those of actualizors as follows:

MANIPULATORS	ACTUALIZORS
1. Deception (Phoniness, Knavery). The manipulator uses tricks, techniques, and maneuvers. He puts on an act, plays roles to create an *impression*. His expressed feelings are deliberately chosen to fit the occasion.	1. Honesty (Transparency, Genuineness, Authenticity). The actualizor is able honestly to be his feelings, whatever they may be. He is characterized by candidness, *expression*, and genuinely being himself.
2. Unawareness (Deadness, Boredom). The manipulator is unaware of the really important concerns of living. He has "Tunnel Vision." He sees only what he wishes to see and hears only what he wishes to hear.	2. Aliveness (Responsiveness, Aliveness, Interest). The actualizor fully looks and listens to himself and others. He is fully aware of nature, art, music, and the other real dimensions of living.
3. Control (Closed, Deliberate). The manipulator plays life like a game of chess. He appears relaxed yet is very controlled and controlling, concealing his motives from his "opponent."	3. Freedom (Spontaneity, Openness). The actualizor is spontaneous. He has the freedom to be and express his potentials. He is master of his life, a subject and not a puppet or object.
4. Cynicism (Distrust). The manipulator is basically distrusting of himself and others. Down deep he doesn't trust human nature. He sees relationships with humans as having two alternatives: to control or be controlled.	4. Trust (Faith, Belief). The actualizor has a deep trust in himself and others to relate to and cope with life in the here and now.[24]

Both types are seen in the churches but "the change from manipulation to actualization is in general on a continuum *from* deadness and deliberateness to aliveness and spontaneity."[25] Therefore, manipulators are generally thought to be unethical and actualizors are viewed to be ethical.

---

24. Everett L. Shostrom, *Man the Manipulator: The Inner Journey from Manipulation to Actualization* (Nashville: Abingdon Press, 1967), pp. 50-51.

25. Ibid.

COERCION

Traditionally, persuasion and coercion have been thought of as opposite positions on an ethical continuum. They would look something like this:

Persuasion	Coercion
Ethical	Unethical

Some modern scholars, however, argue that such terms are relative, depending upon who uses the force. Thus Herbert W. Simons claims, "Only in relationship to such words as 'coercion,' 'force,' and 'power,' is 'persuasion' ever a 'god' [good] word, and there it seems to depend on whether we are opposed to particular users of force or for them."[26]

Furthermore, these two activities sometimes move together into the center of the continuum and overlap, or at least crop up in a given speech. A dictator like Hitler or Mussolini may deliver a persuasive speech sprinkled with dire threats, leaving his hearers with little or no choice but to comply with his proposals.

Nevertheless, contrasted with persuasion, coercion is thought of in this book as being the use of force that denies listeners the right of free choice. Indeed, Richard L. Johannesen defines coercion simply as ". . . an interference with free choice."[27] The Bormanns clarify the differences between persuasion and coercion as follows:

> Persuasion is not the same as force. We can control human beings to some extent with the use of force or the threat of force. Coercion restricts choice. If you are forced to do something, your options are closed. Coercion eliminates choice, while persuasion influences it. Coercion does not require artistry. "Do this or I will bash in your head" may get results, but requires little skill—only the brute strength and the desire to deliver the blow.[28]

Although coercion in some small degree may appear in persuasive speeches and sermons, the coercion referred to in this work has to do with force (see chapter 4). Coercion involves such actions as terrorism, disruption, conflict, destruction, kidnapping, hijacking, and killing as tactics used to force people to comply. Such tactics are the antithesis of persuasion.

---

26. Simons, *Persuasion,* p. 28.

27. Richard L. Johannesen, *Ethics in Human Communication* (Columbus, Ohio: Charles E. Merrill Publishing Co., 1975), p. 133.

28. Ernest G. Bormann and Nancy C. Bormann, *Speech Communication: An Interpersonal Approach* (New York: Harper and Row, 1972), p. 139.

Other terms and phrases are of special relation to rhetoric, persuasion, and preaching. The context of their usage, however, is intended to clarify their meaning. Readers interested in exploring these concepts should consult the books and periodicals mentioned in the footnotes and bibliography. The above definitions, however, should help the readers to understand how these terms are used in this book.

One

The Focus on Ethics

I once watched a fiery young "evangelist" on the broad screen in a Denver theater. He paced back and forth, sweating profusely, gesticulating wildly, and screaming into his hand microphone at his spellbound, tent-meeting audience. "If you don't feel the Spirit here in this meeting tonight, man, you're dead!"

Any self-respecting worshiper sitting in that meeting, crowded in on all sides, would almost rather die than admit, even to himself, that he did not feel the overwhelming power of the "Spirit" under those circumstances.

The meeting dragged on to a close following a contentless sermon loaded with extreme emotion and hyper-suggestion, a vague and almost meaningless invitation, and of course a high-pressured offering. The next scene showed the "evangelist" sitting cross-legged on his hotel bed counting the evening's financial "take."

I was stunned and dismayed at this carnival-like display because this documentary-autobiography of the rise and fall of a "boy evangelist" was being shown all over the country to curious eyes and sneering critics of Christianity. I understood only too clearly the cheap twentieth-century sophistry, the psychological bag of tricks, the rhetorical manipulation being perpetrated on this and other sincere and innocent audiences. I was stunned and dismayed that the ethics of persuasion should be so grossly debased in, of all places, an ostensibly Christian pulpit.

Thankfully, most preachers are not of the Arthur Dimmesdale variety sketched by Hawthorne in *The Scarlet Letter.*[1] They cannot be likened to Sinclair Lewis's *Elmer Gantry.*[2] And they are not in

1. Nathaniel Hawthorne, *The Scarlet Letter* (New York: Random House, 1937).

2. Sinclair Lewis, *Elmer Gantry* (New York: Harcourt, Brace and Co., 1927).

the image of Marjoe, contemporary youth "evangelist" turned actor.[3] Does this mean that sincere preachers never face problems of ethics in their persuasive preaching? Hardly. In recent years communication scholars have become increasingly concerned with the ethics of persuasion in advertising, in politics, and in the pulpit.

Tremendous advances in the modern mass media coupled with new findings in psychology, motivational research, social sciences, and communication theory have led to extended warnings about the morality of the mass media and the ethics of persuaders. Some university communication departments now offer courses in this field. Most new speech texts have included at least a chapter on the subject.

Curious to know how preachers themselves felt about their own ethics of persuasive preaching, I decided to question them. In the fall of 1974, questionnaires were sent to 102 pastors of various religious denominations across America and Canada and 66 of them responded. No claim is made for statistical significance because the sample is limited. Nevertheless, pastoral concerns about the ethics of persuasive preaching tended to cluster around certain plaguing problems. I was interested in discovering how these problems might compare with ethical concerns of other communicators and how contemporary approaches to the ethics of persuasion might help ministers.

Accordingly, this chapter treats two matters relating to this search for an ethic of persuasive preaching. First, it introduces and briefly describes the most frequently mentioned ethical problems reported by active pastors of our day. These problems will be dealt with later in connection with measuring the ethics of preaching relative to its ends, means, and applications. Second, this chapter sketches some of the principles of the ethics of preaching treated in this book.

SOME ETHICAL PROBLEMS IN PERSUASIVE PREACHING

Although Christian preachers face many ethical issues in common with other public speakers, they also have special problems that might be considered "hazards" of their trade. The

3. See Steven S. Gaines, *Marjoe: The Life of Marjoe Gortner* (New York: Harper and Row, 1973).

following list reveals both similarities and differences with problems faced by other speakers. They are, however, of special concern to ministers as indicated by the responses to the questionnaire.

Hermeneutical Problems

Three major difficulties were listed regarding the interpretation of biblical texts.

Reading into the biblical text. Examples include naming Hitler or Mussolini as the Antichrist; seeing the rapture of the church in the translation of Enoch (Gen. 5:24; cf. Heb. 11:5); or viewing Ezekiel's wheel within a wheel (Ezek. 1:16) as a prophecy of modern flying saucers.

Spiritualizing the biblical text. Examples include seeing Christ and the church in the Books of Ruth and the Song of Solomon or seeing the church in Noah's ark (the floodwaters as the world, salvation pertaining to those within the ark, perdition the lot of those outside the ark).

Giving only one of several interpretations of a text. An example is presenting one's own view while avoiding opposing views.

Distortion of the Truth

Allowing for the difficulty, if not the impossibility, of always telling the whole truth, pastors mentioned some specific problems they face in persuasive preaching.

Exaggeration—overstating or stretching a truth beyond the rhetorical technique of hyperbole.

Toning down or softening the truth—the opposite of exaggeration; goes beyond the use of euphemism or rhetorical understatement. This is often used when dealing with unpleasant or unpopular truth.

Stacking evidence in one's favor—the use of supporting evidence and the avoidance of damaging evidence. This practice is similar to giving only one of several possible interpretations of a text.

Overgeneralization—the use of universal terms such as *all, always, every, whole, total, none,* and *no such* in value judgments when they do not account for all cases. Equally problematic is the use of superlatives such as *greatest, best, worst, highest, most,* or *least* when these superlatives cannot be supported.

Personal Preparation

Unlike many public speakers, preachers must speak three or four times (or more) a week for most of their lives. Adequate preparation, then, becomes an ethical problem to the minister. Responses to the questionnaire at this point revealed three major difficulties.

Procrastination or avoidance of preparation. Some preachers admitted to putting off sermon preparation until the latest possible moment. Preachers suffer plaguing guilt over this problem. Some have left the ministry because of it.

Failure to prepare to preach at one's best. This is a problem frequently mentioned by pastors. Contrary to some ministers who relegate preaching to a secondary or tertiary place in the ministry, the respondents to the questionnaire felt preaching had top priority, though they did not always support their conviction with commensurate practice.

Using other men's materials without giving credit. This ministerial form of plagiarism is rather widespread, although some have argued that the nature of preaching does not always demand giving credit.

Personal Ethical Practices

Investigation of actual ethical problems in preaching revealed some difficulties that lie beyond the preparation for and in the practice of preaching.

Preaching for personal glory, power, prestige, or money. Some respondents admitted that their motives for preaching were less than the highest. Motives of personal glory, prestige, power, and money (in that order, last two tied) were mixed with nobler motives.

Preaching what one fails to practice. Preachers were honest in admitting to this problem, one of the most frequent ethical issues in their responses.

Acting as an authority in a field where one isn't an authority. Although the pastors were about evenly divided over their involvement in this problem, the practice of it was admitted frequently enough to merit mentioning.

Audience Adaptation

Preachers recognize the importance of preaching sermons that fit their congregations' needs. They also understand the ethical problems involved in pandering to popular demands. Questions in the survey that were directed at the ethical problems involved in audience adaptation uncovered four major concerns.

Avoiding unpleasant, controversial, or troublesome subjects. This practice seemed to be a frequent one. The nature of it was not described, but a number of pastors admitted to doing it.

Avoiding audience feedback. Closely related to the avoidance of troublesome subjects was the failure of many pastors to pick up any palpable feedback from their congregations.

Using entertaining rather than needful content. The respondents were about evenly divided over this practice.

Preaching what people want rather than what they need. Again, the pastors were evenly divided over this practice. It probably is a more serious problem than many realize.

Postsermon Invitation

The practice of extending a postsermon invitation to potential believers, church members, or other auditors seeking spiritual help, is common among American evangelical preachers and evangelists. The postsermon invitation has been a point where unethical techniques abound. The questionnaire revealed that most respondents overwhelmingly rejected these techniques, though perhaps one-fourth to one third of the pastors admitted practicing some of them.

The use of psychological pressures. Though apparently not extensively, some pastors use psychological techniques such as suggestion, emotional appeal, confusing invitation purposes, and proselytizing instead of evangelizing.

The use of crowd pressures. The respondents showed a slight tendency to use crowd pressure techniques such as using decoys (believers moving forward during the invitation to encourage non-believers), singling people out, and wearing people out with extended invitations.

Promising oversimplified solutions to complex human problems. This was one of the most frequently mentioned problems. About one-third of the pastors admitted that at least sometimes they promised oversimplified solutions to complex problems if people would respond to their invitation to come forward for help.

Other Ethical Problems

Without a doubt preachers face other ethical problems. Many commit ethical errors without knowing it. Lack of rhetorical training and awareness of unethical means and ends contribute to their problems. Thus, most of the respondents to the questionnaire claimed that they never used unethical rhetorical methods like smear tactics; harmful labeling; propaganda devices (see chapter 5); excessive emotional appeals; suggestion; and unethical appeals to tradition, authority, majority opinion, or prejudice. Most of the preachers denied that they used such logical fallacies as false analogies, unsound statistics, invalid causal reasoning, begging the question, specious reasoning, and belief that ends justify the means of attaining them. And yet most of these ethical problems crop up in the average preacher's ministry even though he may not be aware of them. These rhetorical and logical problems have been around for a long time.

In recent years, communication scholars have made us aware of new and demanding ethical dimensions with which pastors must cope. For example, how are ministers going to handle the growing charge that dialogical, two-way communication is ethical whereas monological communication (traditional preaching, speaking) is unethical? What are the ethics of pleasing the majority groups and thwarting the minority groups? How is the church going to view the ethics of protest or confrontation rhetoric with their use of obscenity, uncompromising demands, and even terrorism?

Pondering these many issues may distress and discourage ministers. They may even ask themselves a few more penetrating questions. They may wonder, How do I know my views are right and others' views are wrong? They may query whether the average man is capable of determining his own future. The question, Should one man try to persuade another? may plague conscientious ministers. They may ask themselves, Do we as ministers have an ethical responsibility to always preach at our best?

Confronting the above-mentioned issues is a goal of this book, although morbid introspection will be avoided.

ETHICAL PRINCIPLES OF PERSUASIVE PREACHING

Christians cherish values, truths, and experiences upon which they agree. They form a "fellowship forged by faith." They have, over two millennia, succeeded in spreading Christianity among roughly one-third of the world population.

Individualism, however, has also led Christians to differ among themselves on many issues. These differences of opinion have caused doctrinal controversies, denominational divisions, church splits, and even family fights. Such dissension is often criticized and maligned, but many Christians would prefer theological differences to one great superchurch or loss of individual freedom.

Ethics, of course, is one of those disciplines wherein wide differences of opinion exist among Christian individuals. And the ethics of persuasive preaching is a field of thought and action where scholars differ greatly on such matters as the nature, sources, standards, and applications of ethical performance. Such difference of opinion can be healthy. But it is healthy only insofar as all parties understand the premises upon which debate proceeds.

To acquaint the readers of this book with its basic assumptions, the following principles are set forth to undergird my convictions about the ethics of persuasive preaching. These principles are general and not exhaustive. They are simply a preliminary statement of premises, most of which will be expanded later.

Preaching and Persuasion

Obviously, not all persuasion is preaching, but the opposite comes close to universal truth. There may be in preaching, as in most other human activities, exceptions to this premise, but I cannot recall observing them.

The persuasive character of preaching is consonant with the evangelistic and edifying purposes of the church. John Ker states:

> They [the apostles] had two kinds of preaching. The one was "missionary," for bringing men to a knowledge of Christ; the other was "ministerial," for building them up in the faith and in the practice of it. The first of these we have in the book of Acts; the second we have in the epistles.[4]

Edwin Charles Dargan, using slightly different terminology in tracing the nature of biblical preaching, states, "The two permanent elements of Christian preaching appear: evangelism and instruction."[5]

Some theologians seem to argue that evangelism is just preaching the gospel, proclaiming the good news of Jesus Christ

---

4. John Ker, *Lectures on the History of Preaching* (New York: Hodder & Stoughton; George H. Doran Company, n.d.), p. 38, see also T. Harwood Pattison, *The History of Christian Preaching* (Philadelphia: American Baptist Publication Society, 1903), pp. 34-35.

5. Edwin Charles Dargan, *A History of Preaching,* vol. 1 (Grand Rapids: Baker Book House, 1954), p. 25.

without persuasive accouterments.[6] Others claim that New Testament evangelism, both in precept and example, was persuasion.[7] Thus the great commission passages (Matt. 28:19–20; Mark 16:15),[8] the preaching situations in the Book of Acts (e.g., Peter's sermon at Pentecost, Acts 2:14–41 and Paul's sermon on Mars Hill, Acts 27:22–34), references to persuasive activities (e.g., Acts 13:43; 18:4, 13; 19:8, 26; 26:28; 28:23; II Cor. 5:11), and commands to preach (Matt. 10:7 and parallels; Acts 10:42; II Tim. 4:2; and others) all carry the strong notion of persuasion.

Most theologians would accept the persuasive nature of evangelistic preaching. Some, however, might question whether expository, doctrinal, or other teaching types of sermons should be persuasive. But can anyone interpret Jesus' Sermon on the Mount as not being persuasive? Paul and Barnabas at Pisidian Antioch used persuasion, urging believers there "to continue in the grace of God" (Acts 13:43). And Paul's Epistles often are cited as models of his teaching method. These are highly persuasive in content and appeal.

It is difficult to conceive of any communication that is not at least to some degree persuasive. Some of the leading contemporary communication scholars affirm such a premise. Richard M. Weaver, a respected rhetorician, argues that language is sermonic.

> Language, which is thus predicative, is for the same cause sermonic. We are all of us preachers in private or public capacities. We have no sooner uttered words than we have given impulse to other people to look at the world, or some small part of it, in our way.[9]

David Berlo asserts: "All language utterances have a persuasive dimension. *No statements can be said to be nonpersuasive.*"[10] All

---

6. J. I. Packer has been charged with holding this view in his book, *Evangelism and the Sovereignty of God* (London: Inter-Varsity Fellowship, 1961). But a careful study of his position indicates that he believes persuasion (conversion of the unsaved) is the object of evangelism and preaching (see pp. 48-51).

7. See on this view, C. Peter Wagner, *Frontiers of Missionary Strategy* (Chicago: Moody Press, 1971), pp. 127-34.

8. Although the "long ending" of Mark's Gospel (16:9–20) is questionable, the great commission contained there is in keeping with its expression in other locations (cf. Matt. 28:19–20; Luke 24:47–49; John 20:21; Acts 1:8).

9. Richard M. Weaver, *Language Is Sermonic: Richard M. Weaver on the Nature of Rhetoric,* ed. Richard L. Johannesen, Rennard Strickland, and Ralph T. Eubanks (Baton Rouge: Louisiana State University Press, 1970), p. 224.

10. David K. Berlo, *The Process of Communication* (New York: Holt, Rinehart and Winston, 1960), p. 234.

communication is affective, that is, change seeking. Charles U. Larson points out, "Even the most selfless kinds of communication contain within them the kernels of persuasion—they are motivated in some way."[11]

Some preachers and their critics may be wondering whether preaching ought to be persuasive at all—that whether to be ethical, preachers ought to confine themselves strictly to proclaiming the facts of the gospel, thereby fulfilling their responsibility.

Biblical teaching, however, supports preaching as persuasion. And communication theory raises the question whether preaching is even possible without persuasiveness. For these reasons preaching and persuasion are virtually synonymous. Whether persuasive preaching is always ethical is another matter.

Human and Divine Elements

The conviction and conversion of individuals is ultimately the work of the Holy Spirit. Jesus clearly taught:

> And when he [the Holy Spirit] comes, he will convince the world of sin and of righteousness and of judgment: of sin, because they do not believe in me; of righteousness, because I go to the Father, and you will see me no more; of judgment, because the ruler of this world is judged (John 16:8–11).

And in his famous conversation with Nicodemus Jesus warned the Pharisee:

> Truly, truly, I say to you, unless one is born of water and the Spirit, he cannot enter the kingdom of God. That which is born of the flesh is flesh, and that which is born of the Spirit is Spirit. Do not marvel that I said to you, "You must be born anew" (John 3:5–7).

Nevertheless, God also uses men. Matthew says:

> These twelve Jesus sent out, charging them, "Go nowhere among the Gentiles, and enter no town of the Samaritans, but go rather to the lost sheep of the house of Israel. And preach as you go, saying, 'The kingdom of heaven is at hand' " (Matt. 10:5–7).

And Paul voiced the proper balance between both human and divine elements in communicating the gospel when he wrote to the Corinthians:

> God was in Christ reconciling the world to himself, not counting their trespasses against them, and entrusting to us the message of

---

11. Charles U. Larson, *Persuasion, Reception and Responsibility* (Belmont, Calif.: Wadsworth Publishing Co., 1973), p. 2.

> reconciliation. So we are ambassadors for Christ, God making his appeal through us. We beseech you on behalf of Christ, be reconciled to God (II Cor. 5:19–20).

Accordingly, this book proceeds on the assumption that preaching is neither wholly human nor wholly divine. God takes a dedicated human being, fills that person with his Holy Spirit, and uses him with all his talents and training to communicate the gospel. Preachers should consciously and deliberately dedicate their persuasive talents to the Holy Spirit for His use.

Immunity to Ethical Problems

Just because a public speaker is ordained to the ministry, or because he "preaches the Word," or because he proclaims "sound" doctrine does not mean that he is automatically invested with a religious version of "senatorial immunity" to ethical distortions of communication. In Old Testament times, false prophets prophesied in the name of religion—but they were not approved by God (Deut. 13:1–5; 18:17–22). In New Testament times, Simon the sorcerer sought to duplicate the charismatic abilities of Peter and John, apparently from selfish motives, but was rebuked by the apostles (Acts 8:14–24). And Paul allowed for the activities of certain preachers who preached Christ out of envy, rivalry, selfish ambition, and trouble making (Phil. 1:15–18).

Although preaching inherently involves persuasion, this persuasive character must confront a preacher with ethical responsibility. Jesus blistered the Pharisees for failing to practice what they preached (Matt. 23:1–36). Paul cried out, "Woe is unto me, if I preach not the gospel!" (I Cor. 9:16b, KJV). He worried about the possibility of inconsistency in his own ministry, writing, "but I pommel my body and subdue it, lest after preaching to others I myself should be disqualified" (I Cor. 9:27). And the apostle carefully warned Timothy to "avoid disputing about words, which does no good, but only ruins the hearers" (II Tim. 2:14).

Secular writers recognize the ethical problems that persuasion poses. Richard M. Weaver, claiming that "language is sermonic,"[12] nevertheless warns:

> No one can live a life of direction and purpose without some scheme of values. As rhetoric confronts us with choices involving values, the rhetorician is a preacher to us, noble if he tries to direct our passion toward noble ends and base if he uses our passion to confuse and

---

12. Weaver, *Language Is Sermonic,* p. 224.

> degrade us. Since all utterance influences us in one or the other of these directions, it is important that the direction be the right one, and it is better if this lay preacher is a master of his art.[13]

Thomas R. Nilsen includes preachers when he observes:

> One concern is with the ethics of speech. Every act of speech is essentially a social act, influencing the attitudes or behavior of others. Therefore, rather than attempt to divide communication into moral and nonmoral, we will think of every communicative act as having an ethical component—as carrying some degree of ethical charge. Virtually every act of speech, then, involves an ethical obligation.[14]

And Richard Johannesen feels that, regardless of the objectives of speaking, communication has ethical obligations. He writes:

> Whether a communicator seeks to present information, increase someone's level of understanding, facilitate independent decision in another person, persuade about important values, demonstrate the existence and relevance of a societal problem, advocate a solution or program of action, or stimulate conflict—potential ethical issues inhere in the communicator's symbolic efforts.[15]

Therefore preaching is Christian persuasion, but Christian persuasion is not immune to unethical practices. The various ends, means, and standards of persuasive preaching must be considered.

Classical and Contemporary Contributions

The study of ethics is not new. Henry Ford may have thought of history as "bunk!"[16] but those scholars who have laboriously studied the biblical prophets and apostles, or who have pondered the rhetoric of Aristotle, Cicero, and Quintilian, can truly appreciate the observation of the forgotten wit who moaned, "The ancients have stolen all of our best modern thoughts." Ancient ethical roots have fed today's trees of the knowledge of life.

Equally vital to the Christian preacher is a growing knowledge of what is happening now. Confrontations, terrorism, riots, strikes, and minority demands have all jarred and influenced modern rhetoric and its ethical standards. Pragmatic motivations,

---

13. Ibid., p. 225.

14. Thomas R. Nilsen, *Ethics of Speech Communication,* 2d ed., (Indianapolis: Bobbs-Merrill Co., 1974), p. 17.

15. Richard L. Johannesen, *Ethics in Human Communication* (Columbus, Ohio: Charles E. Merrill Publishing Co., 1975), p. 12.

16. As reported by J. Jeffery Auer, *An Introduction to Research in Speech* (New York: Harper and Brothers, 1959), p. 122.

situation ethics, political upheaval, and many other social changes threaten to destroy the church's communication methods and in some cases, its value judgments.

Chapter 2, "The Ethical Situation," expands on the contributions of both the Hebrew-Christian and the classical rhetorical traditions. These will then be updated by a brief overview of contemporary attitudes toward the ethics of persuasive communication. Contemporary views on the subject are also discussed in later chapters.

The Christian preacher cannot exclude the ethical ideas from these sources. Robert T. Oliver accurately focuses upon our situation when he writes:

> Ethics are of vital concern in all our activities—including persuasive speaking. The ethical problems of persuasion may be isolated only in part from the broader question of morality in general.[17]

Absolute and Relative Truth

The great central doctrines of the Christian faith are revelations of God. Moreover, these doctrines are absolute and binding for the Christian.

Nonetheless there are some biblical teachings, laws, customs, promises, and doctrines that are not dogmatically clear or applicable. The passing years, changes in customs and cultures, and even the reversal of meaning in some words mean that we cannot always interpret these truths the same today as when they first were given. Idol worship, eating things strangled, and drinking blood had great significance to the church in 50 A.D. (Acts 15:1–20) but mean little to Christians today. Thus, the literal command is not considered an absolute one for all Christians for all time unless the same problems should again arise. This does not mean that the underlying principle in the Jerusalem Council's command—do nothing that would cause a brother to fall—is not absolute, for it is. Nevertheless, incidents like this, as well as the vagueness of certain doctrines (i.e. details of eschatology) argue for a tolerant attitude in interpretation.

Applied to the ethics of persuasive preaching, then, certain principles, truths, or guidelines must be held as absolute and binding. But other rules, laws, and suggestions are regarded as relative to the

---

17. Robert T. Oliver, *The Psychology of Persuasive Speech.* 2d ed. (New York: Longman Inc., 1957), p. 23. Previously published by the David McKay Company. Reprinted by permission of Longman.

people, time, and places involved in the particular occasion. These attitudes are especially important regarding ethical guidelines not specifically spelled out in the Bible. This means that the Bible is to be regarded as absolute in its overall authority, though some of its details should be interpreted and applied relatively.

Contributions of Secular Communication and a Biblical Standard

This book draws from many sources—biblical and nonbiblical. The phenomenal growth of communication methodology in our generation should not be ignored. Research in rhetoric, persuasion, semantics, psycholinguistics, cybernetics, and other aspects of interpersonal communication has provided a vast resource of material from which the preacher may profitably draw.

The Christian theologian and preacher, however, takes the Bible as his ultimate and final source of authority and guidelines. He believes this source to be the divinely inspired Word of God. Thus, in matters where secular and sacred theories clash, the Christian persuader is committed to the authority of the Bible. Such occasions are not infrequent in the Bible, for God's people were often moving against the currents of popular opinion. In early church history Peter and John were forbidden by the Sanhedrin to preach in the name of Jesus. The apostle's reply was: "Judge for yourselves whether it is right in God's sight to obey you rather than God. For we cannot help speaking about what we have seen and heard" (Acts 4:19–20, NIV).

Accordingly, this book will intertwine secular and sacred communication theory to build its view of an ethics of persuasive preaching. Some ideas will overlap. This should not be surprising inasmuch as ethics in general has been greatly influenced by the Judeo-Christian tradition. Both similarities and differences between the sacred and secular will be apparent. But conclusions, essentially, will remain biblically oriented.

The Open-ended Process of Christian Communication

This book is neither the complete nor final word on the ethics of persuasive preaching. The process character of communication is one of its major tenets.[18] At times the speed of this process is almost breathtaking. Since this book was started several years ago brash new rhetorical theories have demanded our attention.

---

18. See Berlo, *Process of Communication.*

Dialogical vs. monological theories are competing for dominance. Confrontation or protest rhetoric has forced itself upon us. Intentional ambiguity, obscene words, and even terrorist tactics find extended treatment in academic research. Traditional monological preaching is the target for more concentrated attacks than ever before.[19]

In such a rapidly changing world of ideas and experiences this book cannot claim the distinction of being the last word on the subject. Nevertheless, the ideas and the recommendations of the book are intended to have long-range durability. They will serve, hopefully, to stimulate thought, probe consciences, and be put to use in the present and in the future.

SUMMARY AND CONCLUSION

The ethics of persuasion have been the focus of much concern and study in recent years. Preaching, as a form of persuasion, has been part of this focus and study. Research indicates that contemporary preachers view their ethical problems of persuasive preaching to fall mainly in the areas of *hermeneutics* (biblical interpretation, reading into biblical texts, spiritualizing texts, or giving only one interpretation); *distortion of the truth* (exaggerating, softening truth, stacking evidence, or overgeneralizing); *personal preparation* (procrastination, failure to prepare to preach at one's best, or failure to credit others' materials); *personal ethical practices* (preaching for personal glory, power, prestige, or money, failure to practice what is preached; or acting as authority when not an authority); *audience adaptation* (avoiding unpleasant subjects, avoiding audience feedback, using entertaining rather than needful material, or preaching what people want rather than what they need); and the *postsermon invitation* (using psychological pressures and crowd pressures or offering oversimplified solutions to complex problems).

This book is built upon certain convictions. These convictions are: (1) preaching and persuasion are virtually synonymous; (2) preaching is dependent upon both human and divine elements; (3) preaching is not immune to ethical problems; (4) both classical and contemporary communication methodology contribute to our

19. See Clyde Reid, *The Empty Pulpit* (New York: Harper and Row, 1967); Reuel L. Howe, *Partners in Preaching: Clergy and Laity in Dialogue* (New York: Seabury Press, 1967); Pierre Berton, *The Comfortable Pew* (Philadelphia: J. B. Lippincott Co., 1965).

ethics of persuasive preaching; (5) both absolute and relative factors are involved in our ethical approach; (6) although the ethical position of this book draws deeply from secular sources its ultimate source of authority is the Bible; (7) the process character of communication demands that the views set forth in this book be open-ended and receptive to new developments.

For the most part ministers of the gospel deeply desire to preach, not only effectively, but ethically. This book is submitted for the purpose of acquainting these preachers with the tools and the motivation that will help them accomplish these objectives.

Two

The Ethical Situation

The Christian preacher interested in the ethics of his persuasive task ought to acquaint himself with what ancient and modern men think about it. Although not all sacred and secular thinkers address themselves directly to the issue, many deal with it either explicitly or implicitly. Consider briefly the ancient Hebrew-Christian, the classical rhetorical, and the contemporary rhetoricians' attitudes toward the ethics of persuasive communication.

THE HEBREW-CHRISTIAN VIEW

The ethics of persuasive proclamation receive little formal treatment in the Bible. The ethical spirit, however, is abundantly clear. Good prophets are extolled and false prophets are criticized. Human wisdom and rhetoric, though used, were viewed suspiciously whereas preaching in the power and demonstration of the Spirit was encouraged.

In Old Testament times the people of Israel were forbidden to follow the abominable practices of pagan nations. They were not to listen to soothsayers, augurs, sorcerers, charmers, mediums, diviners, wizards, or necromancers (Deut. 18:9–14). God promised to raise up prophets like Moses and put his words in their mouths. Israel was to heed these divinely inspired prophets. The classical biblical attitude concerning true and false prophets is summed up by Moses:

> And the Lord said to me, "They have rightly said all that they have spoken. I will raise up for them a prophet like you from among their brethren; and I will put my words in his mouth, and he shall speak to them all that I command him. And whoever will not give heed to my words which he shall speak in my name, I myself will require it of him. But the prophet who presumes to speak a word in my name which I have not commanded him to speak, or who speaks in the

> name of other gods, that same prophet shall die." And if you say in your heart, "How may we know the word which the Lord has not spoken?"—when a prophet speaks in the name of the Lord, if the word does not come to pass or come true, that is a word which the Lord has not spoken; the prophet has spoken it presumptuously, you need not be afraid of him (Deut. 18:17–22).

Obviously there were false as well as true messages and messengers in that day. The true prophet and the people ought to know the differences between true and false messages. They should shun the false, and listen to the true. Not only should the prophet be raised up by God himself, but he should speak only those words put into his mouth by the Lord.

One test of a prophetic message was the fulfillment test. If the prophecy was fulfilled in history as predicted, it was God's message. If the prophecy was not fulfilled in history as predicted, then it was only a man's message and not to be heeded.

An equally crucial test of prophetic messages was the consistency test. Again Moses warned:

> If a prophet arises among you, or a dreamer of dreams, and gives you a sign or a wonder, and the sign or wonder which he tells you comes to pass, and if he says, "Let us go after other gods," which you have not known, "and let us serve them," you shall not listen to the words of that prophet or to that dreamer of dreams; for the Lord your God is testing you, to know whether you love the Lord your God with all your heart and with all your soul. You shall walk after the Lord your God and fear him, and keep his commandments and obey his voice, and you shall serve him and cleave to him. But that prophet or that dreamer of dreams shall be put to death, because he has taught rebellion against the Lord your God, who brought you out of the land of Egypt and redeemed you out of the house of bondage, to make you leave the way in which the Lord your God commanded you to walk. So you shall purge the evil from the midst of you (Deut. 13:1–5).

The moral integrity of the true prophet was often seen in his insistence on speaking God's message to man regardless of its popularity.[1] Such integrity is illustrated in an incident in the life of the prophet Micaiah. According to the narrative (I Kings 22), Jehoshaphat, king of Judah, wanted to battle the Syrians at Ramoth-gilead. In his concern about whether he was doing the

---

1. On the prophetic situation see such works as Edward J. Young, *My Servants the Prophets* (Grand Rapids: Wm. B. Eerdmans Publishing Co., 1952); Alexander F. Kirkpatrick, *The Doctrine of the Prophets* (London: Macmillan and Co., 1907); and George Adam Smith, The Book of the Twelve Prophets, 2 vols. (New York: Harper and Brothers, 1929).

right thing, he requested the advice of four hundred of the prophets of Ahab, king of Israel. Their advice was favorable, but Jehoshaphat was wary of it. He asked Ahab if there were any other prophets available to advise. Ahab grudgingly replied, "There is yet one man by whom we may inquire of the Lord, Micaiah the son of Imlah, but I hate him, for he never prophesies good concerning me, but evil" (I Kings 22:8). For his report in the face of the false advice of the four hundred prophets, Micaiah was jailed. But Micaiah held to the truth and the subsequent battle vindicated his advice. One is reminded of the petulant cry of Agamemnon against the seer Kalchas: "Thou seer of evil, never yet hast thou told me the thing that is pleasant. Evil is ever the joy of thy heart to prophesy, but never yet didst thou tell any good matter nor bring it to pass."[2] One thing is certain. The ancient Hebrew prophets were expected to deliver truthful messages regardless of the consequences—messages that could be verified by subsequent history. Any other prophet or prophecy was considered false and unworthy of human response.

Each prophet had his own distinctive personality and message, and yet there was a central core of prophetic characteristics which was so significant that it has extended, not only through their own line, but on into every subsequent age of the true Christian ministry. Yates suggests an excellent list of these marks that distinguish a prophet of God.

> 1. He is an uncompromising individualist. He cannot be bound by conventions or by public opinion or be restrained by the caution of diplomats.
>
> 2. He is conscious of a divine call that holds him to the task set forth by his God. Always he must realize that he is God's mouthpiece. The divine compulsion must be obeyed.
>
> 3. He is conscious of the privilege of access to the inner counsel of Yahweh. He is in immediate contact with God. He is the bearer of precious secrets from the throne of God to needy men.
>
> 4. He is usually a man of action with a certain ruggedness of body and character that commands attention in any gathering. Being intense and keyed to a high pitch he will be apt to stir up antagonism and opposition.
>
> 5. He is conscious of God's authority and backing in all emergencies. It is usually true that he stands alone against practically all of his contemporaries. Even the religious leaders (priests and conventional prophets), who usually find time for social intercourse, are constantly challenging the strange stand of God's prophets.

---

2. Homer *Iliad* 1.105-8.

6. He is very definitely a man of prayer and communion. His lonely, solitary life gives him plenty of time to keep in touch with God.

7. He is clean and consecrated in life and character. In all the long line of genuine prophets we do not find a single breath of criticism of the moral life of any one of them. Each lived a separated life.

8. He is an outspoken critic of specific evils in the social order. Kings, priests, princes, nobles and judges are denounced fearlessly. He does not deal in abstractions. Guided by the will of God he raises his voice in violent protest against any person or institution meriting denunciation.

9. He is God's agent to reveal the future to the people. It is quite true that his main work is that of preaching to his own age. We must not, however, lose sight of the part the prophet plays in revealing the purpose of Yahweh for the future. He is given peculiar insight into the will of God for the generations yet unborn.[3]

Jesus directed some acid criticism at false prophets, saying:

> Beware of false prophets, who come to you in sheep's clothing but inwardly are ravenous wolves. You will know them by their fruits. Are grapes gathered from thorns, or figs from thistles? So, every sound tree bears good fruit, but the bad tree bears evil fruit. A sound tree cannot bear evil fruit, nor can a bad tree bear good fruit. Every tree that does not bear good fruit is cut down and thrown into the fire. Thus you will know them by their fruits (Matt. 7:15–20).

Often Jesus directed bitter criticisms toward the Pharisees and scribes for their inner attitudes as well as their outward messages.

> You brood of vipers! how can you speak good, when you are evil? For out of the abundance of the heart the mouth speaks. The good man out of his good treasure brings forth good, and the evil man out of his evil treasure brings forth evil. I tell you, on the day of judgment men will render account for every careless word they utter, for by your words you will be justified and by your words you will be condemned (Matt. 12:34–37).

Again, in an extended and scathing rebuke, Christ accused the scribes and Pharisees of hypocrisy because they laid upon the people heavy legalistic burdens that they themselves did not keep, thus perpetrating a dramatic contradiction between their preaching and their practice (Matt. 23).

From these and other words of Christ it is obvious that he was deeply concerned about the moral integrity of his contemporary prophets, as well as the intrinsic content of their messages. He related the content of the message to the attitude of the messenger.

---

3. Kyle M. Yates, *Preaching from the Prophets* (New York: Harper and Brothers, 1942), pp. 3-4.

The apostles, in their preaching and teaching, insisted upon a high level of ethical living and communicating. James wrote, "Everyone should be quick to listen, slow to speak, and slow to become angry" (James 1:19, NIV). Concerned about harmful talk, he warned, "If anyone considers himself religious and yet does not keep a tight rein on his tongue, he deceives himself and his religion is worthless" (1:26, NIV).

Peter, aware of the persecution and suffering of scattered believers, warned:

> Who is going to harm you if you are eager to do good? But even if you should suffer for what is right, you are blessed. "Do not fear what they fear; do not be frightened." But in your hearts acknowledge Christ as the holy Lord. Always be prepared to give an answer to everyone who asks you to give the reason for the hope that you have. But do this with gentleness and respect, keeping a clear conscience, so that those who speak maliciously against your good behavior in Christ may be ashamed of their slander (I Peter 3:13–16, NIV).

Although Peter, James, and other apostles clearly expressed themselves on the integrity of messages and messengers,[4] Paul was probably the most influential. Accordingly, a few of his observations should clarify the contribution of the Hebrew-Christian tradition.

Paul presented what must seem to some a baffling, almost contradictory, view of persuasion. On the one hand, it is uncertain whether or not he ever received classical rhetorical training. In addition, he is sometimes represented as critical of persuasion in his Corinthian correspondence (I Cor. 1:17—2:5).

On the other hand, a study of Paul's speeches in the Book of Acts, his literary work, and certain of his specific statements are strong evidence that he used rhetoric or persuasion skillfully, whether trained in it or not. This is only a seeming paradox. A glance at the major points of controversy will be sufficient to clarify his view.

Paul is sometimes represented as being critical of persuasion. The key Scripture cited is I Corinthians 1:17—2:5 in general and I Corinthians 2:4 in particular. The latter verse reads: "And my speech and my message were not in plausible [persuasive] words of wisdom, but in demonstration of the Spirit and power." The question is: Did Paul criticize and reject persuasion in this verse and its

4. See, for example, the apostolic speeches in the Book of Acts plus the writings of James, Peter, John, and the Epistle to the Hebrews.

context? A close examination of the text (2:4) and of the context (1:17—2:5) shows that even though he did use the New Testament word for persuasion [πείθω, translated "plausible" in v. 4, RSV], this word was used to modify the phrase, "words of wisdom." In this verse Paul was contrasting "persuasive words of wisdom" with the "demonstration of the Spirit and power." He claimed that he preached to the Corinthians in the latter, not the former.

The context supports the above assertion. Paul sets in opposition "preaching the gospel" and "words of wisdom" (1:17). He censures "the wisdom of the wise and the cleverness of the clever" (1:19). He denounces the "debater of this age" and the "wisdom of the world" (v. 20), pointing out their failure to bring people to a knowledge of God (v. 21). He rounds out his argument by showing that it was through the folly of the kerygma, the preaching of the crucified and resurrected Christ, that God chose to save those who believed (vv. 21 ff.). Thus, it appears that Paul was more concerned about the content of the message than about its form and presentation, although the latter must not be ruled out completely. When he said, "For I decided to know nothing among you except Jesus Christ and him crucified" (2:2), he was talking about the content of his message. Content was also in his mind when he claimed, "and my speech and my message were not in plausible [persuasive] words of wisdom" (2:4a). When he claimed that his speech was "in demonstration of the Spirit and power" (2:4b), however, he probably was referring to its presentation. This latter statement is not a rejection of rhetoric; it is, rather, a statement concerning how a Christian ought to use it.

Some theologians claim that because Paul used pagan rhetorical methods and wisdom in his sermon on Mars Hill (Acts 17:22–34), the response to that sermon was ostensibly poor. As a result he supposedly forsook that approach in Corinth. But an examination of Paul's Mars Hill sermon does not support such a claim. For even though Paul admittedly used rhetorical methods and devices in that sermon, the heart of the content of the sermon was the same resurrected Jesus Christ he proclaimed in Corinth (cf. Acts 17:31 and I Cor. 2:2). Furthermore, nowhere in Scripture is there a direct statement that his approach in the Mars Hill sermon was either wrong or unfruitful. It would seem that even though the response to his sermon at Athens was not numerically as great as it was in other cities, the Spirit of God apparently saw fit to bless it with the conversion of some Athenians, including Dionysius the Areopagite and the woman named Damaris (Acts 17:34). Thus the Mars Hill sermon, far from being evidence against Paul's use of persuasion, is one of the strongest evidences for his use of it.

There is a second phase of Paul's seeming paradox. Those who claim that Paul disdained persuasion must somehow explain his endorsement and use of it. In his second letter to the Corinthians, Paul vigorously claimed that he and his coworkers persuaded men. He writes, "Therefore, knowing the fear of the Lord, we persuade men" (5:11a). Here again the apostle chose the word *πείθω*, which is used in both secular and sacred literature with such wide meanings as "to convince," "to persuade," "to seduce" (by persuasion), or "to corrupt."[5] In the context of II Corinthians 5, it simply means "to persuade," "to convince," or "to win men." That Paul bore out this claim is attested throughout his missionary tours recorded in the Book of Acts. Luke reports that even in Corinth Paul "argued in the synagogue every sabbath, and persuaded [from *πείθω*] Jews and Greeks" (Acts 18:4).

In addition to Paul's direct endorsement of persuasion, a brief mention of recorded examples of his rhetoric and persuasion is in order. Of course, examples of his rhetoric can be observed in all of his writings, but two passages in particular illustrate his use of classical rhetoric.

The best example is Paul's sermon on Mars Hill (Acts 17:22–34). The recorded speech is, of course, condensed. Nevertheless, one can identify its classical structure of proem (introduction), its body with repeated use of the enthymeme (a Greek form of shortened logic), and its movement toward a climax and application. This peroration, or conclusion, however, was not completed. For when Paul turned the thrust of his message to the theme of the resurrected Christ, he divided his listeners. Some could not bear his doctrine and mocked him. Others procrastinated. But, some believed.

Besides the classical structure of the speech one can see other rhetorical devices. Lane Cooper cites Paul's use of the enthymeme, rhetorical "sign," and appeal to witness.[6] The speech also contains simile, illustration, and example.

---

5. For a helpful discussion of the meaning and uses of *πείθω* and its variations see Geoffrey W. Bromiley, trans. and ed., *Theological Dictionary of the New Testament* (Grand Rapids: Wm. B. Eerdmans Publishing Co., 1968), 6.1-9.

6. Lane Cooper, trans., *The Rhetoric of Aristotle* (New York: Appleton-Century-Crofts, 1932), pp. xxvii-xxix.

The other model of Paul's rhetoric is the passage on love in I Corinthians 13. Although not a speech, the passage has organized movement, partition, and climax. Again Lane Cooper cites Paul's "use of negative expressions in his praise of charity" in the passage—that is, what love is not.[7] In addition, Paul uses copious stylistic devices such as comparison, contrast, repetition, parallelism, balanced constructions, words in series, simile, and metaphor. The whole passage is clear, logical, dramatic, and beautiful. Not even the ancient Attic orators provided more vivid examples of classical rhetoric.

A study of Paul's other writings reveals similar, if not as concentrated, use of logic, rhetoric, and persuasion. The above examples, however, are sufficient to show that his view of persuasion was consistent, not paradoxical, and that Paul frequently used rhetoric.

The Hebrew-Christian tradition thus provides a high level of ethical concern. This ethical concern is revealed both in precept and example in the Bible. To be true to the Christian ministry, the prophetic-apostolic tradition must be followed. This tradition may be summarized under the two general categories: the man and his message.

The preacher (the man) must follow the characteristics exemplified by the prophets, Christ, and apostles. (1) They possessed high moral character. (2) They had good reputation and respect. (3) They revealed clean, rugged manliness. (4) They showed courage, fearlessness, and a noncompromising spirit. (5) They were in some cases men of wisdom and training, such as Isaiah and Paul. (6) They were men of spiritual sensitivity and maturity, although the prophets, Christ, and apostles went beyond the normal preacher at this point and became recipients of supernatural endowments and revelation. (7) Little is known about their abilities of delivery, such as vocal quality and bodily action.

The message must show these biblical features. (1) The content of the message was the "Word of the Lord," and later the kerygma, or gospel of the crucified, risen Christ. Doctrinal and polemical material was included. (2) Although primarily intended for the culture to which delivered, the messages of the prophets, Christ, and the apostles contain transcultural, or eternal, truth. (3) The purposes of the messages were mainly evangelism and edifica-

7. Ibid., p. 197.

tion. (4) Though not disorganized, the messages seldom stressed formal, or classical, arrangement (i.e., introduction, body, and conclusion). Paul's sermon on Mars Hill (Acts 17:22–34) was an exception. Prophetic books such as Isaiah or Ezekiel, however, show careful planning, organization, and literary excellence. (5) Little attention was given to memory of messages as such. They were frequently spontaneous and drew on whatever Old Testament literature could be remembered. (6) The messages are often rich in literary style and provide admirable models for the preacher to study.

The Hebrew-Christian attitude toward persuasion was generally favorable. It approved of true prophets and true prophecy. It eschewed false prophets and false prophecy. It related the moral quality of the messages to the inner conditions of men's hearts. It condemned sophistic forms, presentations, and content. But it approved and used spiritual content and power presented in classical form and style.

THE CLASSICAL RHETORICAL VIEW

The ancient rhetoricians began to clarify, in an embryonic form, the various philosophies of communication. These philosophies were not so much stated as implied. They gradually evolved, through trial and error, observation and practice, study and criticism, and can be seen in the contemporary world of communication, both sacred and secular. Each of these philosophies finds some parallel in the Scriptures.

The first philosophy of communication was that of *results.* It was emphasized by the Sophists of ancient Greece. Corax of Sicily, a Greek of the fifth century B.C., is generally credited with the formulation of the first system of rhetoric. After the tyrants were driven from Sicily, property disputes arose which had to be settled by the landowners themselves arguing in the law courts. Corax observed the speakers and their speeches, noting those factors which seemed to be most persuasive. He arranged them into a system of oratory which stressed the importance of three factors in speaking, namely:

1. Rhetoric was the art of persuasion that sought response from the listeners. This gave speech a push toward a philosophy of results.
2. Arrangement of ideas was important. This initiated what later became a philosophy of methods.

3. Probability was an important part of rhetoric. Thus, if the probability of truth were not present, the speech would be unconvincing. This factor was strong in the subsequent development of the "truth" philosophy of communication.

While Corax himself may not have been a Sophist, his rhetoric was an ideal tool used by sophistic philosophers and orators.

Opinion is somewhat divided over the perils of sophistry, but it seems certain that a host of early opportunists saw the pragmatic possibilities inherent in eloquence and exploited them. Critics have censored these charlatans for their preoccupation with results at any price. Sophists have been accused of manipulating speech for speech's sake, of indifference to truth, of passion for heady oratory, and of preference for persuasion rather than knowledge. Although some scholars have challenged this view, there can be little doubt that sophists of this character, under this or some other label, have always existed and will continue to do so. They operate within Christendom as well.

Results are a legitimate factor of persuasion, whether sacred or secular. The Bible clearly expects results from the labors of Christians. Jesus said: "I am the vine; you are the branches. If a man remains in me and I in him, he will bear much fruit; apart from me you can do nothing" (John 15:5, NIV). Later, he added, "This is to my Father's glory, that you bear much fruit, showing yourselves to be my disciples" (John 15:8, NIV). Early in his ministry Jesus "appointed twelve, to be with him, and to be sent out to preach and have authority to cast out demons" (Mark 3:14–15). These words along with the great commission given at the close of his ministry (Matt. 16:18–20, cf. Acts 1:8) indicate that Christ expected results from his followers.

Paul expected Timothy to preach for results when he charged:

> Preach the Word; be prepared in season and out of season; correct, rebuke and encourage—with great patience and careful instruction. For the time will come when men will not put up with sound doctrine. Instead, to suit their own desires, they will gather around them a great number of teachers to say what their itching ears want to hear. They will turn their ears away from the truth and turn aside to myths. But you, keep your head in all situations, endure hardship, do the work of an evangelist, discharge all the duties of your ministry (II Tim. 4:2-5, NIV).

Many other Old and New Testament passages urge Christians to win souls, baptize believers, and build up the faithful in the body of Christ, which is his church. But when results dominate a speaker or preacher to the point where he compromises his soul through the employment of a bag of rhetorical or psychological tricks, he is guilty of prostituting oratory to undesirable sophistry.

Fortunately, the rhetoric of Corax and his pupil Tisias also was widely used by responsible orators. They contributed significantly to the art of rhetoric and directed later students to the study of persuasion, arrangement, and probability in effective speech.

A second philosophy of communication appeared to develop around Plato (427-347 B.C.), who insisted on the importance of truth in discourse. His dialogues entitled *Gorgias* and *Phaedrus* indicate his conviction as to what speech ought to be.[8] In the *Gorgias* he criticizes the empty sophistry of his day as being separated from truth, questionable in its techniques, and pernicious in its influence. In the *Phaedrus* he set forth more clearly his notion of the ideal orator. Plato felt that the speaker must know the truth of his subject, present it in an orderly manner, be sensitive to audience reaction, have a high moral purpose, and be willing to submit to cross-questioning. Willingness to defend one's ideas was important in establishing the truth. Plato's philosophy of communication was a salient contribution to the art of oratory, and its influence is still with us.

The parallel of Plato's emphasis on truth is evident in Scripture. The prophets were men of high integrity. Jesus claimed to be the truth, saying, "I am the way, and the truth, and the life; no one comes to the Father, but by me" (John 14:6). And, speaking to believing Jews, he said, "and you will know the truth, and the truth will make you free" (John 8:32).

Paul warned the Roman Christians, "For the wrath of God is revealed from heaven against all ungodliness and wickedness of men who by their wickedness suppress the truth" (Rom. 1:18). Paul's communicative ministry seemed to be both preaching, as in Salamis (Acts 13:5), Pisidian Antioch (Acts 13:14 ff.), Iconium (Acts 14:1), Derbe and Lystra (Acts 14:6 ff); and dialogue, as in Thessalonica (Acts 17:2), Athens (Acts 17:17 ff.), Corinth (Acts 18:4 ff.), and other places. The apostle never seemed to shrink from debate or the defense of the gospel.

A third philosophy of communication, sometimes called the methods approach, developed around Aristotle and his great treatise, *The Rhetoric.* Deeply influenced by Plato, yet recognizing

8. See Benjamin Jowett, trans., *The Dialogues of Plato,* 4th ed. (Oxford, England: Clarendon Press, 1953), 1, 3.

the value in some of the techniques of the Sophists, Aristotle included both points of view in his system. *The Rhetoric,* generally thought to be the most important and influential work in the field of public speaking, reveals Aristotle's passion for a scientific analysis of persuasion. His stress on the Platonic idea of responsibility for truth, therefore, is not surprising. Aristotle's treatment of *invention* in speaking with its stress upon the *ethos* (character) of the speaker, and *logos* (logical appeals) in the material of the speech, illustrates the importance he attached to responsibility. Although he considered *pathos* (emotional appeals) incidental, one should not think that his treatment of it is inferior, for it is not.

Aristotle considered speech *method* as vital. His oft-quoted definition of rhetoric, ". . . the faculty of discovering in the particular case what are the available means of persuasion,"[9] indicates this conviction and is the central proposition of *The Rhetoric.* The three books of *The Rhetoric* treat the speaker, the audience, and the speech itself, in that order. Each subject is studied in terms of its contribution to the central proposition. He discusses most of the traditional divisions of speech, invention, arrangement, style, and delivery. Although he gives no explicit attention to memory, it is implied throughout.

Aristotle's *Rhetoric* has been described as being built upon four philosophical postulates: (1) rhetoric is useful to society; (2) rhetoric can be taught; (3) rhetoric should be practiced with balance—avoiding excesses; and (4) rhetoric should emphasize logic as the truest method of persuasion.[10] Aristotle's approach is sane and practical. He was interested in giving "effectiveness to truth."

To describe Aristotle's philosophy of communication with one word, *methods,* is to oversimplify. Yet the great philosopher was the first to systematize rhetoric into a careful and practical method. And this method has become classic. It is not too much to claim that if one's methods are sound, one's results will be sound. By the same token, if one's methods are unsound, distorted, unethical, or irresponsible, then one's results may be equally unsound. Aristotle firmly advocated moral integrity and social responsibility. Without a doubt he influenced all subsequent principles of speechmaking.

---

9. Cooper, *Rhetoric of Aristotle,* p. 7.

10. See on this Lester Thonssen, *Selected Readings in Rhetoric and Public Speaking* (New York: H. W. Wilson Co., 1942), p. 35; and Lester Thonssen and A. Craig Baird, *Speech Criticism* (New York: Ronald Press, 1948), pp. 70-75.

His influence upon homiletical theory and Christian preaching is incalculable.

Although not preoccupied with rhetoric, Christian proclamation concurs with Aristotle's philosophy of methods. We have previously shown the Bible's support of *ethos* (character of the speaker) in the prophetic-Christian-apostolic ministries. These same sources would advance Aristotle's view that if the preacher's methods are sound his results will be sound. Jesus, for example, applied this principle, in a general way, to the influence of men's words. Criticizing certain Pharisees he charged:

> Either make the tree good, and its fruit good; or make the tree bad, and its fruit bad; for the tree is known by its fruit. You brood of vipers! how can you speak good, when you are evil? For out of the abundance of the heart the mouth speaks. The good man out of his good treasure brings forth good, and the evil man out of his evil treasure brings forth evil. I tell you, on the day of judgment men will render account for every careless word they utter; for by your words you will be justified, and by your words you will be condemned (Matt. 12:33–36).

And Paul, though not commenting on rhetoric, set forth a similar principle that could apply to the discipline when he wrote to the Galatians:

> Let him that is taught in the word communicate [Greek, "share with"] unto him that teacheth in all good things. Be not deceived; God is not mocked: for whatsoever a man soweth, that shall he also reap. For he that soweth to his flesh shall of the flesh reap corruption; but he that soweth to the Spirit shall of the Spirit reap life everlasting (Gal. 6:6–8, KJV).

Sophistic preachers should heed the above words of Jesus and Paul.

A fourth philosophy of communication is usually associated with Quintilian (A.D. 35-95), the great Roman teacher of rhetoric. In his *Institutes of Oratory* he expressed the key characteristics of the ideal orator—"the good man speaking well."[11] Quintilian stressed two basic imperatives for the ideal speaker: (1) moral character and (2) speech skill. With these two tenets Quintilian followed the rhetoric of Aristotle rather than developing a new theory. He expanded the theory into a complete course of public speaking contained in the twelve books of his *Institutes.* As such, it

---

11. H. E. Butler, trans., *The Institutio Oratoria of Quintilian* (Cambridge, Mass.: Harvard University Press, 1953), 1.9.

provides us with one of the finest and most complete speech textbooks ever written. Quintilian treated the traditional five areas of speaking: invention, arrangement, style, memory, and delivery. His stress upon the good man speaking well gave to all ages of communication the classical balance of integrity and skill.

Lofty *ethos* (character) of the Christian preacher has always been demanded in the Bible. From the confession and purification of Isaiah:

> Woe is me! For I am lost; for I am a man of unclean lips, and I dwell in the midst of a people of unclean lips; for my eyes have seen the King, the Lord of Hosts!
>
> Then flew one of the seraphim to me, having in his hand a burning coal which he had taken with tongs from the altar. And he touched my mouth, and said: "Behold, this has touched your lips; your guilt is taken away, and your sin forgiven" (Isa. 6:5–7).

to the ministerial standards demanded by Paul:

> The saying is sure: If any one aspires to the office of bishop, he desires a noble task. Now a bishop must be above reproach, the husband of one wife, temperate, sensible, dignified, hospitable, an apt teacher, no drunkard, not violent but gentle, not quarrelsome, and no lover of money. He must manage his household well, keeping his children submissive and respectful in every way; for if a man does not know how to manage his own household, how can he care for God's church? He must not be a recent convert, or he may be puffed up with conceit and fall into the condemnation of the devil; moreover, he must be well thought of by outsiders, or he may fall into reproach and the snare of the devil (I Tim. 3:1–7; cf. Titus 1:5–9; II Tim.).

The minister is expected to be a "good man," as Quintilian put it. Skill in the Quintilianic tradition of great speaking was not demanded in the Bible. God was willing to use Moses though he was not eloquent (Exodus 4:10–17). The Bible does expect that the servant of God be trustworthy (I Cor. 4:2), persuasive (II Cor. 5:11), and diligent in correctly handling the word of truth (II Tim. 2:15).

Each of the above philosophies of communication—results, truth, methods, and the good man speaking well—has found expression in Christian preaching. At times they have been stressed in an unbalanced way to the harm of the church. In more responsible hands they have been applied in sound balance to the edification of Christendom. Each of the philosophies has a place, and none should be dropped. Judiciousness and balance in their use is the key to their integrity and effectiveness. They have provided a significant contribution to Christian preaching.

CONTEMPORARY ATTITUDES

Modern views of the ethics of persuasion are more direct, specific, and organized than in ancient times. They may be seen in current writings on persuasion as well as in contemporary political oratory, newscasting, advertising, publications, and preaching. Some view all persuasion as intrinsically bad. Others consider it intrinsically good, even though it is used unethically at times. Still others see persuasion as neutral, or amoral—neither good nor bad but potentially good or bad depending on how it is used. A brief look at these three views follows.

Persuasion Is Bad

Those who hold that persuasion is bad point to the "tyranny of words" over susceptible humanity. Persuasion, they say, puts a powerful set of tools into the hands of unscrupulous tyrants to subjugate helpless victims. Hitler is cited as a prime example of such despotism. Emotionally laden words, subliminal motivation, suggestion, and other "questionable persuasive tricks" form the perfect weapons to manipulate an unsuspecting and naive society, say persuasion's critics. Political oratory, high-pressure television commercials, magazine and mail advertisements, and door-to-door salesmen frequently exemplify the proposition that persuasion is an evil weapon.

Nor is religion exempt from such criticism. High-powered invitations, psychological gimmicks, and crowd pressures have been known to manipulate audiences by short-circuiting their normal reasoning powers, causing them to make decisions they otherwise would not have made.

Existentialist theologians, especially Sören Kierkegaard, argue that because the subjective life is the domain of ethico-religious beliefs—traditional lecturing, arguing, and persuading may produce results opposite to those sought by the persuader.[12]

In sharp contrast to psychological persuasion, Kierkegaard urges "edifying discourse" as the form of communicating ethico-religious truth. Edifying discourse stresses *indirect* communication. Some techniques of indirection are ambiguity, absolute paradox, contradiction, parables, pseudonyms, imaginary characters, and dialogue between these characters. The sermon, in this view, should

12. See Raymond E. Anderson, "Kierkegaard's Theory of Communication," *Speech Monographs* 30 (March 1963): 1-14.

confront the listener with the "offense" of Christianity, sin as a uniquely Christian concept, and contemporaneousness. Kierkegaard maintains that these edifying discourse techniques will elicit a subjective, existential response from the listener. They are humanitarian in that they protect the individual's right and ability to make his own decision.

Many rhetoricians and homileticians would agree with most of the above criticisms of persuasion. Some, however, would protest that Kierkegaard draws too fine a line between edifying discourse and persuasive communication, and that edifying discourse is merely one of a number of forms of persuasion. This charge is admitted and the difference made one of degree.[13] The desirability of many of Kierkegaard's techniques is recognized. They have been used for many decades by able speakers and rhetoricians. The wise preacher will use both edifying discourse and persuasive speech where they best fit the situation.

Nevertheless, the view that persuasion is intrinsically bad must be rejected. History is replete with persuaders who have elevated mankind to sublime heights. Moses, Jesus, Paul, Luther, and many contemporary preachers have used persuasion effectively and responsibly. Demosthenes, Cicero, Pitt, Lincoln, Churchill, and Roosevelt are among statesmen who have been persuasive and ethical rhetoricians.

Ethical speakers cannot forsake rhetoric in a day when it is greatly needed. To do so would be to leave this powerful tool only in the hands of unscrupulous tyrants. It would provide no recourse to responsible leaders. No ethical voice would be raised to stay the flood of hucksters hawking their wares to a naive public. There may be alternatives to the use of persuasion, but most, if not all, of these alternatives fall into the category of force—authoritarianism, bribery, torture, and war. The alternatives are far worse than persuasion itself.

Persuasion Is Good

Ancient and modern rhetoricians have contended that a close bond exists between ethics and rhetoric. Aristotle is generally represented as an objective or dispassionate observer of speech practices. He set forth what he considered rhetoric to be: "the faculty of discovering in the particular case what are the available

13. Ibid., p. 5.

means of persuasion."[14] Although he is sometimes represented as holding the neutral position because he recognized that rhetoric could be used unethically, his *Rhetoric* seems to indicate that it was good and useful.[15] He mentions four reasons for believing this: (1) truth and justice are superior to their opposites, and if wrong decisions are made it is because advocates of truth and justice fail; (2) knowledge alone does not persuade some people, it needs the instrument of instruction—rhetoric; (3) rhetoric aids an orator to argue both sides of a question, thus promoting the discovery of truths; and (4) rhetoric is needed to help defend oneself.[16]

Further, Aristotle argued strongly for the character (*ethos*) of the speaker himself. His famous lines are:

> It is not true, as some writers on the art maintain, that the probity of the speaker contributes nothing to his persuasiveness; on the contrary we might almost affirm that his character [*ethos*] is the most potent of all the means of persuasion.[17]

Thus, it is not strange to hear him say, "Rhetoric is a kind of offshoot, on the one hand, of dialectic, and, on the other, of that study of ethics which may properly be called political."[18]

Quintilian, the Roman teacher of rhetoric, also linked ethics with rhetoric.

> My aim, then, is the education of the perfect orator. The first essential for such an one is that he should be a good man, and consequently we demand of him not merely the possession of exceptional gifts of speech, but of all the excellencies of character as well.[19]

This is not an isolated and happenstance statement by the ancient Roman teacher, for later in his text he pursues the idea further: "But above all he [the orator] must possess the quality which Cato places first and which is in the very nature of things the greatest and most important, that is, he must be a good man."[20]

Quintilian was concerned lest rhetoric be debased through usage by evil men. Such a tragedy would mean that the great teacher's

---

14. Cooper, *Rhetoric of Aristotle,* p. 7.

15. Ibid., p. 5.

16. Ibid., pp. 5, 6.

17. Ibid., p. 9.

18. Ibid.

19. H. E. Butler, *Institutio Oratoria,* 1.9.

20. Ibid., 12. Intr. 3-1.1.

labor would have rendered the worst of services to mankind. Nature would have proved herself a stepmother instead of a mother regarding the greatest gift to man—the power of speech. And it would have been better that men be born dumb than to turn the gifts of providence to their mutual destruction.[21] The ancient master enlarges upon his point by rebuking the orator who robs his study time by indulging in such distractions as the development of one's estate, excessive anxiety over household affairs, devotion to hunting, or the sacrificing of whole days to the theatre.[22]

Some modern rhetoricians would not go as far as Quintilian. Nevertheless, many agree with his general point of view. Donald K. Smith rejects the idea that speaking skill is ethically neutral.[23] He maintains that ethics and rhetoric are somehow intertwined and that public speaking is intrinsically a moral action. He argues that rhetoric involves the well-being of others and announces, either explicitly or implicitly, certain values. Thus the speaker, in choosing to act in one way or another, affirms or denies certain ethical standards. Professor Smith goes on to say: "Skill in speaking does not assure moral action. But ineptness forestalls the possibility of moral achievement in the vast number of situations in which men talk to one another."[24]

Erwin P. Bettinghaus meets the questions usually put by objectors to persuasion and proceeds to argue in favor of persuasion research and usage.[25] He maintains that persuasive effects are limited, but that he prefers to know what he is doing to people. Persuasion, furthermore, is applied to problems most people agree need solving, and acquiring knowledge including persuasive knowledge is necessary if people are going to understand the world surrounding them.[26] Bettinghaus urges the development of a set of ethics, a knowledge of persuasion, and some criteria for decision making. Persuasion, he claims, should be protected by law and custom. An open society and the development of the mass media are needed to contribute to man's progress.

---

21. Ibid.

22. Ibid.

23. Donald K. Smith, *Man Speaking: A Rhetoric of Public Speech* (New York: Dodd, Mead, and Co., 1969), pp. 228 ff.

24. Ibid., p. 248.

25. Erwin P. Bettinghaus, *Persuasive Communication,* 2d ed. (New York: Holt, Rinehart and Winston, 1973), pp. 280 ff.

26. Ibid.

Jane Blankenship points out that rhetoric should not be confined to a few leaders in a democracy. All citizens should cooperate in decision making. Furthermore, she writes, "The speaker, as a participator in a liberal democracy, should not be misled by the contention that rhetoric is solely a technique and as such has no inherent morality."[27] Blankenship argues that because they involve the value judgments of the speaker as well as the ends and means of discourse, persuasion and ethics cannot be separated.[28]

Among theologians and homileticians persuasion is for the most part considered moral, even mandatory. The list of protagonists is almost endless.

John A. Broadus, one of the most influential homileticians of modern times, wrote:

> But the chief part of what we commonly call application is *persuasion.* It is not enough to convince men of truth, nor enough to make them see how it applies to themselves, and how it might be practicable for them to act it out,—but we must "persuade men."[29]

So convinced was Broadus of the value of persuasion that he added:

> Do we not well know, from observation and from experience, that a man may see his duty and still neglect it? Have we not often been led by persuasion to do something, good or bad, from which we were shrinking? It is proper, then, to persuade, to exhort, even to entreat.[30]

Harry Emerson Fosdick, one of America's most able liberal theologians and preachers, was a great pulpit orator. He advocated what he called cooperative dialogue, or preaching that was counseling. He wrote:

> It certainly takes more than a preacher alone in the pulpit to make an effective sermon. If, however, the people can be there too, so that the sermon is not a dogmatic monologue but a cooperative dialogue in which the congregation's objections, questions, doubts and confirmations are fairly stated and dealt with, something worthwhile is likely to happen.[31]

---

27. Jane Blankenship, *Public Speaking: A Rhetorical Perspective* (Englwood Cliffs, N.J.: Prentice-Hall, 1966), p. 28.

28. Ibid., p. 29.

29. John A. Broadus, *On the Preparation and Delivery of Sermons,* rev. Jesse Burton Weatherspoon (New York: Harper and Brothers, 1944), p. 215.

30. Ibid.

31. Harry Emerson Fosdick, *The Living of These Days: An Autobiography* (New York: Harper and Row, 1956), p. 97.

Fosdick accomplished this dialogue effect in the pulpit by himself. He would raise the questions, objections, and problems with the content of his sermon and then proceed to answer them. Such a practice was not a case of setting up a "straw man" which he could easily demolish. Fosdick tackled real problems and handled them effectively.

One cannot suppose that Fosdick therefore did not believe in persuasion. In his own words he added:

> My own major difficulty sprang from the fact that starting a sermon with a problem, however vital and urgent, suggests a discussion, a dissertation, a treatise. A sermon, however, is more than that. The preacher's business is not merely to discuss repentance but to persuade people to repent; not merely to debate the meaning and possibility of Christian faith, but to produce Christian faith in the lives of his listeners; not merely to talk about the available power of God to bring victory over trouble and temptation, but to send people out from their worship on Sunday with victory in their possession. A preacher's task is to create in his congregation the thing he is talking about.[32]

George Sweazey, formerly of the Presbyterian Department of Evangelism, now a professor of preaching at Princeton Theological Seminary, claimed that no other method could replace preaching as the supreme evangelistic opportunity.[33] He equated warm evangelistic preaching with a healthy church and a lack of it with a weak church. "One clear advantage in preaching, as an evangelistic method," he wrote, "is the time it gives for persuasion."[34]

Richard R. Caemmerer, a Lutheran theologian and homiletician, likened the ancient art of persuasion to Christian preaching for repentance. "Persuasive speech," he claimed, "isn't just for entertainment. It makes a difference in people."[35] Henry Grady Davis defined the proclamation of the gospel as speech controlled by the nature of the gospel. Wary of high pressured forms of persuasion, he nevertheless saw the purpose of proclamation as reaching and reclaiming the lost. He stated: "It takes the form of an announcement that waits to be heard and believed, a direct call

---

32. Ibid., p. 99.

33. George E. Sweazey, *Effective Evangelism* (New York: Harper and Brothers, 1953), p. 159.

34. Ibid., p. 160.

35. Richard R. Caemmerer, *Preaching for the Church* (St. Louis: Concordia Publishing House, 1959), p. 35.

from God to be answered, a personal offer to be embraced, a personal promise to be trusted and acted upon."[36]

Thomas V. Liske, Roman Catholic theologian and speech teacher, pointed out that no profession utilizes speech more than the priesthood. Talking is one of the chief instruments in doing the work for which the priest is ordained. Liske wrote:

> Not only must he convince people of the truth of Christ's teachings and persuade them to live those doctrines, he must also by well-delivered instructions dispose the souls of prospective converts for the grace of divine faith, he must teach children in the classroom, he must speak effectively, and briefly, to persuade sinners in the confessional to change their lives, he must give persuasive advice in an effective way to those who seek his solution of their problems. . . .[37]

When Aristotle claimed that all public speaking should be ultimately persuasive, Liske felt he was speaking directly for the benefit of Catholic priests.[38]

And finally, in a penetrating book, *The Urgency of Preaching,* Kyle Haselden pleads for the improvement and utilization of effective persuasive preaching.[39] He asks, ". . . why turn over to the enemy the best weapons, the spoken word?"[40] He frankly avows, "In the communication of the gospel the spoken word is the best weapon, the superlative tool; in this area it has superiority over all other forms of communication."[41]

Although the opinions cited above are few in number they are representative of much theological and homiletical thought today. Some contemporaries, of course, disagree, but it is safe to say that the majority of Christian theologians and preachers consider persuasive preaching valuable and essential to the task of the ministry. Most recognize its weaknesses and abuses, but they refuse to forsake it just because some demean it.

Persuasion Is Neutral

A third position sometimes presented is that persuasion is really neutral or amoral—neither good nor bad. It becomes good if used

---

36. Henry Grady Davis, *Design for Preaching* (Philadelphia: Muhlenberg Press, 1958), p. 111.

37. Thomas V. Liske, *Effective Preaching* (New York: Macmillan Co., 1951), p. 1.

38. Ibid., p. 207.

39. Kyle Haselden, *The Urgency of Preaching* (New York: Harper and Row, 1963).

40. Ibid., p. 24.

41. Ibid.

ethically. It becomes bad if used unethically. Persuasion is likened to shooting a gun (to defend oneself or to murder another), flying an airplane (as a hospital ship or as a bomber), or discovering how to split an atom (either for peaceful or war-like purposes). Any of these activities can be used for moral or immoral purposes.

It is difficult to discern how much the neutral position differs from the view that persuasion is intrinsically good, although sometimes used in evil ways or for ignoble ends, or both. A few scholars, reputable and respected, who share this view nevertheless assume at least a shading of difference.

Long ago Augustine treated rhetoric as indifferent, available to moral and evil men alike.

> For since by means of the art of rhetoric both truth and falsehood are urged, who would dare to say that truth should stand in the person of its defenders unarmed against lying, so that they who wish to urge falsehoods may know how to make their listeners benevolent, or attentive, or docile in their presentation, while the defenders of truth are ignorant of that art? Should they speak briefly, clearly, and plausibly while the defenders of truth speak so that they tire their listeners, make themselves difficult to understand and what they have to say dubious? Should they oppose the truth with fallacious arguments and assert falsehoods, while the defenders of truth have no ability either to defend the truth or to oppose the false? Should they, urging the minds of their listeners into error, ardently exhort them, moving them by speech so that they terrify, sadden, and exhilarate them, while the defenders of truth are sluggish, cold, and somnolent? Who is so foolish as to think this to be wisdom? While the faculty of eloquence, which is of great value in urging either evil or justice, is in itself indifferent, why should it not be obtained for the uses of the good in the service of truth if the evil usurp it for the winning of perverse and vain causes in defense of iniquity and error?[42]

In spite of its indifferences, he concluded, persuasion should not be surrendered to evil forces. It should be used for the good in the service of truth.

Lester Thonssen and A. Craig Baird approached their criticism of speech on the assumption that "the techniques of rhetoric are amoral, capable of both enlightened and evil use, depending upon the character of the speaker."[43] They further contended that the

---

42. D. W. Robertson, Jr., trans., *Saint Augustine, On Christian Doctrine,* Book 4 (New York: Liberal Arts Press, 1958), 2.3.

43. Thonssen and Baird, *Speech Criticism,* p. 471.

amoral character of rhetoric should not keep critics from considering the ethical implications of public statements.

A slight variation of the neutral position is offered by James C. McCroskey, who claims his view of the ethics of rhetorical techniques to be an amoral one. By this he means that ethical considerations must refer to the speaker himself rather than to his act of communication.[44] Furthermore, according to McCroskey, this ethical judgment turns on the intent of the communicator toward his audience.[45] If the speaker's intent is for the good of other people, then he is ethical. If the speaker's intent is to harm or bilk people, then he is unethical.[46]

Wayne C. Minnick is sometimes represented as holding the neutral position concerning the ethics of rhetoric. If so, this position refers only to certain methods of rhetoric. It is more accurate to relate his attitude as he himself does, i.e., that some of the means of persuasion are generally agreed to be unethical; some means of persuasion appear to be sound; and certain means of persuasion may be good or bad, depending upon their usage. As he says, "From an ethical viewpoint, they appear to be intrinsically neutral."[47] Under the neutral category Minnick includes such persuasive methods as suggestion; rousing the emotions; name-calling; use of personal prestige; appeals to testimony, tradition, or majority opinion; and appeals to needs, wants, or motives.[48] His ethical and unethical list of methods will be discussed later.

Finally, Robert T. Oliver, an influential contemporary teacher of rhetoric, maintains that ethical criticisms of rhetoric should not be lightly dismissed. Oliver reminds us that writing skill may produce both a Machiavelli and a John Locke. Scientific acumen may produce hydrogen bombs and bacteriological warfare as well as profitable goods and life-saving medicine. He writes: "What must not be lost sight of is that persuasion is an art, which may be used for either good or evil."[49] Therefore, he maintains, we should not

---

44. James C. McCroskey, *An Introduction to Rhetorical Communication,* 2d ed. (Englewood Cliffs, N.J.: Prentice-Hall, 1972), p. 272.

45. Ibid., pp. 268, 272.

46. Ibid., p. 269.

47. Wayne C. Minnick, *The Art of Persuasion,* 2d ed. (Boston: Houghton Mifflin Co., 1968), pp. 285-86.

48. Ibid.

49. Robert T. Oliver, *The Psychology of Persuasive Speech,* 2d ed. (New York: Longman, 1957), p. 22.

be tricked into the negative attitude toward rhetoric to the sacrificing of its profitable aspects.

Oliver insightfully reminds us that ethics confront us in virtually all of our activities. Ethics should not be confined to rhetoric but considered part of the broader problem of morality in general.[50]

CONCLUSIONS ON THE ETHICAL SITUATION

The view that persuasion is intrinsically bad must be rejected. Most rhetoricians agree with the condemnation of certain distortions of persuasion. Moreover, responsible rhetoricians, homileticians, and preachers favor the type of communication labeled "edifying discourse" by Sören Kierkegaard and the existentialists. At the same time they would perpetuate the traditional form of speech such as lecturing, arguing, and persuading as part of the preaching act.

Ancient and contemporary writers believe in the intrinsic value or "goodness" of persuasion, although at the same time they recognize that false prophets, sophists, and charlatans exist, and they sometimes use rhetoric for selfish and evil purposes. Some view persuasion as a neutral or amoral tool available to ethical and unethical communicators alike.

A form of the last two views—that persuasion either is intrinsically good or at least neutral—is probably the soundest view. Arguing about the superiority of one of these views over the other seems irrelevant. We know that persuasion, whether good or neutral, is too often used by unethical communicators. Of more concern to us is the question, How does one determine when persuasion is ethical or unethical? It appears that the ethics of persuasion is usually measured by two factors: the ends of persuasion and the means of persuasion.

---

50. Ibid., pp. 22-23.

Three

The Ethical Measure of Persuasive Preaching: Measuring Ethics by the Ends Sought

Most rhetoricians approach the study of the ethics of persuasion in terms of the *ends* sought, *means* used, or both. Obviously, achieving good ends by using good methods is considered ethical. The problem comes into focus, however, when good ends are achieved through bad means, or when either good or bad means are used to achieve bad ends.

MEASURING ETHICS BY THE ENDS SOUGHT

Most speakers have both specific and general purposes or goals. Specific goals would be to inform, to stimulate, to convince, or to actuate. In secular speaking, entertainment may be the object. Specific goals may be broken down into even more sharply defined purposes.

There are, however, certain larger ends of communication by which men measure the ethics of persuasion and under which the specific purposes operate. These may be studied under the general categories of social-effects (or utilitarian) ends; scientific and rational ends; political ends; and theological ends. These are briefly described as follows.

Social-Effects Ends

Virtually all rhetoricians, except unethical sophists, use as their ultimate purpose the good of individuals in particular and society in general. The ethics of rhetorical methods and techniques, they contend, should be measured in terms of whether they help or hurt people.

Individual Ends

Albert Schweitzer, who measured ethics by reverence for life, wrote, "Reverence for life affords me my fundamental principle of morality: namely, that good consists in maintaining, assisting and embracing life, and that to destroy, to harm or to hinder life is evil."[1] Sören Kierkegaard objected to traditional persuasive techniques on the grounds of what Raymond E. Anderson called "a protest against the dehumanization of modern man."[2] Everett Lee Hunt had the well-being of society in mind when he defined rhetoric as "the study of men persuading men to make free choices."[3] Robert T. Oliver, although recognizing the problems connected with the "audience-centered" speech, gave his support to the social-effects principle.[4] Describing this view as "what is good for society as a whole, in the long run is ethical; what is detrimental to society is unethical,"[5] he claims that this principle "readily lends itself for application to persuasive speaking."[6] Winston L. Brembeck and William S. Howell advocate "the social context" or "social utility" theory as the most desirable end of persuasive speaking.[7] They ask of the persuasive process: "Will the social group concerned benefit? Is there a revealed or concealed penalty to be paid? Could injury to one or a few individuals outweigh the group gains?"[8]

Group Ends

A variation of the social effects theory, relating to the group basis of ethical standards, is described by Professor Donald K.

---

1. "Schweitzer's Words: Light in the Jungle," *The New York Times Magazine,* 9 January 1955, p. 73.

2. Raymond E. Anderson, "Kierkegaard's Theory of Communication," *Speech Monographs* 30 (March 1963): 13.

3. Everett Lee Hunt, "Rhetoric as a Humane Study," *Quarterly Journal of Speech* 41 (April 1955): 114.

4. Robert T. Oliver, *The Psychology of Persuasive Speech,* 2d ed. (New York: Longman, 1957), pp. 24 ff.

5. Ibid.

6. Ibid.

7. Winston L. Brembeck and William S. Howell, *Persuasion: A Means of Social Influence,* 2d ed. (Englewood Cliffs, N.J.: Prentice-Hall, 1976), p. 245.

8. Ibid.

Smith.[9] He points out that one approach to the ethical analysis of persuasion is "observing the relationship between particular public speeches and the social institutions supported and served by these speeches."[10] Thus one needs to study the situation surrounding the ethics of teaching, preaching, courtroom speaking, and salesmanship in terms of the ethical standards set up by their respective institutions—the school, church, court of law, and business.

In this view a lawyer, for example, would be judged ethically by the laws and customs of courtroom procedure and not by general standards of the ethics of communication. Stacking evidence in a client's favor while deliberately omitting evidence damaging to that client is not only ethically permissible in the courtroom, it is expected.

In this sense certain preaching ends and means, which might be ethically permissible in the institutional church, might seem reprehensible to observers outside the church. The Christian preacher, however, must remember that his ethical standards should be at least as high as those of the secular world's standards. The success or failure of a preacher's gospel message may depend upon whether it fulfills minimal or maximal ethical standards.

Communication ends that benefit society as a whole, whether of racial, privileged, or ethnic groups, are important. America, as well as other countries, functions on the parliamentary procedure that the majority should prevail in establishing laws, in ruling, and in voting. We also believe, however, that the rights of the minorities should be protected.

Ends of persuasion that violate the rights of others are not only unethical, they may also be illegal. Because minority groups have sometimes been denied basic rights, some revolutionaries have turned from the traditional rhetorical ends and means of negotiation to attain their goals. Whereas once they spoke at rallies, debated, discussed, dialogued, lobbied, or otherwise talked or wrote, now they have turned to nonverbal action. Both their ends and means of attaining those ends have changed dramatically. Once they had a vague goal of "freedom and equality." Now they specifically want equal job opportunities, better education, improved living conditions, and human dignity. Once they spoke for these rights. Now they may burn, loot, take over schools or

---

9. Donald K. Smith, *Man Speaking: A Rhetoric of Public Speech* (New York: Dodd, Mead, and Co., 1969), pp. 238 ff.

10. Ibid.

churches, demand uncompromising settlements, hijack airliners, or kidnap political figures or prominent persons.

The church has not been spared from some of these tactics. On Sunday morning, 4 May, 1969, James Forman of the National Black Economic Development Conference stood up in the Riverside Church of New York City and issued a "Black Manifesto" to the Christian churches and Jewish synagogues of the land.[11] Forman demanded $500 million in reparations from the "racist" religious establishment for Blacks, whom churches and synagogues had allegedly subjugated for years.[12]

The Rev. Ernest T. Campbell, pastor of the Riverside Church, answered the challenge ten weeks later in a sympathetic sermon entitled, "The Case for Reparations."[13] The "Black Manifesto" confrontation at Riverside Church was only the beginning of disruptions of worship services, denominational conventions, and religious institutions.[14]

Both secular government and religious institutions need to settle the question of the "tools of rhetoric" that will be used to solve men's problems in the future.[15] Radical extremists already seem to have set their course. They seem to feel that in using the rhetoric of violence they have nothing to lose—nowhere to go but up. Robert L. Scott and Donald K. Smith list four reasons why extremists feel their cause will succeed:

1. *We are already dead.*
2. *We can be reborn.*
3. *We have the stomach for the fight.*
4. *We are united and understand.*[16]

These reasons sound strangely religious. Perhaps if the rank and file membership of the establishment, leaders and followers alike,

---

11. See "The 'Black Manifesto' Declares War on Churches," *Christianity Today,* 23 May 1969, p. 789.

12. See "Itemizing the Reparations Bill," *Christianity Today,* 6 June 1969, p. 839.

13. See Ernest T. Campbell, *Christian Manifesto* (New York: Harper and Row, 1970), chap. 12, "The Case for Reparations."

14. Howard Schomer, "The Manifesto and the Magnificat," *The Christian Century,* 25 June 1969, pp. 866-67.

15. See Franklyn S. Haiman, "The Rhetoric of the Streets: Some Legal and Ethical Considerations," *Quarterly Journal of Speech* 53 (April 1967): 99-111.

16. See Robert L. Scott and Donald K. Smith, "The Rhetoric of Confrontation," *Quarterly Journal of Speech* 55 (February 1969): 5-6.

would work on humanity's problems with similar dedication, violence and terrorism would not be necessary to accomplish goals. But because the great mass of people and the majority of age-old institutions seem satisfied with "things as they are," radical minority groups may continue to utilize coercion instead of persuasion to attain their goals. At least these are some of the underlying motives for dissatisfaction with the church and its sacred rhetoric—preaching. Christians need to familiarize themselves with the criticisms of these hallowed traditions.

Scientific and Rational Ends

Some men measure the ethics of persuasion by scientific and rational ends. Thus Leonard Doob, a social psychologist, maintained that ends are right if, at a given time, they are scientific and of value to society. Conversely, ends are wrong if they are unscientific and of doubtful value to society.[17] Alfred Korzybski, Polish mathematician, scientist, and general semanticist, voiced a form of the scientific ends of communication theory when he wrote: "Any map or language, to be of maximum usefulness, should, in structure, be similar to the structure of the empirical world."[18] Korzybski argued that language forms that do not correspond to their "fact territories" are misleading and potentially dangerous,[19] whereas language forms that do correspond to their fact territories are reliable and helpful.

Other men think of the ethics of persuasion in terms of the rationality of the content and process. Aristotle began his *Rhetoric* by saying, "Rhetoric is the counterpart of Dialectic."[20] Of his three modes of proof, *logos* (or logic) received favored treatment. His extended treatment of logic is found in *The Organon,* the *Prior Analytics,* and the *Posterior Analytics.*[21] Plato's dialogues are

---

17. Leonard Doob, *Public Opinion and Propaganda* (New York: Henry Holt, 1948), p. 240.

18. Alfred Korzybski, *Science and Sanity: An Introduction to Non-Aristotelian Systems and General Semantics,* 2d ed. (Lancaster, Pa.: International Non-Aristotelian Library Publishing Company, 1941), p. 11. See this notion expanded in this same work, chap. 4, "On Structure." See also the writings of Stuart Chase, S. I. Hayakawa, Wendell Johnson, Irving J. Lee, and others who followed Korzybski in the discipline of general semantics.

19. Ibid., p. 59.

20. Lane Cooper, trans. *The Rhetoric of Aristotle* (New York: Appleton-Century-Crofts, 1932), p. 1.

21. For these see works such as Richard McKeon, ed., *The Basic Works of Aristotle* (New York: Random House, 1941).

examples of ancient logical argument. Today, Franklyn S. Haiman affirms that the development of man's ability to reason is one of the goals of our democracy. He condemns as unethical any persuasive method that aims at circumventing man's reasoning process in order to elicit "nonreflective, semi-conscious responses."[22]

Keep in mind that the view of scientific and rational ends is held in connection with its effects on people and not as an end in itself. As such, it is also related to the social-effects category.

Political Ends

The American political system and democratic society form a widespread and influential end of communication. Thus Professor Karl R. Wallace bases his ethics of communication on the values of our democratic society.[23] He lists these as: (1) the dignity and worth of the individual; (2) the equality of opportunity for all; (3) the freedom to act as long as we do not infringe upon the freedom of others; and (4) the capability of each individual to understand the nature, goals, values, procedures, and processes of democracy.[24] Professor Wallace's methods of persuasion, suggested in light of these democratic tenets, are:

1. Inasmuch as a communicator during a speech is the sole source of argument and information, he must know his subject thoroughly. The speaker should ask himself: "Can I answer squarely without evasion, any relevant question that a hearer might ask?"[25]
2. The communicator must distinguish clearly between fact and opinion.
3. The communicator will invariably make public the sources of his information and opinion. This will include the revelation of any bias, prejudice, or motives—both personal or in his sources.
4. The communicator will always accept and respect difference of argument and opinion.[26]

---

22. Franklyn S. Haiman, "Democratic Ethics and the Hidden Persuaders," *Quarterly Journal of Speech* 44 (December 1958): 385.

23. Karl R. Wallace, "An Ethical Basis of Communication," *The Speech Teacher,* 4 (January 1955): 1-9.

24. Ibid.

25. Ibid.

26. Ibid.

The great latitude provided for freedom of speech by the American Constitution has opened the door to the most extreme examples of political dissent and social protest rhetoric. For example, even though Saul Alinsky, social agitator and protest organizer, believed deeply in the American democratic political values mentioned above, his set of rules for ethical judgment of communication means and ends could lead to the overthrow of these values. Framed in a situational ethics context of speaking and acting, these rules are:

1. One's concern with the ethics of means and ends varies inversely with one's personal interest in the issue.
2. The judgment of the ethics of means is dependent upon the political position of those sitting in judgment.
3. In war the end justifies almost any means.
4. Judgment must be made in the context of the times in which the action occurred and not from any other chronological vantage point.
5. Concern with ethics increases with the number of means available and vice versa.
6. The less important the end desired, the more one can afford to engage in ethical evaluations of the means.
7. Generally, success or failure is a strong determinant of ethics.
8. The morality of a means depends upon whether the means is being employed at a time of imminent defeat or imminent victory.
9. Any effective means automatically is judged by the opposition as unethical.
10. You do what you can with what you have and clothe it with moral garments.
11. Goals must be phrased in general terms like "Liberty, Equality, Fraternity"; "Of the Common Welfare"; "Pursuit of Happiness"; or "Bread and Peace."[27]

Although not all radicals adopt Alinsky's rules, most of them function in the spirit and application of them as their standard of ethics of the means and ends of persuasion.

In contrast, Karl Wallace's set of democratic values and his guidelines for persuasive communication have been widely used as

---

27. Saul D. Alinsky, *Rules for Radicals* (New York: Random House, 1971), pp. 26-47.

an ideal standard for measuring the ethical goals of communication in the American political society. However, the American political system with its democratic processes "represents a minority view"[28] in our world today.

The Nazi political philosophy in Germany under Adolf Hitler during World War II was built upon the simple ethical principle that the ends of national survival and of National Socialism justified any means of persuasion. The test of success was the pragmatic test of results. Not only did Hitler's speeches contain lies, deceptions, distortions, and inaccuracies, his whole propaganda and ministry were built around such methods.[29]

A favorite persuasive method pressed constantly upon the German people was the two-valued, either-or technique. Hitler and his propagandists made everything either "Aryan" (everything that was good, helpful, Nazi), or "non-Aryan" (Jewish, bad, harmful, anti-Nazi).[30] Complete agreement with and support of Nazism meant that one was Aryan. Disagreement with or opposition to any part of Nazism meant that one was non-Aryan. Hitler's two-valued orientation extended to people, greetings ("Heil Hitler"), literature, religion, physics, and even animals. Rabbits and Jewish-owned chickens, dogs, and cats were weak and timid—therefore non-Aryan. Lions and other strong animals were considered Aryan.[31] With such persuasion, Nazism led a whole world into a devastating war and Germany into tragic disaster.

Communism in our day approaches a similar political orientation. Like Nazism, Communism demands absolute loyalty to the state, complete trust in the party, and suspicion and hatred of all enemies. Objectivity, impartiality, and normal interpretation of terms are not mandatory in their communication. Their political ends justify any means of attaining them in persuasion, international mediation, or war. Thus they measure the ethics of persuasion by its contribution to the success of the social struggle.[32]

---

28. Richard L. Johannesen, *Ethics in Human Communication* (Columbus, Ohio: Charles E. Merrill Publishing Co., 1975), p. 30.

29. See Adolf Hitler, *Mein Kampf,* trans. Ralph Manheim (Boston: Houghton Mifflin, 1953); and Haig Bosmajian, "Nazi Persuasion and the Crowd Mentality," *Western Speech* 29 (Spring 1965): 68-78.

30. See S. I. Hayakawa, *Language in Thought and Action* (New York: Harcourt, Brace and Co., 1949), pp. 223-27.

31. Ibid.

32. See on this Jack H. Butler, "Russian Rhetoric: A Discipline Manipulated by Communism." *Quarterly Journal of Speech* 50 (October 1964): 229-39; Robert T.

When Christians interact with such ends, they should avoid either/or attitudes on their own part. They should see both values and dangers in any political goal and not condemn any political philosophy wholesale without study. For example, even though the above listed rules of ethical judgment drawn up by Saul Alinsky are radical, they do contain some truth.

Alinsky's rules of ethics are sometimes the only effective tools of rhetoric available to minority groups and underdogs of society and are the methods that have successfully jolted the entrenched establishments of our day. Like it or not, these principles and actions have sometimes produced results for their users where more traditional verbal persuasive methods have not. Also, some Christians have used a few of these radical ethical rules more than they might be willing to admit. What else could explain Calvin's persecution of Servetus, the church inquisitions, some of the ancient Crusades, the battles between Catholics and Protestants in Ireland, and the religious wars in Lebanon? Christians must not excuse their own ethical injustices while condemning the ethics of others.

But neither can Christians blindly approve the radical political philosophies or goals of Nazism, Communism, or any other worldwide radical political terrorism. Their situation ethics should not be approved. (See discussion of situation ethics in chap. 5.) For example, the tenet, "In war the end justifies almost any means" (Alinsky's Rule 3, listed above) must be rejected.

Radicalism's appeal to man's baser motives rather than his higher ones is deplorable. We must not lie, cheat, steal, kidnap, murder, or destroy to attain our goals.

Radicalism's "immediacy" oriented goals should be questioned. Rapid, disruptive overthrow of people, groups, institutions, or governments may be widely destructive. Immediate goals are important, of course, but long-range goals and methods are probably longer lasting.

Radicalism's dependence upon subjective feelings rather than objective rules should be repudiated. They measure ethics by how a person feels at the moment rather than by any outside tradition or objective laws. Therefore, such relative and radical standards of ethics can lead to hopeless anarchy.

Our world faces a sinister rise in radical and vicious terrorism. *Newsweek* pinpointed thirteen specific terrorist groups and their

---

Oliver, *Culture and Communication* (Springfield, Ill.: Charles C. Thomas, 1962), pp. 88, 104; and others.

world-wide locations.[33] The article concluded that "terrorism is by no means dead," but that individual terrorists can be halted if people are willing to fight them.[34]

Time magazine warned that "the potential for evil will soar if terrorists get their hands on new biological, chemical and radiological—to say nothing of nuclear—arms with which to frighten the innocent."[35]

Almost daily one can observe in the mass media the most recent outbreaks of terrorism. There also appear the fears and warnings of those who are trying to stop it. But terrorist groups, motivated by radical political philosophies, will undoubtedly persist. One shudders at the vision of a nation like America brought to its knees under the threats of even limited atomic attacks from within its own borders.[36] The only alternative to such anarchy is to resist the kind of radical principles that foster it.

Political ends or goals of communication are widespread today. Election promises, political oratory, and national and international diplomacy are all oriented to political ends. As such they are legitimate objects of ethical judgment.

Making the good of society, scientific and rational soundness, and beneficent political ends a measure of the ethics of a free and just society seems sound enough. Only one higher end is imaginable —that of glorifying God. This brings us to a brief consideration of the theological ends of persuasive preaching.

Theological Ends

The Christian persuader should approve and use the legitimate ends of persuasion described above, assuming moderation and balance. Obviously violence, terrorism, and totalitarian political

---

33. These included (1) the Irish Republican Army in Ulster and Ireland, (2) the Red Army Faction in West Germany, (3) FALN in New York, (4) the Japanese Red Army in Western Europe and Lebanon, (5) the Society Against World Imperialism Organization—base unknown, (6) the South Mollucans in Holland, (7) the Ananda Marg in India, (8) the CORU in Miami, (9) the Croation Separatists in Europe and the United States, (10) the Palestinians in Lebanon and Iraq, (11) the Basque Separatists in France and Spain, (12) the Montoneros in Argentina, and (13) the Carlos group in Europe. See "The New War on Terrorism" *Newsweek,* 31 October 1977, pp. 52-53.

34. Ibid.

35. See "War Without Boundaries," *Time,* 31 October 1977, p. 41.

36. See "Terrorist Takeover of Cities Seen," *The Denver Post,* 13 November 1977, p. 9.

ends are not his goals. Nevertheless he preaches for results. He seeks to communicate the truth of God. Scientific accuracy, semantic soundness, and logical rigor are considered part of his responsibility. Certainly the redemption, edification, and benefit of humanity are the objects of his preaching. Furthermore, his ministry is carried out in the social milieu of the church and democratic society.

In addition to his humanity-centered ministry, however, the Christian persuader has an even higher responsibility. He represents another. He follows in the tradition of the ancient herald who spoke a message not his own, but in behalf of his master. As Robert H. Mounce points out concerning the herald in the ancient world, "The proclamation must be delivered exactly as it was received. As the mouthpiece of his master he dare not add his own interpretation."[37] So it is with the Christian herald. He is sent to preach by divine commission: "And how can men preach unless they are sent?" (Rom. 10:15a). So Paul and Barnabas were "set apart" by the Holy Spirit to do the work He had called them to do (Acts 13:2). And they were sent out to preach by the church at Antioch (Acts 13:3). That their message was not their own was attested by Paul when he said to the Corinthians, "For what we preach is not ourselves, but Jesus Christ as Lord . . ." (II Cor. 4:5).

With a divine commission and a prescribed message Paul and his fellow workers preached the gospel fearlessly, always toward the end of pleasing God, not men. He wrote to the Galatians: "Am I now seeking the favor of men, or of God? Or am I trying to please men? If I were still pleasing men, I should not be a servant of Christ" (Gal. 1:10). And similarly he wrote to the Thessalonians, "But just as we have been approved by God to be entrusted with the gospel, so we speak, not to please men, but to please God who tests our hearts" (I Thess. 2:4).

These statements should not be construed to mean that Paul did not care for people and thus did not make them an end of his preaching. Of his own Jewish brethren he cried: "I have great sorrow and unceasing anguish in my heart. For I could wish that I myself were accursed and cut off from Christ for the sake of my brethren, my kinsmen by race" (Rom. 9:2, 3). And of others he

---

37. Robert H. Mounce, *The Essential Nature of New Testament Preaching* (Grand Rapids: Wm. B. Eerdmans Publishing Co., 1960), p. 13.

wrote, "Knowing the fear of the Lord, we persuade men" (II Cor. 5:11a).

Today, Christian preachers are challenged to adhere to the purposes of preaching: to please God, to reconcile men, to build men up in the faith, and to build up the body of Christ. In the words of Paul to the Corinthians, preachers testify: "So we are ambassadors for Christ, God making his appeal through us. We beseech you on behalf of Christ, be reconciled to God" (II Cor. 5:20). And from the Epistle to the Ephesians they learn to use their gifts

> for the equipment of the saints, for the work of ministry, for building up the body of Christ, until we all attain to the unity of the faith and of the knowledge of the Son of God, to mature manhood, to the measure of the stature of the fulness of Christ (Eph. 4:12–13).

The above described theological ends are not exhaustive. They will be discussed more thoroughly in chapter 5, "Ethical Standards for Persuasive Preaching." These ends are biblical, comprehensive, and binding upon Christian persuaders. They are the ends against which all persuasive preaching should be measured.

DO THE ENDS JUSTIFY THE MEANS

Rare is the rhetorician or homiletician who would unreservedly argue that the ends of persuasion justify any means used. But even here, one cannot establish an absolute and claim that the end never justifies the means. For example, to save a life, to protect the dignity of an individual in an extreme case, or to safeguard national security in a time of war or impending war, lying is sometimes justified as the lesser of two evils.

Courts of law expect lawyers to stack evidence in favor of their clients, deliberately avoiding the introduction of facts damaging to their case. Cross examination is provided to ferret out buried evidence. As Brembeck and Howell ask, "If the end does not justify the means, what can?"[38] There is no answer to that question in a relativistic society. Kenneth Andersen, however, comments on Brembeck and Howell's question by saying, "This is not to suggest

---

38. Brembeck and Howell, *Persuasion,* 1st ed., p. 453. See also on this Joseph Fletcher, *Situation Ethics: The New Morality* (Philadelphia: Westminster Press, 1966), p. 120; and Fletcher, *Moral Responsibility: Situation Ethics at Work* (Philadelphia: Westminster Press, 1967), p. 22.

that any means is justified by any given end or that every means possible could be justified by any end."[39]

As a general rule, then, many reject in persuasion the "end justifies the means" philosophy. Exceptions for extreme circumstances are usually cited and accepted, but falsification, distortion, or deception are normally rejected as ways of life. Most scholars are wary of the philosophy of the end justifying the means because they know the vicious results of it in witch hunts, inquisitions, and character assassinations. Accordingly, Christians reject the idea that the end justifies the means, except in certain extreme circumstances where it clearly applies. Because the ends-means controversy is crucial in contemporary society we will develop it more thoroughly in chapter 5, "Ethical Standards for Persuasive Preaching," along with the absolutist-relativist problem and situation ethics.

"WHAT YOU CAN GET AWAY WITH"

A close companion to the philosophy of "the end justifies the means" is the ethic of "what you can get away with."[40] Although the idea is repulsive, its practice is widespread. Some business sharks, public relations practitioners, political manipulators, and advertising marketers seem content to make this the major if not sole end of their persuasion.[41] Spurred by the tremendous influence of the mass media and the glittering potential of huge profits, these persuaders do not hesitate to stimulate impulsive buying habits, manipulate small children, exploit deeply seated sexual desires, and develop wastefulness of natural resources by encouraging planned obsolescence in the commodities people buy.[42] These practices continue because their proponents know they can get away with them.

Tragically, the philosophy of using any means "you can get away with" has found some adherents in preaching, primarily through playing upon human emotions in an unethical way to get money. Radio and television pitches, the offering of anointed handkerchiefs for healing purposes for "freewill donations," and

---

39. Kenneth E. Andersen, *Persuasion Theory and Practice* (Boston, Mass.: Allyn and Bacon, 1971), p. 319.

40. See on this Brembeck and Howell, *Persuasion,* 2nd ed., pp. 239-40.

41. See on this Vance Packard, *The Hidden Persuaders* (New York: David McKay Co., 1957), pp. 255-66.

42. Ibid.

other questionable persuasive tricks used for personal gain, all seem to have one thing in common. These means continue because too many listeners believe in such preachers, and so the manipulators get away with their practices.

Social pressure and legal barriers are usually the only major deterrents to the philosophy of doing "what you can get away with." Business boycotts and peer pressure often work together to keep unethical business practices under control. That failing, federal and state laws have to enforce fair trade practices.

Few laws exist controlling religious persuasion because of the constitutional guarantee of freedom of speech, and this is proper. But Christians everywhere should show their opposition to "preachers" who operate toward the end of doing "anything they can get away with."

ENDS OF PERSUASION AS A MEASURE OF ITS ETHICS

Other than the goals of sheer selfish results, political demagoguery, violence, or "what you can get away with," it would be difficult to brand any of the above purposes or ends of persuasion as unethical. Although difference of opinion exists as to the relative importance of these goals, most rhetoricians would accept them as valid and valuable. But does this mean that the adoption of any or all of these goals makes a persuader ethical? Regardless of the nobility of one's purposes, may he use any method, process, or technique to attain them? This brings us to a consideration of the other half of the measure of persuasion—its means.

Four

The Ethical Measure of Persuasive Preaching: Measuring Ethics by the Means Used

Methods of persuasive speaking and preaching are voluminous. And most of these methods have been criticized at one time or another. This chapter will refer to those that have come under most frequent attack.

THE *ETHOS* OF THE SPEAKER

Ever since Aristotle set forth a speaker's *ethos* (character) as one of the three major sources of "proof," or persuasion, rhetoricians have seriously considered the place of the speaker in the communication process. But these rhetoricians have not always agreed on what constitutes a speaker's *ethos.* Aristotle described it as being the persuader's sagacity (wisdom), high character, and good will.[1] Cicero, the great Roman orator, claimed that the morals, principles, conduct, and lives of forensic pleaders contributed greatly to their success in speaking.[2] Quintilian listed two characteristics of the ideal orator—he ought to be a good man, and he ought to have speaking skill.[3]

Both ancient and modern rhetoricians have expanded these general characteristics and have listed many aspects of them. For our purposes, however, *ethos* will be treated in terms of the general categories of wisdom, moral character, good will (toward self, subject, and audience), and speaking skill.

---

1. Lane Cooper, trans., *The Rhetoric of Aristotle* (New York: Appleton-Century-Crofts, 1932), 2.1 ff.

2. J. S. Watson, *Cicero on Oratory and Orators* (Philadelphia: David McKay, 1897), 2.43.

3. H. E. Butler, trans., *The Institutio Oratoria of Quintilian* (Cambridge, Mass.: Harvard University Press, 1953), 1.9.

Accordingly, the reader may well ask: What could be wrong or unethical about using this kind of *ethos* to persuade people? The answer to this question lies not so much within the intrinsic qualities of *ethos* as in the way they are used. Kierkegaard charges that the persuasive speaker seeks to build up his *ethos,* prestige, or image for the purpose of capitalizing upon it. In contrast, he claims, the edifying speaker should minimize his *ethos.* The persuader channels the existing desires of the listener, the edifying speaker advocates the renunciation of such desires.[4] And, unlike the persuader, the edifying speaker should refrain from techniques such as suggestion, gesticulation, wiping of sweat from the brow, strength of voice, and vigor of fist deliberately employed to put psychological pressure upon the auditors. These techniques, according to Kierkegaard, may succeed only in short-circuiting the very process of valuation the speaker hopes to elicit.[5]

The Christian preacher can hardly challenge Kierkegaard's objection. But neither can the preacher forsake *ethos* as an integral part of his life. He must utilize all of his ethical powers—wisdom, moral character, good will, and speaking skill—in the preaching of the gospel. But he must never prostitute these qualities as cheap tools of persuasion. The preacher must never consciously and deliberately seek to build up or have anyone else build up his personal *ethos,* prestige, or image to overpower an audience.

THE *LOGOS* OF THE SPEAKER

The logical appeal (*logos*), or appeal to reason used by the speaker, has been the focus both of praise and criticism. In the traditional form it involved two general categories:

1. inartistic proof, or what we would call facts, because, as Aristotle explained, we do not furnish them ourselves. In Aristotle's *Rhetoric,* inartistic proof included such things as witnesses, tortures, and contracts.[6] Today this kind of proof would include all matters falling under the definition of facts.
2. artistic proof, or the process of reasoning. Although classical rhetoricians went into great detail expounding the laws of logic, it will suffice merely to say that the logical appeal was generally

4. Raymond E. Anderson, "Kierkegaard's Theory of Communication," *Speech Monographs* 30 (March 1963): 5.

5. Ibid., pp. 5, 10.

6. Cooper, *Rhetoric of Aristotle,* 1.2.

pursued either *inductively* (as in examples) or *deductively* (as in enthymemes—a rhetorical form of syllogistic reasoning).

Controversial Methods of Logical Appeal

Distortion or Falsification

Most rhetoricians consider distortion or falsification of material unethical. Although exceptions may exist in extreme cases, lying is generally condemned. Brembeck and Howell sum up the views of many rhetoricians when they write, "The decision to lie is a weighty one, a burden not to be taken lightly by the persuader."[7]

Propaganda Devices

In the years around World War II the Institute for Propaganda Analysis published a list of what it called "propaganda devices" often used to deceive listeners. They included: (1) the name-calling device, (2) the glittering generalities device, (3) the transfer device, (4) the testimonial device, (5) the plain-folks device, (6) the card-stacking device, and (7) the bandwagon device.[8] Although it is true that these devices are instruments with which the unprincipled propagandist may distort information, it would be erroneous to assume that they are invariably wrong. As Wayne C. Minnick suggests, Judas was a traitor and Thomas Aquinas a saint in spite of the name-calling involved.[9] The stacking of evidence and use of testimonials by lawyers is considered not only ethical but often mandatory in courts of law today. Adapting a message to one's audience and citing majority opinion in support of one's argument seems reasonable and ethical, if it is not distorted, in spite of the plain-folks and bandwagon labels put upon them. In all fairness it must be realized that these devices may be used ethically or unethically, depending upon the speaker.

Communication Barriers

Other communication barriers may distort information. Allness or overgeneralization, the building of small incidents into

---

7. Winston L. Brembeck and William S. Howell, *Persuasion: A Means of Social Control* (New York: Prentice-Hall, 1952), p. 461.

8. Clyde Raymond Miller, "Propaganda Analysis" *Institute for Propaganda Analysis,* 1.2 (November 1937): 1-3.

9. Wayne C. Minnick, *The Art of Persuasion,* 2d ed. (Boston: Houghton Mifflin Co., 1968), p. 283.

catastrophic events; the two-valued either/or statement that reduces many alternatives into one or two oversimplified choices; invalid cause-and-effect reasoning; lying with statistics; distorted definitions; false analogies; appeals to authority; begging the question; *ad hominem* logic, or attacking a man instead of his arguments; guilt or innocence by association; and appeal to the crowd are some of the ways information can be twisted and thus deceive people.[10]

Confusion of Facts with Inference

Statements of fact can be verified, such as, There are mountains in Colorado. Inferences, on the other hand, are statements made about the unverified based upon a sampling of that which is verified: for example, The sun will rise tomorrow. It is true that the sun has risen every morning throughout the past year. But a prediction that it will rise tomorrow, though extremely probable, cannot be made with the same absolute truth as the former statement that it has risen every day last year. This matter may seem absurd, and probably is as it relates to the rising of the sun, but confusion of fact with inference in the realm of beliefs and values has led to deception and distortion in business, politics, and even religion. A responsible preacher, therefore, will be careful about assigning the label "fact" to his unverified statements of inference. He will recognize the difference between experimental and nonexperimental beliefs. Experimental beliefs cannot be reasonably challenged. Nonexperimental or unverified beliefs have led to a multitude of controversies.

Concealment of Purpose, Organization, or Institution

Persuaders, whether door-to-door salesmen or religious sect evangelists, are considered unethical when they try to hide the true purpose of persuasion or the organization they represent in reams of introductory verbiage. Most rhetoricians insist that a persuader "lay his cards on the table" early in his communication. This gives the listener a fighting chance to sort out the speaker's bias, angle, or personal stake in his persuasive talk. After understanding the speaker's purpose and the organization he represents, the listener can make up his mind accordingly. The responsible preacher will

---

10. For a fuller treatment of these and other barriers, see Raymond W. McLaughlin, *Communication for the Church* (Grand Rapids: Zondervan Publishing House, 1968), chap. 4, "Barriers to Communication."

not conceal his purpose or organization for unethical reasons. This does not mean that purpose may not be approached indirectly as a rhetorical device of surprise, but only that it should be done within ethical bounds.

Other Controversial Methods

Although criticism could be extended almost indefinitely to minor content details, the ploys listed above receive the brunt of objection. Adapting messages to the whims and preferences of the audience, advisability of complete and absolute honesty, the slipping of personal value judgments into objective descriptions, and the use of tact and sincerity, however laudable they may seem, can be used unethically.

Criticism of Logical Appeal

Although appealing to the listener's reasoning powers seems unassailable, it has been attacked. Kierkegaard took a dim view of trying to elicit subjective ethical and religious responses through logical demonstration. He claimed that logical proof should not be used to establish belief because belief is a product of volitional action, not assent, and values cannot be probed through empirical demonstration. Thus, he claims, beating the listener down through rigid logical demonstration prevents belief by removing the occasion of choice.[11] The weakness of this attack is in its assumption that logic cannot be used to argue for probabilities, even if not claimed as proof of absolutes. The Christian persuader cannot use logic as an absolute proof for the existence of God. He can merely use it to assert a high degree of probability that God exists.

A broader attack upon traditional Aristotelian reasoning is made by Alfred Korzybski and the general semanticists. Korzybski and his followers struck deeply at the roots of Aristotelian logic—the three laws of thought.

1. The law of identity—whatever is, is.
2. The law of contradiction—nothing can both be and not be.
3. The law of the excluded middle—everything must either be or not be.[12]

---

11. Anderson, "Kierkegaard's Theory of Communication," pp. 4 ff.

12. On this criticism see Alfred Korzybski, *Science and Sanity,* 2d ed. (Lancaster, Pa.: International Non-Aristotelian Library Publishing Co., 1941), p. 404, et passim; Wendell Johnson, *People in Quandaries* (New York: Harper and Brothers, 1946), pp. 7 ff; Irving J. Lee, *Language Habits and Human Affairs* (New York:

From these three laws of thought Aristotle and Aristotelians erected their system of logic, so widely used by mankind. Korzybski's non-Aristotelian approach to life and language stressed what seems to be the opposite of these three laws. Thus he taught:

1. The law of nonidentity—the word is not the reality.
2. The law of nonallness—the word is not all of reality.
3. The law of self-reflexiveness—the word can be used in statements about itself.

A number of scholars charge that Korzybski and the general semanticists have misrepresented Aristotle, applying his laws to language representations when actually he meant them to apply to existing things and to thought.[13] The implications of this Aristotelian point of view is that were he alive today Aristotle would remain true to his three laws as they apply to objects and thinking, but that he would doubtless agree with Alfred Korzybski that the word is not the object, that the word does not tell all about the object, and that language is self-reflexive. Aristotle's laws are distorted when made to mean that the word *table* is identical with the object table, which the label is being used to represent. His law of the excluded middle is distorted when used to shrink a many-valued set of alternatives into a two-valued, either/or set of alternatives. And Aristotle probably never believed that language was not self-reflexive. The Christian persuader then can use Aristotelian logic where applicable. These two disciplines should not be considered mutually exclusive or contradictory.

Finally, some rhetoricians, though favorable to logical appeal, object to those who would insist that it is the only or even the predominant appeal in discourse. They maintain that even though strong logical appeals be structured into a speech, logic does not always persuade listeners. Man's prejudices, biases, and social and emotional conduct do not always allow him to respond to discourse in a logical way. Man sometimes responds to emotion, social influences, suggestion, and other appeals when logic does not convince him. In such situations, a speaker that refuses to use appeals

---

Harper and Brothers, 1941), pp. 87-91, 100-109, et passim; Stuart Chase, *The Tyranny of Words* (New York: Harcourt, Brace and Co., 1938), pp. 226 ff; and other writers on general semantics.

13. For criticism of the general semantics approach see such works as Barrows Dunham, *Man Against Myth* (Boston: Little, Brown and Co., 1947), pp. 233-66; and Margaret Gorman, *General Semantics and Contemporary Thomism* (Lincoln, Nebr.: University of Nebraska Press, 1962).

other than logic may be as unethical as a man who uses them wrongly.[14]

More than that, Professor Donald K. Smith questions the possibility of separating logical from emotional discourse.[15] He points out that even the presentation of facts and logic elicits a degree of emotional response. Words in themselves are not emotional. They create emotional response because they get their meaning from their context. The word *strike* may be the only factual and logical word to use in describing labor's refusal to work under certain circumstances. But this word in this context also elicits definite emotional responses both from labor and management alike. Thus it is erroneous to argue that logical reasoning and emotional appeals are mutually exclusive.

Conclusions

Criticisms of logical reasoning and appeal are helpful to students of persuasion. But one ought to be aware of their strengths and weaknesses. The ethical obligation of the persuasive preacher, however, would seem to be in favor of logic's use. Nevertheless, dependence upon facts and reasoning should not exclude the use of other appeals such as emotion, social influence, and suggestion, if used ethically and together with facts and logic. The Christian preacher needs to assess the ethical implications of failure to use the kind of appeal that would move one type of audience, even though such an appeal might fail to reach another type.

THE *PATHOS* OF THE SPEAKER

The appeal to *pathos* (emotion) has received as much, if not more, criticism than the appeals to *ethos* and *logos.* Emotional appeal has a long history. Although it could be traced back through many of the speeches of the Old Testament and doubtless was an integral part of the rhetoric of common property in virtually all ages, its formal treatment was set forth in the classical rhetorical period.

Briefly, Aristotle observed the great speakers of his day adapting their speeches to their audiences. He concluded that one of the major sources of proof, or persuasion, was appeal to the needs,

---

14. See Brembeck and Howell, *Persuasion,* pp. 449-50; and Minnick, *Art of Persuasion,* pp. 284-85, as representative of this view.

15. Donald K. Smith, *Man Speaking: A Rhetoric of Public Speech* (New York: Dodd, Mead and Co., 1969), pp. 236-38.

wants, and emotions of people. In his *Rhetoric* he provided one of the earliest and ablest analyses of human emotions and their opposites, such as anger and meekness, love and hatred, fear and boldness, shame and shamelessness.[16] He treated these emotions according to: (1) their nature, (2) their object, and (3) their exciting causes. He studied the characteristics of people and surveyed the traits usually observed in people of social prominence, wealth, power, and good fortune.

Classical rhetoricians from Aristotle's time to the present have treated emotional appeal. The needs, wants, and desires of people are exceedingly complex and changing, and categories of treatment vary according to the author consulted.[17] Nevertheless, general categorizations include such basic drives as security, belongingness, esteem, and self-actualization. Each of these general categories is broken down into submotives, and rhetoricians develop emotional appeals on the basis of these general and detailed categories.

Although attacks on the ethics of emotional appeal occur more frequently and vehemently than those on the ethical and logical appeals, the criticisms of *pathos* are not as thorough and detailed as the criticisms of the other two appeals. Most critics merely resent a speaker who bypasses the listener's reasoning process and seeks response solely through emotional appeals.

Kierkegaard objected to the religious persuader who would seek to persuade an audience through the channeling of their existing desires. He felt that the preacher, or the edifying speaker, should confront the listener with the ultimate types of values that might require the renunciation of the listener's desires.[18] Franklyn S. Haiman criticized the emotional appeal as often being at odds with the conscious thought processes of the listener.[19] He does allow for the kind of emotional appeal that does not attempt to short-circuit the hearer's thought process.[20]

---

16. Cooper, *Rhetoric of Aristotle,* bk. 2, chaps. 2-17.

17. See works such as Brembeck and Howell, *Persuasion,* chap. 6; Minnick, *Art of Persuasion,* chap. 9; Robert T. Oliver, *The Psychology of Persuasive Speech,* 2d ed. (New York: David McKay Co., 1957), chap. 11; Alan H. Monroe, *Principles and Types of Speech,* 5th ed. (Chicago: Scott, Foresman and Co., 1962), chap. 10; Martin P. Andersen, Wesley Lewis, and James Murray, *The Speaker and His Audience* (New York: Harper and Row, 1964), chap. 6; and other works on rhetoric and persuasion.

18. Raymond E. Anderson, "Kierkegaard's Theory," p. 5.

19. Franklyn S. Haiman, "Democratic Ethics and the Hidden Persuaders," *Quarterly Journal of Speech* 44 (December 1958): 385.

20. Ibid., p. 388.

Professor Thomas R. Nilsen fears that with the advent of such highly developed communication techniques as mass advertising, motivation research, and professional public relations, persuasion runs the risk of violating democratic principles or values, the intrinsic worth of the individual, his reasoning process, his privilege of self-determination, and the fulfillment of his potentialities as a positive good.[21] These values, according to Nilsen, must control the procedures of communication rather than vice versa. The processes of communication, unrestricted discussion and debate, public address, parliamentary procedure, legal processes, and publicly defined rules of evidence and tests of reasoning should continuously recreate our values.

In a similar vein, Professor Karl R. Wallace criticizes the persuasive methods that violate democratic ideals and values, regardless of the ends pursued by the speaker.[22] The dignity and worth of individuals, equality of opportunity, freedom, and every person's capability of understanding democracy (its goals, values, procedures, and processes) must not be violated.

THE DELIVERY METHODS OF THE SPEAKER

Normally, delivery methods in communication are studied under such speech techniques as impromptu presentation of a message (speaking with little or no previous preparation), extemporaneous delivery (speaking from no notes, or from brief notes with thorough preparation), manuscript delivery (reading a speech or sermon from completed manuscript), and speaking from a memorized speech. Any of these delivery methods can be important to a preacher from the point of view of effectiveness, and any of them could be used ethically.

Of more concern to contemporary communicators are the increasingly utilized delivery methods of dialogue vs. monologue and coercion vs. persuasion. Whether or not we agree, in the minds of many communication scholars both of these competitive approaches to message delivery have ethical implications.

---

21. Thomas R. Nilsen, "Free Speech, Persuasion, and the Democratic Process," *Quarterly Journal of Speech* 44 (October 1958): 235-43.

22. Karl R. Wallace, "An Ethical Basis of Communication," *The Speech Teacher* 4 (January 1955): 1-9.

Dialogue vs. Monologue

Traditionally, preaching has been monologue. Following in the Hebrew Christian and classical rhetorical forms it has been a more or less effective model of one-way communication. Preaching has been the proclamation of God's revealed truth, persuading men to accept and follow Christ.

Charges that preaching does not allow for feedback are somewhat erroneous. Preachers have learned to sense audience responses, both negative and positive, and have adjusted their messages accordingly. Furthermore, some preachers build overt audience response into their material and thus approach realistic dialogue in their monological delivery.

Nevertheless, in recent years monological preaching has come under attack, mainly for its ineffectiveness. Reuel L. Howe, director of the Institute for Advanced Pastoral Studies in Bloomfield Hills, Michigan, criticizes preaching for its verbosity and lack of dialogue. He charges:

> The weakness of preaching stems from its wordiness and monological character. The centuries have been filled with words about Christ. When one stops to think about the volumes of words one develops a sense of horror—words, words; words about words, words undoing words; words for the sake of words; words slashing like a blinding blizzard into the face of the world. And at last the world is beginning to cry, "Stop! We can't stand more words. Your words are empty because they are not reinforced by actions that give them authenticity."[23]

What is Howe's remedy for such a situation? Dialogue! He continues:

> But preaching does have power when it is dialogical, when preacher and people become partners in the discernment and proclamation by word and action of the Word of God in response to the issues of our day. Once again the word must become flesh; men must be able to see it as well as hear it.[24]

Criticisms of preaching seem to climax in Clyde Reid's book, *The Empty Pulpit*. Reid, a former student and colleague of Reuel Howe, strongly condemns contemporary preaching and lists seven current criticisms of it:

1. Preachers tend to use complex, archaic language which the average person does not understand.

---

23. Reuel L. Howe, *Partners in Preaching* (New York: Seabury Press, 1967), p. 5.
24. Ibid.

2. Most sermons today are boring, dull, and uninteresting.
3. Most preaching today is irrelevant.
4. Preaching today is not courageous preaching.
5. Preaching does not communicate (failure to help listeners understand the central message of the sermon).
6. Preaching doesn't lead to change in persons.
7. Preaching has been overemphasized.[25]

Reid points out that we are living in a new age. New technology is producing enormous social change, and it is difficult to live in the past. This new age has a new authority structure that has robbed the minister of his prestige. And the new age has produced a new communication structure through the electronic media. This means that pulpit communication is going to have to elicit involvement from listeners.

Reid's suggested remedy for the empty pulpit, like that of Howe's, is dialogical preaching. Monological preaching still has its place according to Reid, but only as it leads to specific feedback of a dialogical nature. Otherwise traditional monological preaching as a method of communication will become as extinct as smoke signals.

Others, as well, have stressed the dialogical approach to communication. Martin Buber advocates the I-Thou relationship as the center of communication.[26] Such factors as honesty, integrity, openness, and love are paramount in the I-Thou bond.

Reuel Howe, John Powell, Ashley Montague, and others are developing additional aspects of the dialogical relationship.[27] Carl Rogers has been influential in psychiatric circles with his client-centered therapy and nondirective approach to counseling, techniques that stress dialogue and nonmanipulative communication.[28]

Various comparisons and contrasts can be made between dialogue and monologue. The dialogical or monological *attitude* as

---

25. Clyde Reid, *The Empty Pulpit* (New York: Harper and Row, 1967), chapter 1.

26. See works by Martin Buber: *I and Thou,* 2d ed., trans. and ed. Ronald Gregor Smith (New York: Charles Scribner's Sons, 1958); *Between Man and Man,* trans. Ronald Gregor Smith (New York: Macmillan Co., 1965); *Pointing the Way,* trans. Maurice S. Friedman (New York: Harper and Row, 1960); and others.

27. See Reuel L. Howe, *The Miracle of Dialogue* (New York: Seabury Press, 1963) and *Partners in Preaching: Clergy and Laity in Dialogue;* John Powell, *Why Am I Afraid to Tell You Who I Am?* (Chicago: Argus Communications, 1969); and Floyd Matson and Ashley Montague, eds., *The Human Dialogue* (New York: Free Press, 1967).

28. See Carl Rogers, *Client-Centered Therapy* (Boston: Houghton Mifflin, 1951) and *On Becoming a Person* (Boston: Houghton Mifflin, 1961).

well as the methods seems to be the focus of ethical judgment. Thus, some current writers tend to characterize dialogue in *positive* terms as having genuineness, accurate empathetic understanding, unconditional positive regard, presentness, spirit of mutual equality, and supportive psychological climate.[29]

Monologue is often characterized in *negative* terms, as incorporating "self-centeredness, deception, pretense, display, appearance, artifice, using, profit, unapproachableness, seduction, domination, exploitation, and manipulation."[30]

Several conclusions have been drawn concerning the ethics of dialogue and monologue based on the above characteristics. Some scholars are moving to the position that dialogue, with its positive attitude and characteristics, is ethical. At the same time, most of these men hold that monologue, which they feel is negative in attitude and characteristics, is unethical. Persuasion and monologue, they say, are to be equated, and all attempts to persuade others are unethical.

A number of other scholars, however, reject such a polarization of ethical judgments. These scholars view both monologue and dialogue as ethical when used ethically. Monologue, in this view, should be used where needed and used ethically. Dialogue should be supplemental to monologue and should be used ethically.

The latter view seems most consistent with Christian persuasion. Earlier chapters of this book have substantiated the biblical basis of monological preaching—the proclamation of God's Word by example and command. Dialogue is also encouraged since it was used prominently and frequently by Jesus, Paul, and others.[31] A combination of both monologue and dialogue was probably utilized in the speeches recorded in the Book of Acts.

---

29. Richard L. Johannesen, *Ethics in Human Communication,* (Columbus, Ohio: Charles E. Merrill Publishing Co., 1975), pp. 45-46.

30. Ibid., quoting Ronald Gregor Smith, trans., *I and Thou* by Martin Buber (Edinburgh: T. & T. Clark, 1937), pp. 34, 38, 43, 60, 105, 107; Maurice Friedman and Ronald Gregor Smith, trans., *The Knowledge of Man* by Martin Buber (London: George Allen & Unwin, 1965), pp. 82-83; Ronald Gregor Smith, trans., *Between Man and Man,* by Martin Buber (New York: Macmillan Co., 1965), pp. 29-20, 23, 29-30, 95; and Maurice Friedman, *Martin Buber: The Life of Dialogue* (New York: Harper Torchbooks, 1960), pp. 57-58, 63, 82, 123-24, 180.

31. For example, see Jesus' dialogues with Nicodemus (John 3:1–21), with the Samaritan woman (John 4:6–30), with the rich young ruler (Matt. 19:16–26 and parallels), and others. Also Peter's dialogues (Acts 2:14–41; 11:1–18). Also Paul's dialogues (Acts 17:2, 10–14, 16–34 and others), the Jerusalem Council (Acts 15:1–29), and others.

Therefore both biblical teaching and modern communication scholarship support monologue and dialogue as methods of delivery in preaching. There is no reason why monological preaching should not be characterized by the positive qualities associated with dialogue. And there is no guarantee that dialogue can always be free from the negative factors sometimes associated with monological delivery. In Christian persuasion, there is ample room for both methods of message delivery if they are used ethically.

Coercion vs. Persuasion

Chapter 3 mentioned violence, terrorism, and other coercive tactics as *ends* of persuasion. Christians have not been familiar with discord, dissension, disruption, conflict, discomfort, and destruction as goals, ends, or actual purposes of communication. In the last decade, however, these tactics have become rather common *ends* and *means* of attaining some personal and group desires. Whereas in previous generations communicators have used traditional means of persuasion to obtain their goals, now many are forsaking verbal persuasion and turning to coercion to get what they want. At one time or another the following methods or means of persuasion have been substituted for verbal persuasion to get things done.

A few years ago, the *sit-in* was a favorite tactic of college and university students to take over administration buildings and hold them until administrators granted student demands or agreed to some compromise.

The *boycott* was effective in Alabama to assure equal busing rights and in California and other states to stop the purchase of grapes harvested by nonunion farm laborers. Students have boycotted classes, housewives have boycotted supermarkets, and minority groups have boycotted restaurants. This tactic has often brought results, even if only temporarily.

Picketing has been used by labor and other groups for many years. Its continued use signifies its effectiveness, at least in the minds of its participants. Unfortunately, picketing has sometimes led to violence and injury.

Disruption is a favorite tool of dissenters at public meetings. Speakers are interrupted and refused the right to continue speaking. Teachers are shouted down by chants and protests. Stink bombs are exploded, driving everyone from a room or auditorium.

Such tactics have mixed results, satisfying participants but alienating others.

Demands of a dogmatic and exaggerated nature have become a popular tool of coercion by extremists. The Symbionese Liberation Army demanded of the Randolph A. Hearst family nearly $400 million worth of free food for California's poor as a ransom for the kidnapped Patricia Hearst.[32] The kidnappers of a Ford Motor Company executive in Argentina in 1973 demanded a ransom of about $1 million in medical equipment.[33] And, as reported in chapter 3, James Forman in his "Black Manifesto," delivered in 1969 at Riverside Church in New York City, demanded of Christian churches and Jewish synagogues $500 million in reparations for the way they had treated Blacks.[34] Regardless of the noble social motives voiced by the extremists, there is doubt whether they ever expected to obtain their demands. Rather, they may well have intended only to expose and embarrass the "tyrannical establishment" who they knew would refuse them.[35] In some cases, however, at least part of the demands were met.

Bomb threats have been used by some dissidents when they discovered that anonymous calls to certain establishments could disrupt business, education, and other types of meetings. In 1970, repeated bomb threats almost closed Rutgers University. Princeton Theological Seminary was emptied on at least one occasion about the same time. Theaters, lecture halls, laboratories, and offices have suffered from similar threats. Motives for such tactics were often mixed. Disruption, demands, attention-getting plans, even avoidance of school examinations figured in these methods. Their effectiveness has been somewhat limited because of the possibility of exposure of the perpetrator.

Obscenities and profanity often accompany some of the tactics described above. Social protesters inject obscenities into public discourse; spray them upon walls of schools, churches, fences, and billboards; and sprinkle their writings with them, obviously for their shock and attention-getting value. Aside from their "barracks

---

32. John Peterson, "Can We Cope with Rising Terror?" *The National Observer,* 23 February 1974, p. 24.

33. Ibid.

34. See "Itemizing the Reparations Bill," *Christianity Today,* 6 June 1969, p. 839.

35. See on this, Howard H. Martin and C. William Colburn, *Communication and Consensus: An Introduction to Rhetorical Discourse* (New York: Harcourt Brace Jovanovich, 1972), p. 4.

room'' identity or back-alley braggadocio, obscenities are used to get public attention, to unify protest groups, and to embarrass and alienate the so-called establishment.

Aircraft hijacking has become popular in recent years and has reached such proportions that stiff federal laws and search procedures at airports have been enacted to curtail it. International laws and cooperation among countries are still needed to stop this tactic completely.

Kidnapping of prominent persons for ransom or political coercion has become a serious ''rhetorical'' tool for extremists and terrorists. The seizure and killing of international ambassadors and the holding of prominent persons as hostages to trade for political and terrorist prisoners has become well known to the contemporary world.

Desecration and destruction of public and private property was recently almost commonplace in news reports and everyday conversations. Desecration of the American flag was prevalent. Burning draft cards and pouring blood on military records were tactics used to dramatize protest against the Viet Nam war. Excrement was dumped in public places and thrown at public officers. The last decade of unrest and protest saw such tragedies as the bombing of a laboratory and killing of a researcher at the University of Wisconsin and the burning of an administration building at Colorado State University. In both incidents, irreplaceable files of life-long research were destroyed. Similar acts of destruction occurred across America and in foreign countries.

Murder and mayhem have been used to further political and social ends. The Palestinian Liberation Organization slew Jewish athletes at the 1972 Olympics held in Munich. The Basque militants in Spain, the French-Canadian separatists of Quebec, the Weathermen and police-hunting Black Liberation Army in the United States have all turned to extreme terrorism to accomplish their goals. In February of 1974, *Newsweek* magazine reported:

> Over the past six years, American intelligence experts have chronicled a total of 432 major acts of international terrorism, including 235 bombings, 94 hijackings and at least 57 kidnappings. All told, at least 196 people died and another 300 were injured as a result of these operations, and the property damage and ransom payments ran to uncounted millions.[36]

---

36. ''The 'Morality' of Terrorism,'' *Newsweek,* 25 February 1974, p. 21.

The effectiveness of such tactics is great. They can be justified only in the minds of their perpetrators. Readers may wonder why the above coercive activities are even considered in a book on the ethics of persuasion. Psychiatrists, social scientists, and legal authorities, however, are not the only ones interested in such behavior. Communication scholars view protest and confrontation tactics as an extension of the range of rhetoric, or persuasion.[37]

The shift in tactics from persuasion to coercion has taken place because radicals are convinced that verbal persuasion no longer works. They believe that talk brings results too slowly. They claim that channels of communication and negotiation are not equally available to all, especially to underprivileged minorities. Radicals do not trust the establishment because, they claim, the establishment refuses to listen, and uses language to perpetuate injustice, to delay action, and to foster compromise. In spite of these criticisms of verbal persuasion, "action tactics" are accompanied in most cases with written or oral persuasive negotiations.

Although some confrontation rhetoric is used unethically, some rhetoricians, judging it in a situation ethics context, view much of it to be acceptable.[38] Few would agree, however, that killing or injuring innocents is ethical.

Whether the Christian persuader could use or even accept such tactics as ethical is another matter. Nonviolent protests, sit-ins, boycotts, and picketing, might be justifiable and even imperative under the right circumstances, but violence, obscenities, desecration, destruction of property, injury, and killing, would seem difficult to justify under almost any circumstances.

---

37. See Martin and Colburn, *Communication,* chap. 1, "The Changing Fortunes of Talk"; Richard L. Johannesen, *Ethics in Human Communication* (Columbus, Ohio: Charles E. Merrill Publishing Co., 1975), pp. 63-65; Herbert W. Simons, "Persuasion in Social Conflicts: A Critique of Prevailing Conceptions and a Framework for Future Research," *Speech Monographs* 39 (November 1972): 227-47; Parke G. Burgess, "Crisis Rhetoric: Coercion vs. Force," *Quarterly Journal of Speech* 59 (February 1973): 61-73; Franklyn S. Haiman, "The Rhetoric of the Streets: Some Legal and Ethical Implications," *Quarterly Journal of Speech* 53 (April 1967): 99-114; and others.

38. See J. Dan Rothwell, "Verbal Obscenity: Time for Second Thoughts," *Western Speech* 35 (Fall 1971): 231-42; Haig Bosmajian, "Obscenity and Protest," in Bosmajian, ed., *Dissent: Symbolic Behavior and Rhetorical Strategies* (Boston: Allyn and Bacon, 1972), pp. 294-306; Franklyn S. Haiman, "The Rhetoric of 1968: A Farewell to Rational Discourse," in Donn W. Parson and Wil Linkugel, eds., *The Ethics of Controversy: Politics and Protest* (Lawrence, Kans.: House of Usher, 1968), pp. 123-42; Simons, "Persuasion in Social Conflicts"; Burgess, "Crisis Rhetoric"; and others.

The choice between coercion and persuasion is not always an easy one, but it has always been a persistent one. Social upheaval, self-defense, war, and revolution may at times seem to justify violence and coercion. But in the long run, these tactics as tools of persuasion are neither socially acceptable nor Christian.

The crucifixion of Christ poses an almost unbelievable contrast. On the one hand there was the Roman Empire, one of history's most devastating forces of coercion. On the other hand there was Jesus Christ, the quintessence of love, gentleness, and humility, saying, "And I, when I am lifted up from the earth, will draw all men to myself" (John 12:32). How could this gentle carpenter of Nazareth win his battle of persuasion against the brutal power of Rome's coercion?

History has shown who won. Rome with all its power crumbled; Jesus Christ still draws men unto himself. Pilate on that fateful day sat in judgment over Jesus; today Jesus sits in judgment over Pilate. Persuasion must triumph over coercion.

MEANS OF PERSUASION AS A MEASURE OF ITS ETHICS

Measuring the ethics of persuasive preaching in terms of the methods used is considerably easier than measuring them in terms of the ends sought. It is easier to observe a preacher's methods than it is to discern his goals.

This does not mean, however, that preaching methods are either right or wrong. Actually, most persuasive means fall into a neutral category and must be judged right or wrong in terms of how they are used. Although this judgment can be difficult, it is necessary, especially if some standard of measurement can be established. This is the intent of the next two chapters.

Five

Current Ethical Standards for Persuasive Speaking

An increased concern for ethics in persuasion has prompted many scholars to work toward adopting a standard of ethics. Kenneth Andersen claims that, "The minimum step in solving the problem of ethics in persuasion is to be willing to accept some degree of responsibility for self and for one's actions."[1] Such responsibility, according to Andersen, devolves upon both persuader and persuadee. And this responsibility must be measured by some specific standard. Andersen continues: "The first step toward acceptance of responsibility would appear to be an effort to form one's ethical standards and values and remain sensitive to their relationship to the many elements in the persuasion process."[2]

Robert T. Oliver places the need for ethical standards of persuasion in the wider context of all our life activities. He claims, "The ethical problems of persuasion may be isolated only in part from the broader question of morality in general."[3] Although Oliver does not advocate any one specific standard of ethics, such as religion or law, he does recognize the validity of such standards as a part of society's function. He writes, "The whole educational process (in the home, school, church and community) has as a central purpose the inculcation of ethical standards."[4]

Brembeck and Howell concur with the feeling that ethical standards are important: "Feeling our way to moral judgments of actions of others and of ourselves is helpful and necessary but

---

1. Kenneth E. Andersen, *Persuasion: Theory and Practice* (Boston: Allyn and Bacon, 1971), p. 323.

2. Ibid.

3. Robert T. Oliver, *The Psychology of Persuasive Speech,* 2d ed. (New York: David McKay Co., 1957), p. 23.

4. Ibid., p. 27.

unreliable. A systematic and conscious process of assessing the ethical quality of persuasive attempts would be better."[5]

Walter and Scott also support this need.

> The speaker needs a set of values applicable to speaking that will help him choose ideas, select supporting material and decide which basic themes are of greatest worth to him and his audience, aside from their utility as persuasive devices.[6]

The question is not whether men feel the need for ethical standards of persuasion. Rather, it is, What standard shall be used? Erwin P. Bettinghaus, for example, says, "I do not believe in legislating any particular set of ethical standards beyond those minimal safeguards provided by criminal laws."[7] And yet, Bettinghaus would strongly support efforts to develop ethics of research and minimum guidelines for various academic disciplines, including persuasion.[8] Fairly representative of speech scholars, Bettinghaus urges:

> Develop some expectations about morality. I am not an advocate for any particular moral code and would not argue strongly for the moral position associated with Christianity, Buddhism, Islam, Unitarianism, or with any of the other religions found in different parts of the world. I do argue that every individual ought to have developed a set of ethics and a set of expectations regarding ethical conduct, and that he should know what they are and how he wishes to apply them in various situations.[9]

Professor Patrick O. Marsh, though not advocating a particular religious standard, at least allows for such guidelines when he suggests:

> It is convenient that our society recognizes and respects individual differences in appraising moral fitness. Our government protects our religious freedom, and what is religion if it is not what one holds to in ultimate seriousness?[10]

---

5. Winston Lamont Brembeck and William Smiley Howell, *Persuasion: A Means of Social Influence,* 2d ed. (Englewood Cliffs, N.J.: Prentice-Hall, 1976), p. 226.

6. Otis M. Walter and Robert L. Scott, *Thinking and Speaking: A Guide to Intelligent Oral Communication,* 2d ed. (New York: Macmillan Co., 1968), p. 226.

7. Erwin P. Bettinghaus, *Persuasive Communication* (New York: Holt Rinehart and Winston, 1968), p. 284.

8. Ibid.

9. Ibid.

10. Patrick O. Marsh, *Persuasive Speaking: Theory, Models, Practice* (New York: Harper and Row, 1967), p. 47.

The need for ethical standards is generally supported. But agreement on what these standards should be is virtually nonexistent. This chapter seeks to acquaint the reader with the current perplexity over standards: the absolutist-relativist controversy and the ensuing question, Relative to what?

PERSUASIVE STANDARDS: THE ABSOLUTIST-RELATIVIST PROBLEM

Inevitably, a discussion of persuasion confronts the age-old problem of absolute vs. relative truth, in spite of Paul Ramsey's caution that such categorizations be avoided if possible. On the problem of ethics from the "rule-agapist" vs. the "act-agapist" point of view, Ramsey pleads:

> For one thing, a rule-agapist should no longer accuse the act-agapist of being a materialist, a relativist, or subjectivist, or a compromiser, when he is only an act-agapist. And the proponent of situational ethics should no longer accuse the proponent of rule-agapism of being a legalist lacking in compassion when he only believes that Christian compassion can and may and must embody itself in certain rules of action.[11]

Although Ramsey makes his point, one should not be blinded to those extremists both of the rightist legalist position and of the leftist relativistic position. They exist today, as always, and any attempt to ignore them must not sidetrack a quest for sound ethical standards.

ABSOLUTISM-RELATIVISM AND STANDARDS OF ETHICAL MEASUREMENT

Few scholars would advocate a single code of law, a specific set of eternal truths, or one book of absolute principles, such as the Bible, as a standard of ethical measurement of communication. Though scholars agree that a standard of ethics is needed, they refuse to designate what that standard should be.

Absolutism as a Standard of Measurement

Absolute truth is generally held as truth that is unchanging and unvarying for all men at all times and under all circumstances. Francis Schaeffer defines an absolute as "a concept which is not

---

11. Paul Ramsey, *Deeds and Rules in Christian Ethics* (New York: Charles Scribner's Sons, 1967), p. 5.

modifiable by factors such as culture, individual psychology or circumstances; but which is perfect and unchangeable."[12] Schaeffer views absolutism as an antithesis of relativism.

Though absolutism as defined above may seem rigid and unbending, men constructively apply the concept in various ways. Norman Geisler, for example, lists several approaches to universal norms that differ from *antinomianism* (the denial of any meaningful ethical norms whatsoever)[13] and *generalism* (a truth which is generally right or wrong, but there are no universal norms).[14] Geisler's list of possible universal approaches is:

There Is One Universal Norm (Agape Love)

Although this position is known as situationism[15] (discussed later in this chapter) and thus generally regarded as relativism, Geisler is correct in observing that it is a form of absolutism because it does allow for one universal and unchanging absolute—namely agape love. According to this position any act done in agape love is morally right. Any act done without agape love is morally wrong.

There Are Many Nonconflicting Norms

This view, called nonconflicting absolutism,[16] holds that there are many valid universal norms, none of which ever really conflict. Thus such acts as lying and killing are always wrong. But lying to save lives is only a seeming contradiction with killing because of a providential third alternative that forbids any overlapping of ethical norms. Therefore, one could tell the truth about the location of hidden prisoners—leading to their capture and execution—but not be held guilty of the death of the prisoners. Only the captors and executors would be guilty of killing.

There Are Many Conflicting Norms

In this view[17] many acts conflict and are wrong, but one must choose the lesser of the two evils. Thus lying is always wrong and

12. Francis A. Schaeffer, *The God Who Is There* (Chicago: Inter-Varsity Press, 1968), p. 177.

13. Norman L. Geisler, *Ethics: Alternatives and Issues* (Grand Rapids: Zondervan Publishing House, 1971), p. 13.

14. Ibid., p. 14.

15. Ibid., p. 15 and chap. 4.

16. Ibid., p. 16 and chap. 5.

17. Ibid., p. 17 and chap. 6.

killing innocents is always wrong. If faced with a dilemma between the two, one must choose the lesser evil. Those who hold this view claim that man's condition in this fallen and evil world forces individuals into such dilemmas. If man were not sinful, such conflicts would not occur.

There Are Higher Norms

This view, called hierarchicalism,[18] holds that there are many universal ethical norms but that they vary in intrinsic importance. Thus, when acts such as lying to save lives occur, the saving of lives is intrinsically more important than lying, and one should choose to lie. Those who hold this view believe that although there are many ethical absolutes, they do exist in some hierarchical form and men must frequently choose between lower and higher forms of acting.

There are other forms of absolutism and variations and combinations of the types listed above, and absolutists must face conflicts of norms in some way. For example, some absolutists oppose law as a rule of life and emphasize the guidance of the Holy Spirit. In this view the leading of the Spirit determines what is good. Acts done contrary to the Spirit's leading are considered evil.

Acts of Christians who are motivated by love for God and neighbor, empowered by the Spirit, and guided by biblical and theological teaching are viewed by some evangelicals as moral acts. Legalistic attitudes in carrying out these acts are rejected. This kind of living by biblical absolutes is best exemplified by Christ.[19] Here one can see the elements of the motivation of love, the energizing power of the Holy Spirit, the guidelines of the Bible, and the example of Christ all working in the spirit of the law rather than by the letter of the law to help people do ethical acts. This latter view turns strongly upon belief in revealed truth—propositional and absolute—contained in the Bible.[20]

Problems of Absolutism as a Standard of Measurement

Two problems the average preacher faces in his daily preparation for preaching are legalism and its opposite, antinomianism.

---

18. Ibid., p. 18 and chap. 7.

19. See Carl F. H. Henry, *Christian Personal Ethics* (Grand Rapids: Wm. B. Eerdmans Publishing Co., 1957), chaps. 6-19.

20. Ibid., chap. 7.

Avoiding Legalism

Legalism is more of an attitude than it is a doctrine. Kyle Haselden defines this attitude.

> Christian legalism . . . assumes that in the teachings of Jesus and his disciples, in the ten commandments, and in the elaboration of these teachings and commandments . . . we have a detailed, inflexible, always appropriate, moral code which, in its minute prescriptions, is adequate for all times, places, persons, and circumstances.[21]

This attitude of legalism codifies in minute detail the biblical laws, commandments, rules, and obligations and then labors to obey and carry them out regardless of circumstances. But Jesus excoriated the Pharisees for such legalism (Matt. 23).

Haselden, concerned about the ethics of communication, finds at least six reasons why legalism fails. Briefly they are:

1. Legalism externalizes morality.
2. Legalism . . . describes the good life in static, restrictive, negative terms.
3. Legalism mechanizes morality.
4. Legalism tends to concentrate on trivialities.
5. When strictly observed as a way of life, legalism binds the future.
6. Legalism precludes the working of the Holy Spirit.[22]

Very few people completely adhere to such an ethical pattern. Nevertheless, this attitude has been evinced too much, both in pulpit and pew. Such legalism cannot be advocated as an ethical standard of persuasive preaching. Such preachers would fall under the divine dictum of Jesus concerning the Pharisees: "They bind heavy burdens, hard to bear, and lay them on men's shoulders; but they themselves will not move them with their finger" (Matt. 23:4).

Avoiding Antinomianism

The opposite of legalism is antinomianism (against law, or without laws), although Haselden maintains that "the opposite of legalism is relativism,"[23] which he identifies with situationism. (Relativism and situation ethics will be considered later.) As with legalism, a thoroughgoing antinomian in action is seldom observed. This does not mean that neither legalists nor antinomians

---

21. Kyle Haselden, *Morality and the Mass Media* (Nashville: Broadman Press, 1968), p. 12.

22. Ibid., pp. 15-20.

23. Ibid., p. 21.

exist, but that they are not as numerous or obvious as other types of absolutists and relativists.

To an antinomian, morality is strictly for the moment, occasion, or situation. The antinomian functions in the moral realm without any rules or principles from past wisdom. As Erickson puts it, "His [the antinomian's] morality arises spontaneously, whether by some form of intuition or by a direct revelation from the Holy Spirit, or something similar."[24]

Such moral action may sound strangely like that of the situationist, and indeed, it is sometimes difficult to distinguish between the situationist and the antinomian. However, at least theoretically, the situationist comes to the moral act "fully armed with all the wisdom of the past, with all its ethical maxims and instruction."[25] The situationist is willing to lay these past helps aside, however, in the interest of love. The antinomian, in contrast, does not bring principles, laws, or maxims to the ethical situation. He will be bound by no ethical establishment. He proffers an ethical solution strictly from the situation itself.

The antinomian standard of measuring the ethics of persuasive preaching is not actually a standard at all. Although some preachers seem to operate by some such standard, more than likely today's preacher faces a more formidable ethical position—that of relativism, especially situation ethics.

Relativism and Situation Ethics as a Standard of Measurement

Probably the most popular modern designation of relativism as a standard of measurement for persuasion is situation ethics. Approaches to this relativistic standard vary, although a central core of general convictions seems common to them.

1. Most situationists reject any objective, eternal, unchanging truths as binding upon everyone for all time.
2. Ethical practices are always to be determined by the context or situation in which the persuasive act occurs.
3. Usually the context or situation in which the act occurs is the good of individuals or the larger group—social utility.
4. With some, like Joseph Fletcher and his followers, the motivating force, or control, of situation ethics is agape love.

---

24. Millard J. Erickson, *Relativism in Contemporary Christian Ethics* (Grand Rapids: Baker Book House, 1974), p. 36.

25. Ibid.

Within these general principles a host of detailed and varying applications are made as determined by individual communicators.

It is not surprising that relativism seems to lead Edward Rogge to allow for such "questionable" rhetorical techniques as lying, exaggeration, selection of material favorable to the speaker, and suppression of material harmful to the speaker's case, on the basis of the standards developed by the society.[26] According to this standard such techniques could at the same time be ethical in one society and unethical in another. Totalitarian and democratic societies are in continual conflict for this very reason.

Again, it should not seem strange that B. J. Diggs would judge a friend, a lawyer, and a salesperson by differing ethical standards as defined by the specific situation, audience, or society and their assigned norms of ethics for each speaker's role.[27] Diggs allows for general rules of ethics such as Do not lie, Do not kill, Do not cheat, and Keep your promises. But in his contextual perspective of ethical standards even these norms depend upon the nature of the persuader's particular role with each audience for their interpretation.[28]

And the world ought not to be shocked by extreme persuasive techniques such as conflict, terrorism, deceit, and force used by the followers of radical writers such as Saul Alinsky. Alinsky advocates strong, "open-ended systems of ethics and values," which can be adapted freely to a constantly changing society.[29] Under a cloak of contextual ethical standards, radicals reject any rules of fair play, use any means to attain their ends, and disguise their efforts in popular and glittering slogans such as "Liberty, Equality, Fraternity"; "The Common Welfare"; and "The Pursuit of Happiness."[30]

Joseph Fletcher's Approach to Situation Ethics

Religious circles have not remained untouched by situation ethics. One of the most popular and celebrated exponents of this

---

26. See Edward Rogge, "Evaluating the Ethics of a Speaker in a Democracy," *Quarterly Journal of Speech* 45 (December 1959): 419-25.

27. B. J. Diggs, "Persuasion and Ethics," *Quarterly Journal of Speech* 50 (December 1964): 359 ff.

28. Ibid., p. 367.

29. See Saul D. Alinsky, *Reveille for Radicals* (New York: Vintage Books, 1969), p. 207, and *Rules for Radicals: A Practical Primer for Realistic Radicals* (New York: Random House, 1971).

30. Alinsky, *Reveille for Radicals,* p. 207.

philosophy has been Joseph Fletcher, professor of social ethics at the Episcopal Theological School, Cambridge, Massachusetts. In a paper read before the Alumni Association of the Harvard Divinity School at its annual meeting in April 1959, Fletcher presented his views on situation ethics.[31] This paper, which was also published in the *Harvard Divinity Bulletin,* became the "seed document" of his famous book on that subject.[32] The book's influence upon recent Christian ethical theory has been widespread, and situation ethics must be reckoned with in any consideration of the ethics of persuasive preaching.

To understand situation ethics as a standard of persuasive measurement, readers should know that Joseph Fletcher writes from the underlying presuppositions of (1) *Pragmatism,* or the principle of expediency;[33] (2) *Relativism,* or the rejection of any laws but love;[34] (3) *Positivism,* "in which faith propositions are posited or affirmed voluntaristically rather than rationalistically";[35] and (4) *Personalism,* in which "situation ethics puts people at the center of concern, not things."[36] Upon these four presuppositions Fletcher proffers six propositions, which are the heart of this situation ethics.[37]

Only One "Thing" Is Intrinsically Good; Namely, Love; Nothing Else at All

By *love* Fletcher means agape love—defined as "goodwill," or "benevolence."[38] It is something people do, not what they are. With agape love, people are always treated as ends, never as means.[39]

The Ruling Norm of Christian Decisions Is Love; Nothing Else

---

31. Joseph Fletcher, *Moral Responsibility: Situation Ethics at Work* (Philadelphia: Westminster Press, 1967), p. 11, footnote.

32. From *Situation Ethics,* by Joseph Fletcher. Copyright © MCMLXVI, W. L. Jenkins. Used by permission of The Westminster Press.

33. Ibid., pp. 40-43.

34. Ibid., pp. 43-46.

35. Ibid., pp. 46-50.

36. Ibid., pp. 50-52.

37. Ibid., chaps. 3—7; also reprinted in his *Moral Responsibility,* chap. 1.

38. Fletcher, *Situation Ethics,* pp. 63-64.

39. Ibid., p. 64.

In this proposition Fletcher replaces law with love, citing Jesus: "The sabbath was made for man, not man for the sabbath" (Mark 2:27). Also, Paul stated that one could eat the kind of food he desired as long as in the situation his act was edifying (I Cor. 10:23–26). Fletcher claims that these men functioned by love, not law.[40]

Love and Justice Are the Same
for Justice Is Love Distributed; Nothing Else

Philosophers and theologians who formerly treated love and justice as separate and balancing truths, now see these truths as identical in Fletcher's view. Fletcher denies that the two can ever be paradoxical, or even in true conflict—"Love = justice; justice = love."[41]

Love Wills the Neighbor's Good
Whether We Like Him or Not

Simply stated, Fletcher claims that loving and liking are not the same. Though he may not be insisting that loving and liking are mutually exclusive, he is distinguishing between the central thrust of each. In Fletcher's view agape is benevolent good will, which is divorced from self-interest, whereas liking is self-centered, partaking of the characteristics of *eros* love.[42]

Only the End Justifies the
Means; Nothing Else

Fletcher baldly asks, "If the end does not justify the means, what does?" and immediately answers "Obviously, nothing!"[43]

Love's Decisions Are Made Situationally,
Not Prescriptively

According to Fletcher, no moral decision is made by consulting codes, laws, rules, constitutions, or Bibles, but by sizing up the immediate situation, the present context of the act, and deciding in the spirit of agape love. An ethical decision, thus made, does not

---

40. Ibid., p. 69.

41. Ibid., p. 95.

42. Ibid., p. 105; Cf. Anders Nygren, *Agape and Eros,* trans. Philip S. Watson (London: S.P.C.K., 1953).

43. Fletcher, *Situation Ethics,* p. 120.

necessarily conflict with the aforementioned laws, but it is not bound to abide by them. Fletcher writes,

> The situationist, cutting himself loose from the dead hand of unyielding law, with its false promises of relief from the anguish of decision, can only determine that as a man of goodwill he will live as a free man, with all the ambiguities that go along with freedom.[44]

Relativistic Ethics' Influence

Relativism and situation ethics are not new. In religious circles men like Dietrich Bonhoeffer, Rudolph Bultmann, Karl Barth, H. Richard Niebuhr, and Paul Tillich have given impetus to this position.[45]

Most secular communicators avoid the extremes of absolutism and relativism. They find them inadequate for an exceedingly complex life. Brembeck and Howell, in the first edition of their book *Persuasion,* describe the problem of locating absolute principles.

> We . . . have searched for rules and principles to guide us. Think about this a moment and you will see that this implies that such rules and principles of a fixed and definite nature exist, or they can be formulated. Is this a true assumption? We are unable to judge its truth categorically; instead we can only turn to inspection of the world around us to look for evidence of the operation of fixed ethical principles manifested in the behavior of people.[46]

Brembeck and Howell's perspective is fairly representative of secular rhetoricians and, of course, rejects any view connected with divine revelation of moral laws such as those contained in the Bible. But lest the reader gets the impression that most rhetoricians, in rejecting absolute standards, see no problems with relativistic standards, consider the observation of Kenneth Andersen.

> All relativistic systems face the problem of answering "Relative to what?" Each individual through experience, and cultural and family conditioning comes to accept certain standards and to hold certain

---

44. Ibid., p. 135.

45. See works such as Dietrich Bonhoeffer, *Ethics,* ed. Eberhard Bethge (New York: Macmillan Co., 1955); Thomas C. Oden, *Radical Obedience: The Ethics of Rudolph Bultmann* (Philadelphia: Westminster Press, 1964); Rudolph Bultmann, *Jesus and the Word* (New York: Charles Scribner's Sons, 1958); Karl Barth, *Church Dogmatics,* 4 vol. (Edinburgh: T. & T. Clark, 1961), especially volumes 2 and 3; H. Richard Niebuhr, *The Responsible Self* (New York: Harper and Row, 1963); Paul Lehmann, *Ethics in a Christian Context* (New York: Harper and Row, 1963); and Paul Tillich, *Love, Power, and Justice* (New York: Oxford University Press, 1954).

46. Brembeck and Howell, *Persuasion: A Means of Social Control,* 1st ed. (New York: Prentice-Hall, 1952), pp. 444-45.

> values. The relativistic approach suggests that one weigh the factors in the situation in order to estimate what is the best ethical decision in that given situation.[47]

Andersen, therefore, recognizes the weaknesses in the relativist position but, like others, moves toward a situation-ethics approach. In doing so he approaches the problem by suggesting some answers to the question, Relative to what?

Relative to What?

Relative standards of ethics of persuasion are usually identified with the goals or ends of persuasion. Thus, having rejected any objective standards such as those in the Bible, Christianity, or even written law,[48] many communication scholars make the ends or goals of persuasion the standards of their ethics; they focus on social utility factors or humanitarian considerations.

Kenneth Andersen suggests that persuasive ethics may relate to the receiver's standards; to the entirety of the communication-binding process; to certain generalized goods or goals of society; or to the means and ends of persuasion.[49]

Wiseman and Barker start with the individual as standard—"to thine own self be true."[50] Wieman and Walter propose the nature of man as the standard of value, that is, his capacity to symbolize and his need of acceptance.[51]

The standard of James C. McCroskey varies slightly from those described above. McCroskey rejects the means and ends of persuasion as standards of ethics, holding that these are amoral or neutral. He advocates an ethic based on the speaker's *intent* toward his audience.[52] Intent, however, must be measured by some standard, and McCroskey measures the intent of the speaker in terms

---

47. Andersen, *Persuasion,* p. 319.

48. For an example of the instability of written law as an absolute standard of ethics, see Brembeck and Howell, *Persuasion,* 1st ed., p. 445, quoting from Vilfredo Pareto, *The Mind and Society,* ed. Arthur Livingston and trans. Borgiomo and Livingston (New York: Harcourt Brace and Co., 1935).

49. Andersen, *Persuasion,* pp. 317-19.

50. Gordon Wiseman and Larry Barker, *Speech-Interpersonal Communication* (San Francisco, Ca.: Chandler Publishing Company, 1967), p. 156.

51. Henry N. Wieman and Otis M. Walter, "Toward an Analysis of Ethics for Rhetoric," *Quarterly Journal of Speech* 43 (October 1957): 266-70.

52. James C. McCroskey, *An Introduction to Rhetorical Communication,* 2d ed. (Englewood Cliffs, N.J.: Prentice-Hall, 1972), pp. 266-70.

of whether it is good or bad for his audience.[53] McCroskey's standard, then, is social utility, a standard held by many communication scholars.

Professor Donald K. Smith asserts that one way of reducing the level of abstraction of ethical norms is to "approach ethical analysis by observing the relationship between particular public speeches and the social institutions supported and served by these speeches."[54] Thus, according to Smith, speeches should be measured against the ethical systems held by institutions such as the school, church, sales force, and courtroom. These ethical systems do not cross one another. One does not measure the ethics of a sales pitch by the ethics of the courtroom or the church.

Smith then proceeds to set forth the American political system, elsewhere called the free democratic society's value system, as the overriding ethical system.[55] Presumably, the ethical practices of the lesser institutions should not violate the ethical system of the higher organization.

In addition to these social and humanitarian standards are those mentioned earlier (in chapter 3). Thus Albert Schweitzer's "reverence for life," Sören Kierkegaard's "dignity of the individual," Everett Lee Hunt's "freedom of choice," and Karl R. Wallace's "tenets of our democratic society" are not just ends of persuasion; they are also the standards of the ethics of persuasion held by their advocates.

In like manner, scientific and rational ends, semantic soundness, and rhetorical factors sometimes function as ethical standards of persuasion by their proponents. A popular example of this approach can be seen in Robert T. Oliver's list of "fundamental ethical standards." He mentions negative prohibitions such as: Do not falsify evidence, Do not speak on subjects on which you are not informed, Avoid "smear" attacks, Do not delude yourself into believing that the end justifies the means.[56]

Relative approaches to the ethics of persuasion fit in well with the contemporary belief in situation ethics, the philosophy that rejects any absolute codes or moral laws as standards of conduct binding in every instance. A persuader committed to situation

---

53. Ibid., p. 231.

54. Donald K. Smith, *Man Speaking: A Rhetoric of Public Speech* (New York: Dodd, Mead, and Co., 1969), p. 239.

55. Ibid., pp. 242-45.

56. Oliver, *Psychology of Persuasive Speech,* pp. 29-31.

ethics determines the morality of his functions in terms of the given factors operative at the time of his persuading. In secular speech circles this total situation is usually seen in relation to the backdrop of the social and humanitarian factors mentioned above. In Christian persuasion, situationists claim only one eternal and universally binding law, the law of agape love. The question that faces the Christian persuader today is, Is relativism, or situation ethics, adequate as a standard for measuring the ethics of persuasive preaching?

Points of Agreement with Situation Ethics

At first glance relativism and situation ethics might appear to be entirely foreign to the Bible and evangelical Christianity. Although much of the situationist's approach justifies such a suspicion, not all of it does. Christian persuaders find themselves in agreement with certain tenets of situation ethics.

The Complexity of Life's Situations

Christians agree with situationists that we are living in an exceedingly complex physical, spiritual, and moral world. No two individuals, objects, disciplines, or moral decisions are exactly alike. Nonidentity, the fact that objects differ, is always present. Yet people tend to join things together, ignoring their differences and magnifying their similarities. In this highly complex situation, general ethical principles, rules, and decisions may apply to everyone, but specific rules and decisions may have to be tailored to fit individual needs. Killing, for example, may be justified in a defensive war but not in peaceful times.

The Process Character of the World

A complicating factor of our universe is that of continual process. Heraclitus, the ancient Greek philosopher, argued that a man could not step into the same river twice. Both the man and the river constantly change. Times and attitudes change. America today is not the America of its birth two hundred years ago. The moral decisions that justified revolution in 1776 now are used by some to condemn it. Social, legal, and ethical standards once held in churches have now been laid aside. Movies, once condemned in some churches as "worldly," are now watched approvingly on television. Attitudes on social issues such as race, abortion, war, equal rights, sex, and drinking have undergone drastic changes, often to the church's consternation and sometimes to its ineffectiveness.

Theological change sometimes moves so rapidly and erratically that ministers and laymen cannot keep up with it. Constant process often makes ethical decisions difficult, but the same changes that sometimes upset people also free them from some of the chains of traditional legalism. The Christian persuader profits from the process character of life.

The Relatedness of Objects

Although we reject unqualified relativity, we agree with situationists regarding the relationship that exists between all things. No man, church, group, race, or country exists in splendid isolation. We are all interdependent upon one another. Churches may disagree theologically, but they need each other to present a united front against social, moral, and spiritual evils in the world. Although the relatedness of things sometimes makes moral decisions difficult, this does not change the reality of relations. Tolerance and love help to relieve the difficulty.

The Abstract Character of Language, Laws, and Rules

Christian persuaders agree with situationists concerning the semantic problems connected with words used to communicate laws, rules, and maxims. We recognize that the laws and the words used to express them are not the objects, persons, or moral situations that the words are describing. We also understand that verbal laws do not describe all of the situations they are being used to describe, curtail, or forbid. Words are abstract, general, limited maps of the situation-territories they are discussing. Because they are abstract they leave out details of the moral situations they are treating. As a result, words and laws cannot always be used to fit every moral situation they are being used to control. For example, Christian persuaders would agree with situationists regarding the difficulty of applying the moral commandment of the aged apostle John when he wrote:

> Do not love the world or the things in the world. If any one loves the world, love for the Father is not in him. For all that is in the world, the lust of the flesh and the lust of the eyes and the pride of life, is not of the Father but is of the world. And the world passes away, and the lust of it; but he who does the will of God abides for ever (I John 2:15–17).

The semantic vagueness of such phrases as "the world," "the things in the world," "the lust of the flesh," "the lust of the eyes," and "the pride of life," though communicating certain forbidden preoccupations, are a long way from defining precisely what those preoccupations are. Preachers have used the above text to flail such things as movies, card playing, ballroom dancing, alcoholic beverages, illicit sexual activities, chewing and smoking tobacco, bobbed hair, bossy wives, and women preachers. But seldom have these same preachers used this text to condemn war, racial prejudice, economic injustice, or sexual inequities. And yet the latter sins are as "worldly" as the former ones. That is the problem all Christian persuaders face, not just situationists. The answer to the problem of the abstractness of language and laws, of course, lies in the advantages of this linguistic characteristic, not in its weakness. Were it not for the elasticity of language and laws, we could not use them at all, for one law would have to apply to one act and nothing else. Interpretation of laws, rules, and maxims may be a tricky endeavor, but it is nonetheless necessary and helpful. It must be done with semantic soundness, with hermeneutical accuracy, and in the spirit of agape love.

The Failure of Extreme Absolutism and Legalism

Who can challenge the situationist's criticism of extreme absolutism and its accompanying evil, legalism? Jesus bitterly attacked the Pharisees for these excesses (Matt. 23:1–36 and parallels). And Paul warned the Corinthians that his ministry was "not in a written code but in the Spirit; for the written code kills, but the Spirit gives life" (II Cor. 3:6).

Therefore Christians can agree with situationists that extreme absolute and legalistic interpretation and application of all laws, rules, and codes is not only reprehensible, it is impossible. Many of the laws of Leviticus binding upon Israel in its early history (i.e., those concerning leprosy, purification, and offerings) were necessary and helpful during those days. The same could be said of some of the commandments for the early church (i.e., the prohibition against eating meat offered to idols or the meat of strangled animals). But these laws mean little to Christians of the twentieth century.

This does not mean that all Old and New Testament laws, commandments, and standards are obsolete and nonbinding. The Decalogue is still the highest and most necessary law of civilization. Jesus said:

> Think not that I have come to abolish the law and the prophets; I have come not to abolish them but to fulfill them. For truly, I say to

> you, till heaven and earth pass away, not an iota, not a dot, will pass from the law until all is accomplished'' (Matt. 5:17–18).

And Paul argued that despite our inability to live up to the law, it is still good. He wrote: ''What then shall we say? That the law is sin? By no means!'' (Rom. 7:7a). And he continued: ''So the law is holy, and the commandment is holy and just and good'' (Rom. 7:12). The law is, however, inadequate for salvation.

The Christian's task, then, is to love, respect, and obey the law but to avoid the excesses of absolutism and legalism. The law cannot be pressed in all its details upon people. The spirit of the law must be maintained rather than insisting upon the letter of the law.[57]

The Difficulty of Moral Decision Making

Because of complexity, change, relatedness, abstractness of language and laws, and the failure of absolutism-legalism, situationists are correct in asserting that moral decision making is difficult. There are no easy answers or oversimplified solutions to complex ethical problems. For this very reason a quick moral decision made in the heat of physical or emotional stimulation, even in the name of love, is a vastly oversimplified and dangerous one. To ignore Christian tradition, family training, and personal moral standards at such a time can be disastrous to human personality. Moral decision making is difficult even when carefully researched and thought out. It is complicated even more when previous guidelines are forsaken.

The Importance of Love

Because moral decision making is difficult, these decisions should be made in the spirit of agape love, a biblical standard that is selfless, people-centered, and God-centered. Agape love should be directed to all people, whether or not they can return that love. This involves loving the unlovely, the unattractive, the uncouth, as well as the lovely, attractive, and gracious. Jesus commanded: ''Love your enemies, bless them that curse you, do good to them that hate you, and pray for them which despitefully use you . . .'' (Matt. 5:44, KJV).

---

57. For a good critique of the extremities of current morality—legalism vs. relativism, see Haselden, *Morality and the Mass Media,* chap. 1, ''Rethinking Morality.''

Persuasive preaching that carries out these principles should be ethically sound as well as rhetorically effective. It cannot stop, however, at these points. Like life in general, it needs further guidelines. Although the above principles are good, they are not enough. Christians agree with situationists on these principles, but there are points of disagreement that should be raised.

Points of Disagreement with Situation Ethics

Situation ethics, though widespread in its influence, is not without its critics, both of the right and left, of the secular and sacred, pro and con.[58] Criticisms are directed at virtually every tenet of this controversial philosophy. In terms of the ethics of persuasive preaching, however, disagreements may be seen at least at three major points.

A Vague Definition of Love

Few would challenge agape love as a necessary ingredient in ethical judgments. But when Fletcher and others advocate agape love as the only standard of ethical judgment without defining how that love should operate, it becomes a weak and useless guide. It is not enough merely to say an act is good because it helps persons, or bad because it hurts persons.[59] Though such a view is plausible, its vagueness does not help a preacher decide whether or not he should preach a sermon on racism when he knows that to do so may split his church. Yet Fletcher's discussion of agape love seldom gives a preacher more guidance than to say "do the loving thing." Such vagueness of definition on Fletcher's part leads James M. Gustafson to write:

> "Love," like "situation," is a word that runs through Fletcher's book like a greased pig. . . . Nowhere does Fletcher take the trouble to indicate in a systematic way his various uses of it. It refers to everything he wants it to refer to. It is the *only* thing that is intrinsically good; it *equals* justice; it is a formal *principle,* it is a *disposition,* it is a *predicate* and not a property, it is a ruling *norm.*[60].

---

58. See works such as Haselden, *Morality and the Mass Media;* John C. Bennett and others, *Storm over Ethics* (Philadelphia: United Church Press, 1967); Harvey Cox, ed., *The Situation Ethics Debate* (Philadelphia: Westminster Press, 1968); Millard J. Erickson, *Relativism in Contemporary Christian Ethics* (Grand Rapids: Baker Book House, 1974); and Erwin W. Lutzer, *The Morality Gap: An Evangelical Response to Situation Ethics* (Chicago: Moody Press, 1972).

59. Fletcher, *Situation Ethics,* p. 59.

60. James M. Gustafson, "Love Monism," in *Storm Over Ethics,* ed. John C. Bennett, p. 33.

Kyle Haseldon senses the same thing in Fletcher's definition of love as "benevolence" and writes: "Fletcher is wrong in reducing love to good will, to benevolence and in making *that* the determinate of right and wrong in a given situation."[61] According to Haseldon, such an appeal "is slippery ground and most people who try to stand on it plunge into the wholly unprincipled libertinism Fletcher disavows."[62]

Millard Erickson charges that the vagueness of the concept of love "suggests that situationism has greater affinity with antinomianism than was initially claimed [by situationists]."[63] Although situationists approach ethical decision making armed with the principles, rules, and maxims of the past and antinomians do not, situationists are willing to drop the rules if love dictates such. Erickson claims that such willingness to drop all rules in the interest of love pushes situationists dangerously close to antinomianism.[64]

Situationism, then, is inadequate at the point where it makes agape love the only standard of ethical judgment and action. People need more specific and helpful guidelines than beneficence in the ethical decision-making process.

A Naive Faith in Man's Judgment

Even if one accepts agape love as binding in ethical decision making, he still must know how to apply that principle. Inasmuch as Fletcher and others have rejected any predetermined or "prefabricated" rules to help in the application of love in an ethical decision, man is left to exercise his choice solely by his own human judgment. Is that human judgment adequate? Any biblical theologian must answer No.

At the outset of his *Nature and Destiny of Man,* Reinhold Niebuhr opined, "Man has always been his own most vexing problem."[65] Even secular writers recognize the distorted nature of man's reasoning process. Brembeck and Howell, in criticizing "The Cult of Reason," say, "This approach assumes that the persuadee is capable of setting aside his prejudices and focusing his

---

61. Haseldon, *Morality and the Mass Media,* p. 22.

62. Ibid.

63. Erickson, *Contemporary Christian Ethics,* p. 100.

64. Ibid., p. 97.

65. Reinhold Niebuhr, *The Nature and Destiny of Man: A Christian Interpretation* (New York: Charles Scribner's Sons, 1949), p. 1.

intellect on an issue. . . ."[66] Later Brembeck and Howell continue this thought, writing:

> There are obvious values in being factual and logical. But much human conduct is nonlogical. Choices are made frequently on bases other than those of evidence and reason, which, though involved, are not deciding factors.[67]

Also, Wayne C. Minnick understands the weaknesses of human judgment, suggesting:

> . . . some people adopt and change their attitudes in response to reason and reality testing, others are motivated to accept and reject attitudes largely because of social influences, and still others are motivated primarily by ego-defensive needs. Thus, only persons inclined to view the world rationally can be moved by appeals to argument and evidence.[68]

Although the latter criticisms of the rational process are directed toward receivers in the communication process, there is no reason to believe that speakers are exempt from the weaknesses of human judgment. This claim is true especially when one turns from human writings to biblical teaching.

No one was committed more to agape love as a lifestyle than were Jesus and Paul. Christ charged his followers, "Love your enemies and pray for those who persecute you" (Matt. 5:44). Later he added: "For if you love those who love you, what reward have you? Do not even the tax collectors do the same?" (Matt. 5:46). He also lifted love to the highest level of the law, saying:

> You shall love the Lord your God with all your heart, and with all your soul, and with all your mind. This is the great and first commandment. And a second is like it, You shall love your neighbor as yourself. On these two commandments depend all the law and the prophets (Matt. 22:37–40).

Nevertheless, Jesus also recognized the weakness of human judgment and found it necessary to say to Peter and the other disciples, "If any man would come after me, let him deny himself and take up his cross and follow me" (Matt. 16:24). And on another occasion, sensing the fickle judgment of a multitude of would-be followers, Christ said, "If any one comes to me and does not hate his own father and mother and wife and children and

---

66. Brembeck and Howell, *Persuasion,* 2d ed., p. 237.

67. Ibid.

68. Wayne C. Minnick, *The Art of Persuasion,* 2d ed. (Boston: Houghton Mifflin Co., 1968), p. 285.

brothers and sisters, yes, even his own life, he cannot be my disciple" (Luke 14:26). Christ knew that self-interest warps human judgment and makes it unreliable.

Paul repeatedly urged believers to love the Lord and one another.[69] His classic poem on agape love recorded in I Corinthians 13 leaves little doubt as to how love is to be applied.

Paul thoroughly establishes his commitment to agape love as a way of life. And yet, at the same time, Paul never claimed that his belief in and practice of love were sufficient to make him a man of unerring judgment. On the contrary, Paul saw man as totally depraved by the power of sin.

> None is righteous, no, not one;
> no one understands, no one seeks for God.
> All have turned aside, together they have gone wrong;
> no one does good, not even one.
> Their throat is an open grave,
> they use their tongues to deceive.
> The venom of asps is under their lips.
> Their mouth is full of curses and bitterness.
> Their feet are swift to shed blood,
> in their paths are ruin and misery,
> and the way of peace they do not know.
> There is no fear of God before their eyes (Rom. 3:10–18).

In this penetrating passage, quoted from the Old Testament,[70] Paul concludes that the whole race is sinful (Rom. 3:10–12) and that the whole man is sinful (Rom. 3:13–18). How can such individuals exercise adequate moral judgment? To show the struggle Paul had with doing right and wrong one needs but to turn to Romans 7:14–25, where Paul records his own testimony of battling with sin. Although some hold that Paul in this passage is describing his struggle with sin prior to his conversion, the context would seem to support the position that he is confessing a struggle he goes through as a Christian. If a Christian of Paul's caliber must confess, "I do not understand my own actions. For I do not do what I want, but I do the very thing I hate" (Rom. 7:15), how, even under the motivation of agape love, can anyone consistently make correct moral decisions? When Paul admits, "For I know that nothing good dwells within me, that is, in my flesh. I can will what is right,

---

69. See passages such as Rom. 8:28; 13:8, 9; I Cor. 2:9; 8:3; Gal. 5:14; Eph. 5:25, 28, 33; Col. 3:19; I Thess. 4:9; and others.

70. Cf. Psalm 14:1–3; 53;1–3; Eccles. 7:20; Psalm 5:9; 140:3; 10:7; Isa. 59:7, 8; Psalm 36:1.

but I cannot do it. For I do not do the good I want, but the evil I do not want is what I do" (Rom. 7:18, 19), does he not reveal the inevitable flaw that mars all human moral judgment? Earlier, Paul admitted his weakness in judgment to the Corinthians.

> But with me it is a very small thing that I should be judged by you or by any human court. I do not even judge myself. I am not aware of anything against myself, but I am not thereby acquitted. It is the Lord who judges me. Therefore do not pronounce judgment before the time, before the Lord comes, who will bring to light the things now hidden in darkness and will disclose the purposes of the heart. Then every man will receive his commendation from God (I Cor. 4:3–5).

Christians should not insist that men never make correct moral decisions, with or without the motivation of agape love. What they should object to is the situationist's naive proposal that mankind, guided only by agape love, will, or can, consistently make right moral decisions in the complex situations of life. Neither Holy Scripture nor human experience supports such a claim.

A Forsaking of Life's Continuities, Traditions, Maxims, and Laws

Although situationists avowedly differ from antinomians (who reject all eternal laws in the decision-making process) in that situationists approach moral decision making armed with the moral wisdom of the past, the difference between the two is so tenuous as to be of little help to persons forced to make ethical choices. The antinomian makes the moral decision without any rules whatsoever. The situationist may draw upon his past moral training as long as he does not rely upon it as legally binding. The situationist readily casts aside laws, principles, or maxims if they seem to contradict or impede the law of agape love. In this way life's continuities, traditions, and laws are so emasculated as to render them virtually useless. For all practical purposes they are rejected as legalistic stumbling blocks that are barriers to making moral decisions by love alone.[71]

According to situationists, by forsaking life's traditions and laws man enters a new freedom bound only by the law of love. That may be true for one partner in moral decision making, but is it true for others who are involved? The relativists are inconsistent at this

---

71. For example, see Joseph Fletcher's systematic derogation of the Ten Commandments as being law in conflict with love, *Situation Ethics*, pp. 71 ff.

point. Such action tends to ignore other people's freedom, dignity, and standards. An act of adultery involves at least three persons, maybe more. Are all involved freely and happily released? An act of thievery involves at least two or more. Are the victims equally freed and blessed with the thief? Likewise, when a preacher financially "fleeces" God's people in a religious meeting, even for high-sounding ends, God is not served thereby, nor are the people's freedom, dignity, and standards honored. In such circumstances, both God and the people are unethically manipulated.

Though legalism may be charged with being a complex, burdensome system, and situation ethics touted as a simplified approach to life's moral problems, the reverse may also be true. Situation ethics by virtue of its simplicity becomes an intolerable burden. To ask anyone to make snap decisions without previously adopted standards is asking too much. Even agape love gets distorted at these times.

Situation ethics views each life act as separate from all others. It decides then and there, untied from any other precedent, experience, or law, except agape love. It turns its back upon the great philosophers and moralists. It forsakes tradition, experience, and revelation if they conflict with human judgment motivated by agape love. The situationist functions as though he alone understands agape love and how it should be administered. On this latter point Bishop Gerald Kennedy of the Methodist church eloquently states:

> The final impression that *Situation Ethics* makes upon me is of an arrogance so overpowering as to be almost unbelievable. Can any man announce that he is capable of deciding any question without help from his brethren? Is any person able to ignore tradition as if everything began with him at this particular moment? Can anyone subscribe to such an idea without being guilty of the pride which the Bible defines as the ultimate sin? Absolutes are for God alone and only the meek inherit the earth.[72]

Though life is marked by constant change and complexity, making ethical decisions difficult, people are aided in these difficult decisions by certain continuities. The Bible sets forth eternal truth. Jesus said, "Heaven and earth will pass away, but my words will not pass away" (Matt. 24:35). The Constitution of the United

---

72. Gerald Kennedy, "The Nature of Heresy," in *Storm Over Ethics,* ed. John C. Bennett, p. 148.

States remains useful, not simply because it can be changed through amendment, but also because it contains abiding laws.

Thus, as soul-binding absolutism and its correlative legalism must be rejected, so also must thoroughgoing relativism be disavowed. While accepting life's changes, moral decisions can nonetheless be made in the light of agape love guided by life's continuities, traditions, and biblical truths.

Effect of Situation Ethics on Persuasive Preaching

Situation ethics is not just an isolated philosophy studied and cited by students as an academic discipline or a justification for loose living. It permeates many activities of our daily lives. Specifically, situationism must be dealt with by preachers in at least two areas of the ethics of persuasive preaching: (1) the ends-justify-the-means controversy; (2) relativism vs. the Bible as standards of ethical measurement.

Do the Ends Justify the Means?

As mentioned in chapter 3, most rhetoricians reject the unqualified idea that the ends of persuasion justify the means of attaining them. Rhetoricians allow for certain exceptions to this rule under extreme circumstances, such as the preservation of life or national security. As a normal practice in life, however, most rhetoricians warn against the ends justifying the means.[73]

And yet, a relativist such as Joseph Fletcher continues to press the question, "If the end does not justify the means, what does?"[74] It is important that we understand clearly what Fletcher does not mean as well as what he does mean by this question and its associated philosophy. Millard Erickson suggests four logical possibilities:

1. A good end justifies a good means.
2. Any old end justifies a good means.
3. A good end justifies any old means.
4. Any old end justifies any old means.[75]

Fletcher's conviction that values are not intrinsically good or bad eliminates numbers one and two above. He writes: "There are no 'values' in the sense of inherent goods—value is what *happens* to something when it happens to be useful to love working for the

---

73. For example, see Oliver, *Psychology of Persuasive Speech,* p. 31.

74. Fletcher, *Situation Ethics,* p. 120.

75. Erickson, *Contemporary Christian Ethics,* p. 57.

sake of persons."[76] Thus, no act has value unless it contributes to the end of love. Again, Fletcher specifically rejects number four listed above saying, "It should be plainly apparent, of course, that not any old end will justify any old means. We all assume that some ends justify some means; no situationist would make a universal of it!"[77]

Fletcher, therefore, is left with the third logical possibility listed above, "a good end justifies any old means." He supports this position by citing Paul in I Corinthians (6:12 and 10:23), where the apostle claims that all things are lawful, but not all things are helpful. But is Fletcher's claim of Paul's rejection of the intrinsicalist position true? Serious question has been raised about Fletcher's confusion of the nature of the good with the lawful. Erickson refutes Fletcher's claim.

> Yet Paul is not necessarily identifying the lawful with the good [in I Cor. 6:12 and 10:23]. To be good means being lawful plus being helpful. Not everything lawful is helpful and therefore good. He is not asserting that what is unlawful can become good by being edifying.[78]

One must remember in connection with Paul's position that he asks the Roman believers, "And why not do evil that good may come?—as some people slanderously charge us with saying" (Rom. 3:8). Again, the apostle questions the Romans, saying: "What shall we say then? Are we to continue in sin that grace may abound? By no means! How can we who died to sin still live in it?" (Rom. 6:1-2). Such statements indicate that Paul did not believe that "a good end justifies any old means."

Furthermore, the ends-justify-the-means view is suspect because of its vulnerability to license. Man's inhumanity to man on the basis that religious ends justify any means argues strongly against this proposition. What other rationalization could John Calvin have used to justify his allowing Servetus to be burned at the stake to preserve trinitarian orthodoxy?[79] What other philosophy could the Roman Catholic Church have enlisted to justify the inquisitions to suppress heresy in the reformation?[80]

---

76. Fletcher, *Situation Ethics,* p. 50.

77. Ibid., p. 121.

78. Erickson, *Contemporary Christian Ethics,* pp. 57-58.

79. See Williston Walker, *A History of the Christian Church,* rev. ed. (New York: Charles Scribner's Sons, 1959), pp. 355-56.

80. Ibid., pp. 231-32.

Ends-and-means relativism is applied to many decisions—from birth control to euthanasia; from white lies to political deception; from hyperbole in preaching to mass manipulation of crowds from the pulpit. Not all of these means claim justification by carefully thought out ends. Sometimes they are perpetrated thoughtlessly by people motivated solely by selfishness or self-preservation. Nevertheless, the ends-justifying-the-means philosophy as developed by Joseph Fletcher and his followers allows for the most extreme actions ostensibly justified by the motive of agape love—nothing else. Love may be a many splendored thing, but it needs more guidelines than a beneficent feeling provides.

Six

The Biblical Standard for Persuasive Preaching

Relativism, Situationism, and the Bible

The Christian persuader is committed to the Bible as his ultimate course of faith and practice. He may study other books, espouse assorted ideas, profit from various ethical systems, but in the final analysis he measures all systems by the standard of the Bible and its theology. Joseph Fletcher and other situationists claim to be biblical. It is doubtful, however, that they would agree that the Bible's propositional assertions are true for all men of all times and places.

Thus, not all theologians, preachers, and laymen agree on how the Bible should be used. Christians as well as non-Christians face the absolutist-relativist problem in biblical interpretation. Although to the outsider theologians might seem to fit better into the absolutist rather than the relativist ethical system, this is not necessarily the case. For theologically oriented communicators represent virtually all the shades of opinion in the absolutist-relativist controversy. Some hold to an extreme absolutist biblical ethic with an attendant system of legalism. Others hold to the situation ethics system of Joseph Fletcher and others, who insist that only agape love is intrinsically good and eternally true.[1] Still other theologians hold a more mediating position, utilizing characteristics of both the absolutist and the relativist.

This latter position seems to offer the most to the concerned Christian persuader. He wants to avoid the extreme absolutist-legalist preoccupation with the minute and manifold details of religious laws. He also rejects the loose and unbridled indulgence of

1. Joseph Fletcher, *Situation Ethics: The New Morality* (Philadelphia: Westminster Press, 1966), pp. 57-68; and John A. T. Robinson, *Honest to God* (Philadelphia: Westminster Press, 1963), pp. 105-21.

the sheer relativist or situationist. The Christian persuader eagerly accepts agape love as his dominant motivation to action, but he also gladly accepts some guidelines that have been laid down for him and have been tested and approved through the centuries. The Christian persuader willingly starts where Christ started.

At the outset of his earthly ministry Jesus was severely tempted by the devil. Faced with three difficult ethical decisions that seemed to call for immediate response, Christ called upon eternal, scriptural laws as guidelines for his decisions. Three times he refused the temptation, answering the devil: "It is written . . ." (Matt. 4:4, 7, 10). If Jesus was disposed to abide by even part of God's laws in moral decision making, we can do no less.

When Jesus openly avowed, "Think not that I have come to abolish the law and the prophets; I have come not to abolish but to fulfil them" (Matt. 5:17), Christian persuaders take him seriously. When Christ pointedly claimed, "If you love me, you will keep my commandments" (John 14:15), Christian preachers obey him—not grudgingly, but gladly; not legalistically, but lovingly.

The entire Bible forms the ethical backdrop for the persuasive preacher—not necessarily as a legalistic catalogue of detailed rules to master and obey to the letter, but as a reference guide that he may consult when needed. It is true that the more the preacher saturates himself with the biblical law and lore, the more sensitive he will be to God's will on at least general ethical matters. Such knowledge frequently will aid him on specific ethical decisions as well. Until the Christian preacher arrives at such a desirable mastery of the whole Bible, however, he should start where Jesus viewed ethical law to be more crucial.

The Two Great Commandments

Because agape love alone does not give us sufficient guidelines to help in the often tense and highly emotional encounters of life in general and persuasion in particular, a discussion of the ethics of persuasion can begin at a point where Jesus judged both love and law to be of supreme importance.[2] In answer to the test question of a Sadducee and lawyer regarding the great commandment, Jesus answered:

---

2. For an excellent treatment of the two great commandments as a foundation for authentic morality, see Kyle Haselden, *Morality and the Mass Media* (Nashville: Broadman Press, 1968), chap. 2.

> You shall love the Lord your God with all your heart, and with all your soul, and with all your mind. This is the great and first commandment. And a second is like it, You shall love your neighbor as yourself. On these two commandments depend all the law and the prophets (Matt. 22:37–40).

Before applying this text to ethical standards of persuasion, some clarifications should be made.

First, agape love is understood as the supreme love discussed in the New Testament. Agape is indifferent to values. It is not motivated by the value of the object. It is the type of love elicited by our Lord when he commanded, "Love your enemies and pray for those who persecute you" (Matt. 5:44).

Second, both love and law are part of the great commandments—not just the love of the situationists, not just the law of the legalists.

Third, love is central and law is peripheral; love is dominant and law is subservient; love is primary and law is secondary.

Fourth, though love is the dominant motive, law is the guideline for the Christian persuader. Law is not destroyed by love but fulfilled by it.

The importance of these observations is underscored by Jesus' brief commentary, "On these two commandments depend all the law and the prophets" (Matt. 22:40).

Building Basic Structure

The structure of ethical standards has agape love as the dominant and continuous motive. Examination of the two great commandments cited by Jesus shows that love, and consequently our ethics, have three goals or ends. Two of these goals are specifically mentioned, one is implied.

Love God
Love Neighbor
Love Self (implied)

A comparison of these biblical objects of agape love against the backdrop of other rhetoricians' ends, goals, or standards reveals both differences and similarities. Like other responsible rhetoricians, Christian persuaders are bound to an ethical system that respects social and humanitarian objects—loving neighbors and loving themselves. But the Christian persuader is also bound to an additional and more demanding standard or goal—loving and pleasing God.

From the two great commandments of the Bible, then, the Christian is obligated to at least two fundamental standards:

Love God - Theological Standard
Love Neighbor } - Social Effects Standard
Love Self }

From the order of these commands it is obvious that regardless of the humanistic implications of the gospel and modern philosophy, God, not man, is the primary object of man's love. The ethics of Christian persuasion must be measured first against everything people can know and learn about God. The more Christians know about God the less apt they are to violate his will and to harm his highest creation—man.

Close to the great commandment to love God is the command to love your neighbor. Jesus said, "And a second is like it," raising the second commandment close to, if not equal to, the first.

Christianity, though not humanistic, is man-centered. Christ is interested in people. Regardless of any seeming sacredness of institutions, methods, creeds, traditions, cultures, laws, or ceremonies, the focus of true love is people. A persuasive ethic, then, must be consistent with the agape love of people. And the agape love of people must be consistent with that of Christ, who said, "I came that they may have life, and have it abundantly" (John 10:10b).

People must not be viewed solely as potential converts, church members, tithers, or leaders to help in the work of the church. People must be seen as persons maturing in the habitat of freedom and in the atmosphere of love, the source of which is God.[3] The words of Paul ought never to be forgotten, "For those whom he foreknew he also predestined to be conformed to the image of his Son . . ." (Rom. 8:29). Persuasive goals must be in keeping with these human concerns.

Love of self is clearly implied in the great commandments: "You shall love your neighbor *as yourself*" (Matt. 23:39, italics mine). Surely God does not ask his people to love either their neighbors or themselves in an unwholesome, selfish, fleshly way. He expects them to love their neighbors and themselves according to the human dignity he has bestowed upon his children through regeneration.

Christian persuaders need to evaluate themselves objectively, to understand their strengths and weaknesses. Interestingly enough, in a context of bearing one another's burdens, the apostle Paul com-

---

3. Ibid.

mands: "But let each one test his own work, and then his reason to boast will be in himself alone. . . . For each man will have to bear his own load" (Gal. 6:4–5).

The biblical view of God's people is a high one. Paul reminded the Corinthians:

> Do you not know that your body is a temple of the Holy Spirit within you, which you have from God? You are not your own; you were bought with a price. So glorify God in your body (I Cor. 6:19–20).

This text clearly shows the value all have in the sight of God. It is not wrong to love one's self in the proper way—to cultivate, develop, educate, and prepare one's self to serve God and neighbor better. There is something radically wrong with the Christian who insists on debasing himself. Self-flagellation may impress outsiders, but it carries little weight with God.

The persuasive preacher must have confidence in himself, in his message, and in his listeners if he is to be effective for his Lord. Nothing less is ethical. Social and humanitarian concerns focus on one's neighbor, but they include one's self.

The great commandments of our Lord, then, form the basic biblical foundation for the Christian's standard of ethics of persuasion. This standard is both God-centered (theological) and man-centered (social). On these two great foundation stones the structure of the Christian persuader's ethics must be built. Any end, goal, or standard of persuasion must be measured first of all against the standard, Will this please God and help mankind? Once committed to these two foundation stones, the Christian persuader can build his superstructure of the ethics of persuasive preaching.

Building a Superstructure of Biblical Ethics

Although no attempt will be made here to develop a broad and detailed system of biblical ethics for the preacher, the Bible certainly provides such a possibility. Harry Emerson Fosdick, the leading liberal preacher of the last generation, wrote:

> The Scripture is an amazing compendium of experiments in human life under all sorts of conditions, from the desert to cosmopolitan Rome, and with all sorts of theories, from the skepticism of Ecclesiastes to the faith of John. It is incalculably rich in insight and illumination. It has light to shed on all sorts of human problems now and always. . . .[4]

---

4. Harry Emerson Fosdick, "What Is the Matter with Preaching?" *Harper's Magazine* 157 (July 1928): 133-41.

With this broad appeal, the Bible also provides a corresponding ethic.

After serious study of the great commandments, the Christian persuader would do well to analyze and apply the agape love taught by the apostle Paul in I Corinthians 13. In these beautiful verses Paul warns that the absence of agape love in life may lead to tragic failure as a communicator, a prophet, a pietist, a philanthropist, or even a martyr.

The apostle suggests that agape love rejects the negative factors of life such as jealousy, boastfulness, arrogance, rudeness, and resentment. At the same time it is patient, kind, all-bearing, all-believing, and all-enduring.

Paul closes his great love poem by setting forth two contrasting laws of life—the law of the temporal, and the law of the eternal. The law of the temporal indicates that some things in life are subject to process, change, and termination. Paul clearly promises, however, that faith, hope, and agape love will abide forever (the law of the eternal). But the greatest of these is agape love.

As part of the superstructure of the Christian persuader's ethic are the driving emotion and the divine objective—agape love and God's highest creation, man.

Beyond the great commandments of the Bible—love God, love neighbor, and love self—and beyond Paul's love chapter (I Cor. 13), the Christian persuader may further enhance the superstructure of his ethical standard by a study and application of Christ's Sermon on the Mount (Matt. 5:1—7:27).

The Sermon on the Mount was spoken specifically to Jesus' disciples, although others apparently were listening (cf. Matt. 7:28–29). Accordingly, the ethical ideal set forth in Jesus' sermon cannot be said to be binding upon non-Christians. Only the Christian persuader should feel the obligation to live toward its "kingdom ideal."

The ethic of the Sermon on the Mount is a present ideal. It is the goal for the people of God in the present age, not just a future eschatological age. The practice of these ethical principles is not viewed as a legalistic method of obtaining divine grace. Obeying the Sermon on the Mount does not bring salvation. The moral ideals set forth therein are general principles rather than minute and legalistic laws that need to be memorized and slavishly obeyed. The sermon advocates more of an attitude than a code of law.

The Sermon on the Mount sets forth the ideal of the kingdom of God in the present age and in the age to come. The Beatitudes

(Matt. 5:3–12) describe the subjects of the ideal kingdom. The parables of the salt of the earth and the light of the world (Matt. 5:13–16) show the influence of the kingdom. The relationship of the kingdom to the law is discussed (Matt. 5:17–48). The nature of worship is described (Matt. 6:1–18). Allegiance to God, relationships with other kingdom subjects, prayer in the kingdom, and a challenge to follow the kingdom standards complete the sermon (Matt. 6:19—7:27).

Jesus left no doubt that his ethical ideals were the only profitable and lasting lifestyle. In his brief and vivid conclusion he said:

> Every one then who hears these words of mine and does them will be like a wise man who built his house upon the rock; and the rain fell, and the floods came, and the winds blew and beat upon that house, but it did not fall, because it had been founded on the rock. And every one who hears these words of mine and does not do them will be like a foolish man who built his house upon the sand; and the rain fell, and the floods came, and the winds blew and beat against that house, and it fell; and great was the fall of it (Matt. 7:24–27).

Although the Sermon on the Mount forms an adequate basis for general ethical principles, certain passages further develop the preacher's specific ethical obligations. Thus, the Christian persuader ought to study Paul's exhortations to the believers in Thessalonica (I Thess. 2) and to Timothy (II Tim. 2).

Paul defends the ministries of Timothy, Silas, and himself among the Thessalonians, writing:

> For you yourselves know, brethren, that our visit to you was not in vain; but though we had already suffered and been shamefully treated at Philippi, as you know, we had courage in our God to declare to you the gospel of God in the face of great opposition. For our appeal does not spring from error or uncleanness, nor is it made with guile; but just as we have been approved by God to be entrusted with the gospel, so we speak, not to please men, but to please God who tests our hearts. For we never used either words of flattery, as you know, or a cloak for greed, as God is witness; nor did we seek glory from men, whether from you or from others, though we might have made demands as apostles of Christ. But we were gentle among you, like a nurse taking care of her children. So, being affectionately desirous of you, we were ready to share with you not only the gospel of God but also our own selves, because you had become very dear to us. For you remember our labor and toil, brethren; we worked night and day, that we might not burden any of you, while we preached to you the gospel of God. You are witnesses, and God also, how holy and righteous and blameless was our behavior to you believers; for you know how, like a father and his children, we

> exhorted each one of you and encouraged you and charged you to lead a life worthy of God, who calls you into his own kingdom and glory (I Thess. 2:1–12).

What do these verses mean to contemporary preachers in their daily ethical decision-making processes? A number of guidelines can be outlined.

Courage Even in Opposition (I Thess. 2:2)

The Christian persuader must be compassionate, empathetic, tactful, and tolerant. But when the time comes that these attributes threaten to compromise his convictions—when they oppose his declaration of the gospel of God with all of its implications—then let him have the courage in his God to preach that gospel without fear. Wealthy church members, antisocial traditionalists, extreme progressivists, family cliques, legalists, and various immature partisans will at times become pressure points of opposition to the preacher. It is then that the Christian preacher must exercise wisdom, judgment, and above all, the courage to confront people with the truth, even if it hurts. Although irrevocably committed to maintaining "the unity of the Spirit in the bond of peace" (Eph. 4:3), and to "building up the body of Christ" (Eph. 4:12), the Christian persuader must remember that "we speak, not to please men, but to please God who tests our hearts" (I Thess. 2:4). Unpopular and controversial as the gospel of God may have been at both Philippi and Thessalonica, Paul and the other missionaries had the courage to preach it (I Thess. 2:2).

Preaching Ethics Based on the Word of God (I Thess. 2:5)

Paul indicates that the missionaries' speaking was grounded in the gospel of God, "but just as we have been approved by God to be entrusted with the gospel, so we speak not to please men, but to please God who tests our hearts" (2:5).

The apostle also points out that the Thessalonians accepted the preaching of the missionaries as the word of God, "when you received the word of God which you heard from us, you accepted it not as the word of men but as what it really is, the word of God" (2:13). Paul was not identifying the Bible as we know it with the word of God. After all, much of the New Testament, including some of his own epistles, was not yet written, let alone canonized by the church. Nevertheless, preachers today find no divinely authoritative source for their preaching other than the Bible. They therefore consider the Word of God and the Bible to be the same.

As a conscientious preacher ponders his preaching and its ethical implications, the Word of God, not the word of men, is his standard of ethics. Appealing as men's philosophies may seem—relativism, situation ethics, positivism, humanism, materialism, or pragmatism—the Christian communicator has taken the Word of God as his final source of authority in ethical matters. This is not to say that the Christian preacher should not study and profit from human philosophers, but that he not make them his final standard of ethics.

Also, the Word of God, not the word of men, is the basic content of the Christian preacher's sermons. This does not mean that every sermon must be textual or expository, but that every sermon should be biblical in thought and spirit. Life situation sermons should not be psychological lectures, but should contain both psychological and biblical insights to life's problems. Moral or ethical sermons should not be philosophical disquisitions, but messages that confront people with God's moral demands as revealed in his Word. Doctrinal sermons should not be human theological speculations divorced from biblical underpinnings, but should arise from the texts of the Bible and be rich in their content and spirit. In preaching on any social, political, or moral issue, the preacher should consult the Word of God to determine *how,* or even *if* the Bible confronts such issues.

Credibility and Persuasiveness Based on Character (Ethos)

In his first letter to the Thessalonians Paul did not hesitate to remind them of the preachers' character: "You know what kind of men we proved to be among you for your sake" (1:5b). Paul's references to preaching the gospel courageously in spite of opposition (2:2), the workers sharing themselves as well as the gospel (2:8), and the missionaries supporting themselves through labor while preaching the gospel (2:9), illustrate the apostle's use of the *ethos* of the preachers. In fact, the whole passage is a careful establishment of the missionaries' ethical character as Paul seeks to defend their ministry and secure the Thessalonians' belief.

Scholars through the years have felt that the speaker is the strongest source of proof or persuasion in the speech situation. Paul understood and appealed to this source of persuasion. This does not mean that the use of *ethos* cannot be debased or corrupted. Paul, in his effort to establish his own and his coworkers' *ethos,* revealed both the negative and positive motives that can underlie this appeal.

Ethos and Motives

Negative Motives. Paul indicates that there were certain negative motives that he and his fellow missionaries avoided in their ministry. They shunned any appeal to error, uncleanness (moral impurity)[5] or guile (2:3). They refused to speak to please men (2:4). They avoided flattering their listeners (2:5). They were not motivated by greed (2:5). They did not seek glory from men despite their status as apostles (2:6).

The church probably faces more trouble with the negative, flattering, glory seeking, autocratic type of minister than it does with the shy, retiring, modest, and self-effacing type. Paul and his fellow ministers were bold but not autocratic.

André Bustanoby writes concerning the dictatorial type of person:

> The Autocratic Personality is characterized by domineering behavior. He compulsively attempts to control and overorganize his life and the lives of those around him. He gives the appearance of competence and efficiency.[6]

Bustanoby applies this type of personality to the pastor who seeks an admiring band of followers to support his dictatorial domination. When his attempt to seize dictatorial control is thwarted he may leave the church in "righteous indignation." Sometimes the situation seriously hurts both pastor and people. Bustanoby continues his discussion by writing:

> When the Autocratic Personality is found in a pastor, the church faces the danger of a power struggle between the pastor and others in the church who also find their security and self-worth in controlling. Such personalities tend to pull support from Docile-Dependent Personalities in the church who will flatter, respect, and obey them. Power struggles between Autocratic people have divided many a church into warring camps. Too often it is not the issues that are

---

5. From ακαθαρσία see G. Abbott-Smith, *A Manual Greek Lexicon of the New Testament,* 3d ed. (Edinburgh: T. & T. Clark, 1937), p. 16.

6. André Bustanoby, *You Can Change Your Personality: Make It a Spiritual Asset* (Grand Rapids: Zondervan Publishing House, 1976), p. 73 and chap. 6, "The Managerial-Autocratic Personality." Used by permission.

> responsible for factionalism; the real problem is with the autocratic personalities who lead the power struggle.[7]

Since pastors have a unique role in the church—that of standing in the pulpit "six feet above contradiction"—it is understandable how easily the pastoral office lends itself to autocratic, dictatorial personalities and functions.

Fortunately the managerial-autocratic personality can change. That kind of *ethos* does not have to remain dominant, dictatorial, and autocratic. Bustanoby suggests changing the behavior of an autocratic personality into more normal managerial behavior by eliminating the following attitudes and actions:

- Domination of others
- Acting impressed with his own importance
- Planning the lives of other people for them
- Acting dictatorial
- Insisting his way is the best
- Expecting others to obey and admire him
- Always engaging in some activity showing off his physical or intellectual strength
- Justifying his behavior
- Planning excessively[8]

And he recommends adding the following submissive behaviors:

- Admit when wrong on important matters
- Apologize when he wronged someone
- Follow the directions of others
- Let others do things for him
- Sit quietly and let others talk
- Occasionally do things spontaneously
- Occasionally sit and do nothing[9]

Although these recommendations were for a specific personality and might be changed for another, most of them would fit the average autocratic person in the churches. Bustanoby would facilitate these changes with personal counseling and family help.

More than the above suggestions, the Bible promises that the inner struggle of the flesh with the Spirit may be subdued victoriously through Jesus Christ (Rom. 7:13–25). Certainly there are

---

7. Ibid., p. 74.
8. Ibid., p. 79.
9. Ibid.

more dictatorial pastors than the church needs. If they choose to remain this way, they are a serious ethical threat to themselves and their congregations. These negative personalities and motives must change.

Positive Motives. The apostle also states that there were certain positive motives that characterized their ministry to the Thessalonians. They were courageous in their preaching of the gospel of God in spite of opposition (2:2); they spoke to please God (2:4); they labored with gentleness (2:7); they yearned after[10] the Thessalonians (2:8); they were unselfish (2:8), self-supporting (2:9), holy, righteous, blameless (2:10), encouraging, and challenging (2:11).

In addition to describing ministerial motives in terms of the rhetorical instrument of positive and negative characteristics, Paul clarified these motives by contrasting some of them.

Contrast of Ministerial Motives
I Thessalonians 1:5–9; 2:1–14

Positive Motives	Negative Motives
1. Be courageous (2:2) a. In spite of opposition (2:2) b. Encouraging (2:11) c. Challenging (2:11) d. Results oriented (1:6–9; 2:13–14)	1. (No contrast)
2. Be God pleasing (2:4)	2. Be men pleasers (2:4) a. Use flattery (2:5) b. Seek glory from men (2:6)
3. Be unselfish (2:8) a. Share self as well as the gospel (2:8) b. Be self-supporting if necessary (2:9)	3. Be greedy (2:5)
4. Be gentle (2:7) and have a longing for people (2:8)	4. (No contrast)

10. From ὁμείρομαι "to desire earnestly, yearn after," Abbot-Smith, *Greek Lexicon,* p. 316.

5. Be ethical (2:10)	5. Be unethical (2:3)
a. Holy	a. Appeal to error
b. Righteous	b. Appeal to uncleanness
c. Blameless	c. Appeal to guile

Paul's discussion of ministerial motives is general rather than specific. Some contemporary applications will be included later in chapter 7.

Results-oriented Preaching (I Thess. 1:6-9; 2:13-14)

Paul was not a sophist who would use rhetorical tricks to manipulate an audience for his own selfish ends. The preacher who would use the passages under consideration to justify such sophistry would be wrong. He would have to ignore such Pauline passages as I Corinthians 2:1–5, where Paul rejects the use of "lofty words or wisdom" (v. 1) and claimed, "My speech and my message were not in plausible words of wisdom, but in demonstration of the Spirit and power" (v. 4). He would also have to overlook Paul's charge to Timothy: "Preach the word, be urgent in season and out of season, convince, rebuke, and exhort, be unfailing in patience and in teaching" (II Tim. 4:2).

Nevertheless, Paul and his coworkers preached for results and got them. Thus in I Thessalonians 1:6–9 he writes:

> And you became imitators of us and of the Lord, for you received the word in much affliction, with joy inspired by the Holy Spirit; so that you became an example to all the believers in Macedonia and in Achaia. For not only has the word of the Lord sounded forth from you in Macedonia and Achaia, but your faith in God has gone forth everywhere, so that we need not say anything. For they themselves report concerning us what a welcome we had among you, and how you turned to God from idols, to serve a living and true God.

And again in I Thessalonians 2:13–14 Paul thankfully reported the results of the missionaries' preaching.

> And we also thank God constantly for this, that when you received the word of God which you heard from us, you accepted it not as the word of men but as what it really is, the word of God, which is at work in you believers. For you, brethren, became imitators of the churches of God in Christ Jesus which are in Judea; for you suffered the same things from your own country men as they did from the Jews.

These two passages leave no excuse for a preacher to justify a lack of interest in results. Too many Christian persuaders try to justify their ineffectiveness by claiming that their only responsibility as servants of God is to faithfully proclaim the gospel. They deny the obligation of fruitfulness.

A conscientious preacher, seeking to maintain an ethical preaching ministry should study these Thessalonian passages as a personal ethical standard. They are rich in practical guidelines for persuasive preaching.

Additional Guidelines from II Timothy 2:14–26

Paul's farewell advice to Timothy (II Tim. 2:14–26) should be etched indelibly on every Christian communicator's mind. Paul urges Timothy:

> Remind them of this, and charge them before the Lord to avoid disputing about words, which does no good, but only ruins the hearers. Do your best to present yourself to God as one approved, a workman who has no need to be ashamed, rightly handling the word of truth. Avoid such godless chatter, for it will lead people into more and more ungodliness, and their talk will eat its way like gangrene. Among them are Hymenaeus and Philetus, who have swerved from the truth by holding that the resurrection is past already. They are upsetting the faith of some. But God's firm foundation stands, bearing this seal: "The Lord knows those who are his," and, "Let every one who names the name of the Lord depart from iniquity."
>
> In a great house there are not only vessels of gold and silver but also of wood and earthenware, and some for noble use, some for ignoble. If any one purifies himself from what is ignoble, then he will be a vessel for noble use, consecrated and useful to the master of the house, ready for any good work. So shun youthful passions and aim at righteousness, faith, love, and peace, along with those who call upon the Lord from a pure heart. Have nothing to do with stupid, senseless controversies; you know that they breed quarrels. And the Lord's servant must not be quarrelsome but kindly to every one, an apt teacher, forbearing, correcting his opponents with gentleness. God may perhaps grant that they will repent and come to know the truth, and they may escape from the snare of the devil, after being captured by him to do his will.

This touching ministerial passage is divided into two distinct sections, which, though related, stress different aspects of the Christian communicator's task: his message (*logos*) vv. 14–19 and his character (*ethos*) vv. 20–26.

The Communicator's Message (Logos) vv. 14-19

Aristotle taught that the speaker's *logos* was one of his strong sources of proof, or persuasion, along with his *ethos* and *pathos* (emotion). The message was built upon two indispensable elements: facts and reasoning.

Paul was concerned about these two elements in his advice to Timothy. Regarding the facts of the communication situation that Timothy would face in the churches, Paul warned his protégé that there would be two ways in which words could be handled: (1) willfully distorting the words of men, and (2) rightly dividing the word of truth. Paul clearly showed the results of each method.

Willfully distorting the words of men (vv. 14, 16–18, 23). What kind of distortion did Paul warn Timothy against? He warned him to avoid disputation about words (v. 14) and to "Have nothing to do with stupid, senseless controversies" (v. 23). These disputations and senseless controversies do no good. They only ruin the hearers (v. 14).

Another form of word distortion Paul warned Timothy to avoid was that of gossip, or godless chatter (v. 16). Gossip, Paul reasons, leads to ungodliness (v. 16); infects like gangrene (v. 17); and encourages false teachers (like Hymenaeus and Philetus, who taught a false doctrine of the resurrection that upset people's faith, vv. 17, 18).

Paul urged Timothy to utilize a different way of handling words—with equally different results.

Rightfully dividing the word of truth (v. 15, KJV*).* The verb "rightly divide" means "to cut straight, as a road," or to plow a straight furrow.[11] Therefore, Timothy was to handle the word of truth with "straightforward exegesis,"[12] and not to bend it to support human biases.

Timothy was to handle the word conscientiously, "Do your best" (v. 15). He was to handle the word unashamedly, "Present yourself to God as one approved, a workman who has no need to be ashamed" (v. 15).

The whole passage presents a contrast between distorted or unorthodox words and straightforward or orthodox words of truth. Paul reminds Timothy that upset faith is the fate of those who preoccupy themselves with unorthodox controversies. But the assurance of those who remain anchored to the rightly divided word of truth is that "God's firm foundation stands bearing this seal: 'The Lord knows those who are his,' and 'Let every one who names the name of the Lord depart from iniquity' " (v. 19).

---

11. See E. K. Simpson, *The Pastoral Epistles* (Grand Rapids: Wm. B. Eerdmans Publishing Co., 1954), p. 137.

12. Ibid.

Second Timothy 2:14–26 suggests several practical applications concerning the ethics of persuasion to contemporary preachers.

There is an ethical problem facing the preacher whose *logos* is preoccupied with verbal distortions (II Tim. 2:14–19, 23).

The facts about these distortions are that they are:

Disputations about words, v. 14.
Stupid, senseless controversies and quarrels, v. 23.
Gossip, or godless chatter, v. 16.

The logical conclusions or results of these distortions are:

They do no good, v. 14.
They ruin the hearers, v. 14.
They will lead people into more ungodliness, v. 16.
They will lead to a "gangrenous" condition, v. 17.

"Stupid, senseless controversies" split denominations, churches, and even families. Quarrels about separation between liberal and conservative constituencies, dialogue between believers of different theological persuasions, involvement in cooperative evangelism (i.e. a Billy Graham evangelistic campaign), the time of the rapture of the church, or whether the millennium described in Revelation 20 will be literal or spiritual, have tragically ruined some believers, hardened partisan disputants, and depressed the spiritual fervor of churches and denominations. The academic study of controversial themes and the presentation of differing points of view are ethical. But allowing controversial themes to ignite senseless controversies, disputation about words, and godless chatter over differences of opinion usually are unethical. Such preoccupation may well be the most harmful indulgence of the church.

There is an ethical character about the preacher whose *logos* is preoccupied with rightly dividing the word of truth (II Tim. 2:15 ff).

The commands about this ethical handling of the words of truth are:

Interpret the word of truth with straightforward exegesis (v. 15).
Do not bend exegesis to fit preconceived biases, or to support stupid, senseless controversies (v. 15 ff).
Handle the word conscientiously—work at one's best—optimum effort (v. 15).
Handle the word unashamedly—God is the one whose approval is important (v. 15).
Handle the word expectantly (v. 25).

The logical results of rightly handling the word of truth are:

The approval of God
An unashamed ministry
Assurance that God's firm foundation has been communicated—both with its promises and with its challenges (v. 19).

Ministers and churches who consistently handle the word of truth well have grown strong and healthy. Concentrating on straightforward preaching and teaching of the word of truth, these preachers and churches enjoy the promises, challenges, and approval of God.

The Communicator's Character (Ethos)

The second section of Paul's counsel to Timothy (II Tim. 2:20–26), presents one of the apostle's main ministerial concerns, that is, the *ethos* of the preacher (cf. I Thess. 1:5; 2:1–12). According to Aristotle, the *ethos* of the speaker, along with his *logos* (message, facts, reasoning) and *pathos* (emotion) were the major sources of his persuasion.

Paul challenges Timothy to a life of high moral character by the use of the analogy of "a great house" (v. 20). In this house there are both noble vessels, represented by gold and silver, and ignoble vessels, represented by wood and earthenware (v. 20). The minister is either a noble vessel or one who would be satisfied to remain as an ignoble vessel, unwilling to purify himself from what is ignoble (v. 21).

The ignoble or negative elements of a minister's *ethos* are "youthful passions" (v. 22); involvement in "stupid, senseless controversies" (v. 23); quarrelsomeness (v. 24); and possibly impatience, unkindness, and ineptness in teaching (implied from v. 24).

On the other hand, the noble or positive elements of a minister's *ethos* are purification from ignoble elements such as youthful passions; consecration to any good work (v. 21), righteousness, faith, love, and peace (v. 22); avoidance of senseless controversies and quarrels (v. 23); commitment to kindness to everyone, aptness to teach, and forbearance (v. 24); and commitment to the correcting of one's opponents with gentleness (v. 25).

The logical results Timothy might expect, according to Paul are: (1) God's granting of repentance and knowledge of truth to backsliding opponents of the truth and (2) the possibility that these backsliding opponents may escape from the snare of the devil, who has captured them (v. 26). As E. K. Simpson opines, "Holding unfeigned repentance to be a work of the Spirit, we need not despair of seeing sound doctrine reinstated in these backsliders."[13]

From Paul's confrontation of Timothy with his ethical obligations (*ethos*) several practical applications can be drawn for today's conscientious Christian persuader.

The Christian persuader's *ethos* is exceedingly important. One hears now and then from arrogant preachers, "I don't care what people think of me, I do what I want to do." A certain detachment from people and indifference to their whims and demands may be justified and even needful at certain times. After all, the apostle Paul did insist to the Thessalonians that his speaking was not to please men, but to please God, who tested his heart (I Thess. 2:4).

Preachers, however, need to understand how persuasive their moral characters are. They also need to realize how destructive their lives can be if they are immoral or lacking in those positive elements of *ethos.* We all have seen the sad spectacle of ministers who have failed because they surrendered to impure passions, quarrelsomeness, impatience, unkindness, and ineptness in teaching and preaching. We are also aware of the winsomeness of preachers who are pure, consecrated, prepared, righteous, faithful, loving, peaceful, not quarrelsome, kind, patient, tolerant, and gentle. The conscientious Christian would be foolish to ignore or avoid such ethical considerations.

The way to change an ignoble or common ministry into a noble or useful one is a willingness to eliminate ignoble elements and to consecrate oneself to God and to those elements that He considers noble and useful.

Why do mediocre and ignoble ministers stay that way? Is it not because their will to purify and consecrate themselves to higher things is weak? One pastor commented, "The trouble with ministers is that they are lazy." Though overgeneralized, this comment is true in many cases.

The motivation for a high level of ministerial *ethos* is the possibility that through it God will grant repentance and knowledge of truth to the hearers.

---

13. Ibid., p. 142.

Expandable Biblical Standard of Ethics

The biblical passages examined form an adequate structure for a beginning standard of ethics for the Christian persuader. They establish a platform of action with the focus on God and man and a lifestyle of interpersonal relationships sketched out by Jesus and Paul as ideal for the kingdom of God, now and in the future. This ethical lifestyle has as its dynamic force agape love.

The passages cited also set forth guidelines for conscientious ministers concerned about the specific elements of their own ethical lifestyle, as well as for the nature of their messages and preparation for them.

These passages free the persuader who wishes to throw off the yoke of religious legalism, yet provide him with at least minimal guidelines. For the persuasive preacher who wants more concrete and detailed ethical principles to guide his conduct, the Bible provides a vast and profound source of ethical instruction, from the Decalogue of Moses to the ethics of Jesus and the apostles.

Accepting this biblical ethic—studying it and living it—is no more demanding or legalistic than adopting the American democratic system. To adopt either is to enter into a lifetime of study and application, of striving and growing. Both are just a beginning.

The Biblical Ethic and Other Standards of Ethics

Orientation to a biblical standard of ethics does not excuse the Christian persuader from the responsibilities of other standards of ethics. Thus the Christian persuader feels free to measure the ethics of his persuasion against the ends, standards, and methods of secular rhetoricians. He accepts the demands of the scientific and rational communicators. He appropriates and uses the classical rhetorical ends—the results, truth, methods, and good-man-speaking-well orientation of the ancient orators. The Christian persuader measures his *ethos, logos,* and *pathos* against the most highly respected standards of both ancient and modern rhetoricians. He strives for semantic soundness. And the Christian persuader merges all of these standards with his biblical-theological-anthropological commitment.

Along with utilizing the well thought out ethical standards of ancient and contemporary rhetoricians, the Christian persuader takes seriously the great commandments of the Judeo-Christian faith. He earnestly cultivates agape love as the dynamic force of all his actions. He devoutly appropriates the kingdom ethic of Jesus' Sermon on the Mount.

Building an effective ethic of persuasion is not easy. But preachers and public speakers alike can learn from the past and from one another. For the Christian persuader, the words of the Lord Jesus Christ are eternally before him: "If you love me, you will keep my commandments" (John 14:15).

Seven

The Christian Persuader's Ethical Obligation: Some Practical Suggestions

Many scholars are reluctant to tell others how to live or act. Accordingly, one will not find an abundance of do's and don'ts in the literature on ethics of persuasion. Reluctance to publish prohibitions and affirmations should not be interpreted as cowardice or evasiveness. Indeed, there are serious reasons why one should be careful about offering such lists. The complexity of life, differences of opinion on what is right or wrong, and the limitations of language all work together to make do's and don'ts difficult to apply to everyone under all circumstances.

The necessity of making his ethics of persuasive preaching practical and of acting out his theology and ethics, demands that the Christian persuader go beyond a discussion of theory. The following suggestions are based on the biblical standards of ethics set forth in chapter 6 and the rhetorical literature developed through the years by secular and religious scholars. Contemporary attitudes toward many of the problems will be cited from the questionnaire described in chapter 1.

HERMENEUTICALLY SOUND BIBLICAL STANDARDS

If the Christian persuader is going to preach by a biblical standard, he is ethically bound to use sound biblical hermeneutics (interpretation). Such a practice would seem to be logical and easy to follow. The questionnaire sent to pastors, however, indicated that a number of them have problems at this point.

The major ethical problem cited was the giving of only one of several possible interpretations of a biblical passage when preaching. Of sixty-six respondents concerning this problem, sixty admitted to this practice. One pastor defended his action by saying that his congregation would not stand for anything else. They wanted only a simple, straightforward presentation of Bible messages, uncomplicated by consideration of rival views. Other preachers may have similar reasons for presenting only one of several views of biblical passages.

Another hermeneutical problem reported was that of reading one's own meaning into a text of Scripture. Although twenty out of seventy-one responding pastors claimed they "never" followed this practice, fifty-one admitted to doing it at least sometimes. Probably there is a positive correlation between this and the above hermeneutical problem.

A third ethical problem of biblical interpretation reported was that of spiritualizing biblical texts. Out of sixty-five answers to this question, forty-six pastors said they sometimes followed this practice. Spiritualizing biblical texts is probably more widespread than one might think. For example, I once heard a preacher spiritualize the story of Jesus and his disciples crossing the Sea of Galilee (Luke 8:22–25 and parallels). Unsatisfied merely to narrate the simple facts of the story, i.e., the command to cross the sea, the rising storm, the sinking boat, the intervention of the Savior, and the arrival at the other side of the lake, this preacher found "deep lessons" in the text. The boat, in his opinion, was the church; the sea was the world. The world surrounded the church and part of the world had gotten into the church, threatening to sink it. But the Savior intervened and the church arrived safely on the other shore (heaven) with its occupants (saints), and so on.

Other hermeneutical problems plague preachers, but the above listed ones are most frequently mentioned. Interestingly enough, many church members approve these practices, attributing to their pastors a special, mystical, deep insight into the Scriptures that other interpreters do not seem to have. Such support, however, is questionable. It does not excuse a pastor from intellectual integrity, diligent study, and courageous confrontation with the truth.

A conscientious pastor will acquaint himself with at least the rudiments of the hermeneutical disciplines and then apply them to his preaching. The following hermeneutic principles are suggested as simple guidelines and should not be substituted for a course in hermeneutics or thorough reading in the subject.[1] These principles are fairly representative of evangelical Protestant hermeneutics.

---

1. For those interested in investigating the discipline of hermeneutics see works such as L. Berkhof, *Principles of Biblical Interpretation* (Grand Rapids: Baker Book House, 1950); A. Berkeley Mickelsen, *Interpreting the Bible* (Grand Rapids: Wm. B. Eerdmans Publishing Co., 1963); Bernard Ramm, *Protestant Biblical Interpreta-*

1. Determine the historical background, the geographical setting, and the chronological period of the Scripture event, saying, or teaching being studied.

2. Consider the relevant socio-economic and cultural factors of the time the event, saying, or teaching occurred or was intended to be heard or observed.

3. Interpret the Bible naturally, normally, or literally unless the language or context suggests otherwise. "Literal" interpretation here means the opposite of figurative, allegorical, or mythical interpretation.

4. Consider the contextual setting of the Scripture passage being interpreted. This should include the immediate context, the book context, the testament context, and finally the whole biblical context. Scripture should be compared with and interpreted by other Scripture.

5. Consider the grammar, syntax, and definition of the words in the text. Knowledge and use of the original languages is most helpful here, but not absolutely necessary. Good Bible translations and exegetical commentaries help immeasurably.

6. Build doctrine rationally, biblically, and systematically. Theology should grow out of the biblical text, be supported by it, and be systematized with the whole of it.

7. In preaching, teaching, witnessing, counseling, or any other practical use of the Bible two rules are important:

   a. Determine the original meaning and intent of the text.
   b. Apply the eternal, transcultural truth of the passage to people today.

As an example of these principles, on several occasions (Eph. 6:5–9; Col. 3:22–4:1; I Tim. 6:1–2) the apostle Paul laid down rules of attitude and conduct for slaves and their masters in early church life. Thankfully, slavery has been abolished. But wouldn't today's laborers and employers profit by applying these principles of conduct to their relationships? Christian laborers would be wise to

---

tion, 3d rev. ed. (Grand Rapids: Baker Book House, 1970); Ramm and others, *Hermeneutics* (Grand Rapids: Baker Book House, 1971); and Milton S. Terry, *Biblical Hermeneutics* 2 vols. (New York: Phillips and Hunt, 1883).

work with obedience, respect, sincerity, integrity, and wholehearted service to their employers as unto the Lord (Eph. 6:5–8). Likewise, Christian employers should treat their employees the same way (Eph. 6:9). They should not threaten them, and they should provide their employees with what is right and fair (Col. 4:1, NIV). The analogy between ancient slave-master and modern employee-employer relations may not be perfect, but the principles involved would go a long way in solving problems between these groups.

A word of warning is due here. Preachers should not use cultural tradition in interpreting the Bible as a convenient excuse for escaping all biblical commands. For example, we may be justified in ignoring the advice of not eating meat offered to idols on the basis that this practice was purely cultural for Paul's day (I Cor. 8). This religious practice does not exist in our society. But are we likewise justified in setting aside Paul's injunction for Christians to avoid taking lawsuits among themselves to pagan law courts (I Cor. 6:1–8)? Although this prohibition was written primarily for the Corinthian church of Paul's day, it has a clear parallel for subsequent ages.

Because determining which practices are cultural and which are transcultural is very difficult, increased diligence in study and objectivity in communicating transcultural principles is necessary for every generation of preachers.

Hermeneutically, then, we are justified in "principling" although we are not justified in allegorizing unless the Scripture itself allegorizes. In the words of Bernard Ramm, "To principlize is to discover in any narrative the basic spiritual, moral, or theological principles."[2] Concerning the more questionable practice of allegorizing, Ramm writes, "Allegorizing is the imputation to the text of a meaning which is not there, but *principling* is not so guilty."[3]

The above hermeneutical principles, though not detailed and exhaustive, form a sound set of guidelines for biblical interpretation. They should be used when building a system of biblical ethics for persuasion, or for preaching the Bible. Preachers are ethically bound to give the Bible the meaning it was originally intended to have. This is only asking as much in biblical interpretation as any literary critic would ask in interpreting nonbiblical literature.

---

2. Bernard Ramm, *Protestant Biblical Interpretation,* pp. 199-200.

3. Ibid., p. 200.

EVALUATING PERSUASIVE METHODS

The following principles of ethical rights and wrongs must be general. Exceptions to almost every rule could be found. Whereas some feel that these rules should not be absolute or eternal, it is difficult to conceive of a society where honesty and integrity are not the norms of life. It is out of the basic laws of honesty and integrity that most ethical methods grow.

Unethical Persuasive Methods

Allowing for certain exceptions of an extreme nature, we usually regard some persuasive methods as unethical. Professor Wayne C. Minnick suggests four such practices:

1. Falsifying or fabricating evidence
2. Distorting evidence
3. Conscious use of specious reasoning
4. Deceiving the audience about the intent of the communication[4]

Robert T. Oliver offers a more extensive list of prohibitions:

1. Do not falsify or misrepresent evidence. . . .
2. Do not speak with assurance on a subject on which you are actually uninformed. . . .
3. Do not seek approval from your audience for a policy or a program by linking it in their minds with emotional values (such as patriotism or sympathy for the underprivileged) with which it has no actual connection. . . .
4. Avoid confusing the minds of the audience about the worthiness of a point of view by "smear" attacks upon the leadership associated with it. . . .
5. Do not delude yourself into feeling that the end justifies the means. . . .
6. If you are activated in advocating a proposal by self-interest or by your allegiance to a particular organization, do not conceal that fact and pretend an objectivity you do not possess. . . .
7. Do not advocate for an audience something in which you yourself do not believe. . . .[5]

---

4. Wayne C. Minnick, *The Art of Persuasion,* 2d ed. (Boston: Houghton Mifflin Co., 1968), p. 285.

5. Robert T. Oliver, *The Psychology of Persuasive Speech,* 2d ed. (New York: Longman, 1957), pp. 29-31.

Measured against the biblical standard, these practices are generally considered unethical. Although the list of negative prohibitions could be extended greatly, such would tend to promote a letter-of-the-law legalism. But if the Christian persuader will get the above principles "under his skin," so to speak, he will be well on the way to avoiding unethical practices.

Distortion of the truth among ministers is not uncommon. Preachers seldom tell "bald-faced" lies, but they will bend the truth a bit. In the questionnaire, forty-one out of sixty-six respondents admitted to exaggeration, a form of truth distortion. At the opposite side of exaggeration, an equal number admitted to "toning down or softening the truth." About an equal ratio, forty-one out of sixty-four respondents, confessed that they sometimes stacked evidence in their own favor when preaching. Another thirty-four out of sixty-five respondents said they would sometimes omit truth damaging to their point of view. Twelve out of sixty-five preachers admitted to telling "white lies," and ten out of sixty-five answered that they deceived audiences about the intent of their messages.

These practices are not confined to ministers, but are part of life on all levels. They indicate how difficult it is to "tell the truth no matter what." And they reveal areas where ministers of the gospel, dedicated to the "truth that makes men free," can improve. The positive expression of these prohibitions are therefore more important.

Ethical Persuasive Methods

1. Tell the truth

Telling the truth seems obviously ethical. Exceptions for the protection of life are sometimes cited. "White lies" used to protect people's feelings may be questionable. But beyond these possible exceptions, the limits of time for research and reporting, the limits of language, and the weakness of human ability make it virtually impossible for anyone to "Tell the truth, the whole truth, and nothing but the truth." Nevertheless, our ceaseless goal and effort must be to tell the truth to the best of our ability.

2. Promote Credibility

Presenting carefully investigated information as truth is generally thought to be ethical. Professor Minnick urges, *"An ethical advocate is obliged to reject propositions which, when tested by his best thinking, prove to have a low truth-probability.*"[6]

3. Be objective

Objectivity and consideration of all possible evidence is thought to be ethical. Stacking evidence in the speaker's favor seems acceptable and legal in law courts where cross examination by opposing lawyers can ferret out neglected evidence, but this practice is questionable in preaching or other monological persuasive activities. Within the limits of time allotted for the sermon, the preacher should speak objectively, logically, and fairly.

This is not impractical in preaching. The preacher can anticipate problems, objections, and differences of opinion and handle them briefly and fairly in the sermon. This was a favorite method of the late Harry Emerson Fosdick, pastor of the Riverside Church of New York City. In his autobiography Dr. Fosdick says:

> If it is well done, however, with no dodging of the difficulties, it can be vitally stimulating and can spoil all somnolent use of sermon time. An auditor, after one Sunday morning service, exclaimed, "I nearly passed out with excitement, for I did not see how you could possibly answer that objection which you raised against your own thought. I supposed you would do it somehow but I could not see how until you did it."[7]

Fosdick's experience shows that, far from being dangerous to the sermon, such objectivity can actually enhance it and make it persuasive to an intelligent audience.

4. Be hermeneutically sound

Christians hold that to be ethical, biblical preaching must be hermeneutically sound. Wild spiritualizing, careless interpretation, or worse yet, making the Bible mean what one wants it to mean to enlist its support in some private point of view, is using the Bible unethically. It is not too much to claim that the biblical preacher must enter the house of homiletics through the door of hermeneutics. Merrill R. Abbey reminds us:

> . . . biblical hermeneutics—a prime responsibility of the pulpit—brings men of extant age into such encounter with the Word spoken

---

6. Minnick, *Art of Persuasion,* p. 286.

7. Harry Emerson Fosdick, *The Living of These Days: An Autobiography* (New York: Harper and Row, 1956), p. 98.

to all ages as to clarify and reshape their life in relation to the living God.[8]

5. Speak clearly

Clarity of presentation is generally thought to be ethical. Circumlocution, burying one's views in a barrage of abstract words, or deliberately speaking over the listeners' comprehension may be forms of deception. This does not mean that a speaker cannot use a wide vocabulary but only that the vocabulary be clear. Profound thought is certainly acceptable if listeners can understand it.

Circumlocution is usually associated with those politicians who, seeking to avoid political pitfalls, speak all around an issue with vague and meaningless rhetoric. In so doing they can avoid committing themselves on controversial issues which might defeat them at election time.

Ministers are not always free from such verbosity and vagueness. Theological terminology provides the Christian communicator with the perfect vocabulary to impress people—but, unfortunately, also to mystify them. One theologian opined, "But if theological thought is significant to the Christian way, all believers must understand for all are travelling together."[9] He felt that it might be scientific to say:

> Scintillate, scintillate, globule vivific,
> Fain would I fathom thy nature specific,
> Loftily poised in the ether capacious,
> Strongly resembling a gem carbonaceous.

But it is more communicative to state,

> Twinkle, twinkle, little star
> How I wonder what you are,
> Up above the world so high,
> Like a diamond in the sky.[10]

Sermon listening experience confirms the idea that many preachers present theological thought more in the style of the former than that of the latter. If, as a result, they mystify or

---

8. Merrill R. Abbey, *The Word Interprets Us* (Nashville: Abingdon Press, 1967), p. 16.

9. Robert L. Saucy, "Doing Theology for the Church," *Journal of the Evangelical Theological Society* 16 (Winter 1973): 5.

10. Ibid.

confuse people rather than illuminate them, an ethical problem exists.

Accordingly, preachers should speak in simple, short, concrete, Anglo-Saxon words, avoiding complex, compound sentences. Abstract thought should be clarified by concrete illustrations. And preachers should strive for preciseness and conciseness rather than vagueness and prolixity. Clarity is not the only matter at stake in preaching. A man's eternal salvation may hang in the balance.

Measured against the standard of loving God, our neighbors, and ourselves, the above positive affirmations are ethically sound and point the Christian persuader in the right direction.

Neutral Persuasive Methods

Experience in persuasive communication shows that lists of prohibitions and affirmations turn out to be relatively short. It should not be surprising, then, to discover that by far, most persuasive methods are placed in a neutral category. They get their "rightness" or "wrongness" from the way they are used or, possibly, from the intent of the speaker. Neutral persuasive methods are numerous and thus cannot all be discussed. The following are methods most frequently encountered.[11]

Propaganda Devices

The propaganda devices, though often listed as unethical, should probably be viewed as neutral. The Institute for Propaganda Analysis names seven of these devices.[12]

The name-calling device. This is usually the use of derogatory value labels. A speaker seeks to influence a listener's judgment by attributing unpleasant characteristics to a person or idea he wants the audience to dislike. Calling a person a liberal, a fundamentalist, a radical, or a neoevangelical, usually with offensive connotations or associations, is considered unethical. The opposite use of labeling is possible too. A person can be called "man of the hour," a dauntless liberator, a prince of the pulpit, or other encomia with eulogistic connotations. Such praise, if undeserved, may be unethical.

---

11. For a more thorough treatment of these methods see Raymond W. McLaughlin, *Communication for the Church* (Grand Rapids: Zondervan Publishing House, 1968), chap. 4, "Barriers to Communication."

12. C. R. Miller, *Propaganda Analysis,* Institute for Propaganda Analysis, I, 2 (November, 1937), 1-3.

In both cases, however, if blame or praise is deserved, such devices should not be considered unethical. Therefore, the name-calling device as such should probably be judged ethically neutral. It takes its ethical or unethical character from the way it is used.

The glittering generalities device. Lumping people or ideas together, exaggerating similarities and ignoring differences, is usually considered unethical. Using terms like *all, always, every, whole, total, none,* and *no such* indicate an all-inclusive generalization. Used with value judgments about people, races, or ideas, these terms may distort the truth. For example: Are all fundamentalists ignorant? Are all liberals skeptics?

A glittering generality may also be a superlative. Extreme degrees of quality may be described as best, worst, highest, most, or least. Thus, a politician may describe himself as the best-qualified, the highest-trained, and the most compassionate candidate for a political office. At the same time he may accuse his opponent of being the least-qualified, the least-experienced, and the most-dishonest pretender to office in the current election. Can such extreme statements be supported? If not, are they not unethical?

Is the glittering generality always unethical? Or is it more accurate to describe it as neutral? After all, there are times when generalities are true. Was Paul not correct when he wrote, "So faith, hope, love abide, these three; and the greatest of these is love" (I Cor. 13:13)?

Therefore, the glittering generalities device can be designated as a neutral rhetorical device. It is ethical or unethical according to how it is used. The Christian persuader, however, ought to exercise great caution in his use of universal and superlative terms, for these terms may distort the truth if they do not square with the facts they suggest.

The transfer device. Transferring the qualities of one idea, object, person, or context to another may or may not be ethical. A communist rally that seeks dignity and respect by displaying the American flag and a glittering cross on its speaker's platform would be suspected of hypocrisy. Churches, however, are seldom thought unethical for displaying both the Christian flag and the American flag together on the same platform inasmuch as the ideologies of both are generally consistent. This is not to claim that Christianity and Americanism should be equated.

In sermons preachers must beware of using the transfer device unethically. For a preacher to say, "Some religions ought to be crucified on the hammer and sickle of communism" seems a deliberate effort to transfer listeners' hatred of communism to a hoped-for hatred of an opponent's theology. If such an assertion cannot be substantiated, its suggestion is unethical.

Such ethical implications are equally true of positive transfer devices. For a preacher to verbally equate the gospel with mother, flag, baseball, and apple pie is to use the transfer device in a most unethical way. On the other hand, it would not be unethical for a preacher to identify himself and his message with such Christian symbols as the cross, the bread and wine of the communion service, the baptismal act, or the Bible. Although Jesus probably used the word *cross* metaphorically when he told his disciples, "If any man would come after me, let him deny himself and take up his cross and follow me" (Matt. 16:24), he clearly intended to transfer the symbolical humility and servitude of Roman crucifixion to Christian discipleship. What he said that day was honest and ethical.

The testimonial device. Some writers view the testimonial as an unethical device.[13] They feel that listeners accept products or ideas on the testimony of others rather than upon a critical evaluation of the products or ideas. Testimonies are often hypocritical—important people urge the public to purchase products and ideas they themselves do not use. Critics resented Joe Namath, a burly professional football player, for advertising pantyhose on national television. It is a product he probably does not use.

This latter type of criticism has been directed toward preachers. Helmut Thielicke, German theologian and preacher, observed that preaching had deteriorated dangerously close to death. He feared that the reason for the decay lay in the credibility gap created by the preachers themselves. "Does the soft drink commercial announcer actually drink the product he advertises?"—or rather—"Does the preacher himself drink what he hands out in the pulpit?"[14] Though not accusing preachers of blatant hypocrisy, Thielicke writes, "What does it mean to be convinced of something and to advocate it as the 'truth'?"[15]

Obviously, testifying to Christian truth that one does not believe or practice is hypocrisy. Deliberately using testimonials to short cut

---

13. Ibid., see also W. H. Werkmeister, *An Introduction to Critical Thinking,* rev. ed. (Lincoln, Nebr.: Johnson Publishing Co., 1957), chap. 4.

14. Helmut Thielicke, *The Trouble with the Church,* ed. and trans. John W. Doberstein (New York: Harper and Row, 1965), pp. 2-3.

15. Ibid.

an audience's reasoning process, to get them to accept truth without thinking it through, would be unethical.

Testimonials need not be misleading or hypocritical. Testimonials to the resurrection of Christ by eye witnesses helped to establish that historical incident and to motivate the early church to amazing exploits (I Cor. 15:3–8; Christian ministries recorded in the Book of Acts). Law courts continually depend upon the testimonials of witnesses. News reporting projects, military intelligence, and other activities depend upon the testimonials of others. Therefore the testimonial is a neutral rhetorical tool. It may be used ethically or unethically by the communicator.

The plain-folks device. Identifying one's self with plain, working people to establish common ground with them for persuasive purposes has been viewed as unethical. But is the plain-folks device inevitably unethical? Harry S. Truman used this device effectively in the 1948 presidential campaign. Truman, however, arose from among the common people and was not misrepresenting himself. If John F. Kennedy or Nelson Rockefeller had ever used this device to identify with Detroit laborers or Iowa farmers, he would have been criticized for being unethical.

Jesus frequently associated with laborers, outcasts, and sinners. His appeal to the common man was legitimate, compassionate, and ethical. The plain-folks device therefore should be thought of as a neutral rhetorical tool—ethical or unethical depending upon how it is used.

The card-stacking device. The stacking of evidence in one's own favor while ignoring or avoiding evidence harmful to one's cause is usually thought of as unethical. There are mitigating circumstances, however, even for card-stacking. Law courts expect lawyers to present their most convincing arguments, ignoring and avoiding evidence harmful to their cases. The courts provide cross-examining for the purpose of uncovering suppressed evidence.

Debate with rebuttal, dialogue, and feedback sessions can provide for discovery of omitted truth in communication. Thus, it is evident that card-stacking may be used either ethically or unethically by communicators.

Preachers given to the predominant use of monological communication should exercise great care in stacking evidence in favor of their favorite beliefs. Research evidence indicates that presenting only one side of an issue does not always bring about desired results.[16]

The bandwagon device. Sometimes speakers seek to persuade listeners by an appeal to the majority. To cry "Fifty million Americans can't be wrong!" may be persuasive, but it may also be wrong. What parent hasn't endured the teen-age argument, "Everyone's doing it, why can't I?" Such examples suggest the reason why the bandwagon technique is often thought of as unethical.

It is inaccurate to brand this technique as always unethical. Wayne C. Minnick derides those who consider the bandwagon technique always evil by asking, "Is it wrong to tell Americans that the majority of Americans are opposed to war? Since this is the bandwagon device, we had better not let that information out, for it is evil."[17]

Preachers can be unethical by urging people to come forward and accept Christ because "everyone is doing it in this revival," when such a statement is not true. They should not be condemned, however, for using the bandwagon appeal for support of a belief or action which in fact is supported by a majority of believers.

The bandwagon technique, then, should be considered ethically neutral. It becomes ethically good or bad depending upon how it is used.

Forty-nine out of sixty-six preachers surveyed by the questionnaire claimed that they never used propaganda devices unethically. Sixteen admitted to using the devices "sometimes," whereas none felt that they used them frequently. The propaganda devices probably are used more often than ministers realize. Although almost fifty ministers denied that they ever used propaganda devices, earlier in the questionnaire forty-one of them admitted to stacking evidence in their favor at least sometimes.

Propaganda devices can be used to deceive listeners, but they do not have to be used that way. After all, the apostle Paul was not just called a saint, he was a saint. Generalities can be substantiated in certain cases. Who could challenge the generality in Romans 3:23 (KJV), "For all have sinned, and come short of the glory of God"?

---

16. Carl I. Hovland, Arthur A. Lumsdaine, and Fred D. Sheffield, "The Effects of Presenting 'One Side' Versus 'Both Sides' in Changing Opinions on a Controversial Subject," in *Experiments in Persuasion,* ed. Ralph L. Rosnow and Edward J. Robinson (New York: Academic Press, 1967), pp. 71-97.

17. Minnick, *Art of Persuasion,* p. 283.

And so it could be demonstrated with the other so-called propaganda devices. They take their ethical character from the way in which they are used.

Audience Analysis and Adaptation

This should be viewed as a neutral method. A speaker would be foolhardy to ignore the nature, intelligence, sex, interests, values, and emotions of the audience he addresses. It might even be unethical not to adapt to them. But at the same time the temptation to pander to audience entertainment rather than needs is a strong one. Many a preacher has prostituted his prophetic and apostolic office to the comedian's platform because jokes get a better response than analytical reasoning. Both jokes and analytical reasoning can be valuable, and audience adaptation can be ethical or unethical, depending on how it is used.

The questionnaire to pastors revealed that about half of them admitted that they sometimes preached what their people wanted to hear rather than what they needed. Three pastors confessed that they did this frequently. Forty-four admitted to avoiding unpleasant, controversial, or troublesome subjects. Thirty-two said that at least sometimes they used entertaining rather than needful content in their sermons. And forty-one admitted that they occasionally avoided audience feedback.

It would seem that one of the more serious ethical problems facing today's ministers is that of confronting the audience with their needs more than with their desires. Today's ministers need to strengthen their prophetic roles. Whether or not parishioners "enjoy" sermons on unpleasant, controversial, or troublesome subjects, they may need such confrontation much more than they need the latest ecclesiastical jokes, magical tricks, or other forms of entertainment.

I was once asked to supply the pulpit for a well-known pastor while he was on vacation. The pastor requested a sermon on the second coming of Christ because such a topic always brought out a better crowd. This group of believers, however, had heard so many sermons on eschatology that their need did not lie in learning more about it. They needed to be confronted with Christian service, human needs, and social obligation.

Contemporary preachers also need to build more feedback opportunities into their preaching situations. Providing time for questions, challenges, corrections, contributions, and testimonies will inevitably strengthen people and pastors alike. It will frequently help the pastor to "scratch a place that truly itches" in the lives of his people.

Serious audience analysis, open feedback opportunities, and sermonic adaptation to human needs can upgrade the preaching situation. Although such approaches could conceivably be harmful, they frequently are helpful. They are neutral tools that can be ethical or unethical according to how they are used.

Ethos, Logos, and Pathos

These forms of audience adaptation should be viewed as neutral.[18] *Ethos,* or personal prestige appeals, may be necessary to establish a speaker's right to speak. If they are used merely to build up egos, they are wrong. *Logos,* or logical appeals, seem beyond the reach of ethical criticism, but Kierkegaard argued that when used to beat the listener down, to remove his powers of free choice, logical appeals may actually be unethical.[19] *Pathos,* or emotional appeals, are generally considered ethically neutral. They appeal to a normal part of man. However, when emotional appeals predominate the sermon and short-circuit the thought processes of the listeners, then they are unethical.

Suggestion

Suggestion should be viewed as neutral. This rhetorical technique is often attacked as unethical because it bypasses the normal reasoning process. We see suggestion in the gas station attendant's cheery question "Fill 'er up?" when we intend to buy only five gallons of gas. We see suggestion in the waitress's question "Are you ready to order dinner?" when we merely intend to buy a cup of coffee.

The evangelist mentioned in the opening of chapter 1 inflated the emotions of his audience close to the point of frenzy, then used suggestion viciously as he cried "If you don't feel the Spirit here . . . you're dead!" The suggestion was so powerful that no one in the emotionally supercharged audience wanted to question it. Suggestion, in this instance, was used unethically.

When used after carefully laying a rational, intelligent, and objective foundation, however, suggestion may be decidedly ethical

---

18. For further treatment of *ethos* and *logos* see chapter 6, "The Biblical Standard for Persuasive Preaching."

19. For this view see Raymond E. Anderson, "Kierkegaard's Theory of Communication," *Speech Monographs* 30 (March 1963): 3-5.

in a sermon. There is serious doubt whether it is possible to speak at all without including suggestion. For example, study the opening words of Paul's sermon on Mars Hill (Acts 17:22–34):

> Men of Athens, I perceive that in every way you are very religious. For as I passed along, and observed the objects of your worship, I found also an altar with this inscription, "To an unknown God." What therefore you worship as unknown, this I proclaim to you (vv. 22–23).

Paul does not come right out and say to the Athenians, "Look, we have a lot in common here. Listen, therefore, to what I say," but the suggestion of this thought is strong. And the religious character of the statement adds more suggestive power to the common ground approach.

An example of suggestion from contemporary preaching is a sermon by Dr. Ralph W. Sockman, "The Roots of the Reconciling Message."[20] Supporting the proposition that the altar of God is the place where we find the roots of our reconciling work—the importance, objects, and resources of it—Dr. Sockman observes, "All thoughtful persons realize that it is reconciliation or ruin."[21] The suggestion that only thoughtful persons see Dr. Sockman's alternatives is surely an innocent one, but it is there. In a similar statement urging reconciliation, Sockman writes, "The critics of the church would admit the sound sense of that command."[22] The suggestiveness of the phrase "sound sense," is subtle, but effective. Few critics would brand Dr. Sockman an unethical manipulator, but the above examples of suggestion illustrate how innocently and easily this rhetorical tool can be included in a speech or sermon. Under such conditions, used in connection with other ethical devices, it is probably ethical.

Most writers feel that suggestion is ethical if it is not used as a substitute for content in the message. If the sermon is weak on facts, reasoning, and exegesis while strong on suggestion and emotion, the preacher may be ethically suspect. Like other neutral methods, suggestion takes its rightness or wrongness from the way in which it is used.

---

20. From G. Paul Butler, ed., *Best Sermons,* Protestant ed. (Princeton, N.J.: D. Van Nostrand Co. 1964), vol. 9, pp. 17-26.

21. Ibid., p. 19.

22. Ibid., p. 20.

Appeals to Tradition

Referring to tradition cannot be fairly designated as either right or wrong. Appeals to audiences to be loyal to such traditional institutions as the church, the state, the schools, and the family may seem outmoded to many of the modern generation, but these institutions provide a stability necessary to society. Therefore appeals based on such values are often ethical. When tradition is used without logic and as a purely emotional appeal to perpetuate obsolete standards, it can block progress and therefore be unethical.

Appeals to Majority Opinion

Our democratic society is built upon the parliamentary law that majority opinion must prevail and that the rights of the minority must be protected. History, however, has shown events where the majority opinion was wrong. Probably the most dramatic incident of this nature occurred when Pontius Pilate asked the crowd, " 'Then what shall I do with Jesus who is called Christ?' They all said, 'Let him be crucified' " (Matt. 27:22). Appeal to majority opinion gets its rightness or wrongness in terms of how it is used.

Appeals to Needs, Wants, and Motives

Closely associated with emotional appeals, this technique should be considered neutral. Sermons pitched strictly at such human characteristics and devoid of other sound rhetorical methods can be unethical. But cold logic, turgid exposition, or even scientific demonstration may leave an audience unmoved toward a vital decision for their own security. In such a case, relating a message to the audience's needs, wants, and motives may be decidedly ethical.

Appeals to Authority

Although it is true that some speakers seek to impress and even persuade their auditors by citing reams of authoritative quotations, authorities may be wrong. Piling up authoritative evidence to support a view may be unethical if opposing views are conveniently ignored. Nevertheless, appeals to authority may be legitimate, helpful, and ethical. We accept the authoritative statements of doctors, lawyers, and mechanics every day. Their statements may be true and ethical or untrue and unethical.

Most of the respondents to our questionnaire (51 out of 66) felt that they did not use the appeal to authority unethically. The appeal to the Bible as the preachers' main source of authority is not considered unethical. Most preachers equate the Bible with the

Word of God and therefore consider it authoritative. The preacher's task is to use appeals to authority fairly and ethically.

Cause-and-Effect Reasoning

As long as the preacher does not attach invalid causes to effects or erroneous effects to apparent causes, this type of reasoning is ethical. Invalid cause-and-effect reasoning may be unethical. It is wrong to accuse a Sunday school teacher of failing in her class if the membership has decreased because part of the class has moved to other locations.

Appeals to Statistics

If proper conclusions are drawn from statistical data, the method can be ethical. Statistics can be distorted, however, and such use of statistics can be unethical.[23]

Definition of Terms

Defining one's terms seems obviously ethical; and if done clearly, objectively, and fairly it is helpful. But defining terms strictly the way a person wants them used may violate not only the semantic character of the terms but also their ethical usage. Common usage, not personal preference, should guide speakers in their definition of terms.

Logical and Semantic Fallacies

Use of false analogy, *ad hominem* attacks (attacking the man instead of his argument), guilt or innocence by association, and begging the question are usually viewed as wrong and unethical. In most cases they are fallacious. As in the case of most rhetorical methods, exceptions to the rule can be found. Ordinarily most of these fallacies are judged unethical *by definition.* Who can argue against that? It would seem more sound to view them as possibly neutral, right or wrong according to how they are used.

Other rhetorical tools could be discussed: the credibility-building devices such as the common-ground method; the "yes, yes" method; the "yes, but" method; and the implicative method.[24] Also, there is an ethical character to attention-getting devices such as variety, intensity, repetition, definiteness or con-

---

23. See Darrell Huff, *How to Lie With Statistics* (New York: W. W. Norton and Co., 1954).

24. Minnick, *Art of Persuasion,* pp. 170-75.

creteness of verbal form, vividness, suspense, proximity, and humor.[25] These and other rhetorical techniques have ethical implications but are generally viewed as neutral.

These methods may be likened to a modern jet plane. In time of war it may be pressed into service either as a bomber to destroy life or a hospital plane to save life. The Christian persuader will quickly see the necessity of measuring his persuasive techniques and methods against his adopted standards of ethics. If his standards are biblical, such as those suggested in chapter 6, then he must ask himself if his methods honor God, edify society, and are consistent with his own highest self-image. Nothing less than this can be considered ethical in persuasive preaching.

EXAMINING PERSUASIVE METHODS IN LIGHT OF BIBLICAL STANDARDS

Readers familiar with the disciplines of rhetoric and homiletics are aware of the close kinship between the two. Although the exact time of the merger of classical rhetoric and Christian preaching is unknown, it was established by the time of Chrysostom and Augustine in the fourth and fifth centuries A.D. and may have existed as early as the time of the apostle Paul. The two disciplines have been closely intertwined ever since.

It should not be surprising, then, that the persuasive techniques discussed above should appear frequently in persuasive preaching. This is true of all three kinds—unethical, ethical, and neutral. But there are certain practices in persuasive preaching that Christian persuaders ought especially to analyze and measure carefully against biblical standards. These practices do appear in nonpreaching speech situations, but the special function of preaching seems too often plagued with them.

Problems That Threaten the Standard of Love for God

The proper attitude in Christian preaching recognizes a healthy balance between divine and human elements. God chooses human beings through whom to speak or record His messages. Biblical and secular history attest to the persuasive effectiveness of Moses,

---

25. On these factors of attention see Winston Lamont Brembeck and William Smiley Howell, *Persuasion: A Means of Social Influence,* 2d ed. (Englewood Cliffs, N.J.: Prentice-Hall, 1976), chap. 12; Robert T. Oliver, *Psychology of Persuasive Speech,* chap. 6; and other works on persuasion.

Amos, Jesus, Paul, Luther, Wesley, and Graham. Paul recognized this divine-human balance when he told the Corinthians:

> . . . God was in Christ reconciling the world to himself, not counting their trespasses against them, and entrusting to us the message of reconciliation. So we are ambassadors for Christ, God making his appeal through us. We beseech you on behalf of Christ, be reconciled to God (II Cor. 5:19–20).

Christian persuaders sometimes violate this method chosen and honored by God.

A *let-God-do-it-alone* attitude may violate our ethical standard. This attitude is reflected in the hyper-spiritual person who spurns preparation as fleshly, stands up in a pulpit to preach, and claims that God puts the proper words in his mouth to speak. Such arrogance is unethical because it presumes upon God and insults the intelligence of the people gathered to hear the sermon.

Closely related to this type of preacher is the man who is an activist, who excessively takes upon himself administrative duties, board and committee appointments, luncheon club memberships, and hobby preoccupations. Instead of hard and earnest prayer, study, and meditation he busies himself with secondary priorities until his sermon preparation time shrinks to almost nothing. When he stands to preach he expects God to stimulate his gift of gab, prod his memory, and inspire him with emotional fire to make his content-deprived message sound convincing. Such practice by ministers is more widespread than it should be. It rejects personal responsibility and thus upsets the divine-human balance of preaching. It is unethical.

But then, a *let-me-do-it-alone* attitude can violate ethical standards as well. This attitude ignores the place of the Holy Spirit in preaching and relies wholly upon personal magnetism, rhetorical techniques, and psychological manipulation. This type of preaching is often accompanied by thorough preparation. Its main problem is substituting human manipulation for divine-human influence.

In a 1950 survey of a number of evangelical pastors the question was asked: "What differences, if any, are there between preaching in the power of the Holy Spirit and any preaching that utilizes thorough preparation, personal magnetism, good psychology and rhetorical persuasion?"[26] Although only twenty-six pastors out of

---

26. Raymond W. McLaughlin, "The Place of the Holy Spirit in Preaching," unpublished doctoral dissertation (Chicago: Northern Baptist Theological Seminary, 1950), pp. 256-58.

the sixty-two who responded to the survey felt that the Holy Spirit uses the above methods (twenty-nine felt there was a difference and seven gave no answer), most Christian preachers would agree with them that God uses preparation, personal magnetism, good psychology, and rhetorical persuasion. But the ethical and theological danger faced by every Christian persuader is one voiced by Dr. W. Theodore Taylor:

> I believe the items mentioned are tools which the Holy Spirit will use when recognized as such and dedicated to Him. The fearful temptation is one of substitution.[27]

The *let-me-do-it-alone* kind of preaching telegraphs the message, I don't need God's help, I've studied persuasion. It rejects spiritual responsibility, and thus upsets the divine-human balance necessary in preaching. It is unethical because the results that accrue will probably be claimed by the preacher rather than credited to God.

The solution to the seeming dilemma of choosing between letting God or the preacher do the persuasion is to strive for a balance between the two. If "God was in Christ, reconciling the world unto himself" and if He "hath committed unto us the word of reconciliation" (II Cor. 5:19, KJV), then the preacher's obligation as a Christian persuader is constantly to seek this scripturally supported divine-human balance.

Preachers must train themselves to the best of their ability in as many related academic disciplines as possible and dedicate whatever gifts and tools they have to the use of God in the persuasion of men. If they are faithful in performing this task, preachers will be working with God in the persuasive act. They will be preaching to the best of their ability in the power of the Holy Spirit, and any results that accrue to such preaching will be God's results through the human instruments he chose to communicate his message. That kind of preaching honors the biblical standard of love toward God and is ethical.

Problems Which Threaten the Standard of Love for Neighbor

There are doubtless many ways in which preachers can and do violate their supposed love of neighbor. Some of these violations have already been mentioned. A few instances, however, seem

27. Ibid., p. 257. Quotation taken from personal correspondence with Dr. Taylor and used by permission.

more open and dramatic than others. Often these violations take place in the use of the evangelistic invitation given at the end of the sermon, but at times they appear during the sermon itself.

Crowd Pressure

The use of psychological crowd pressures may rob an individual of the freedom to make a decision under careful and thoughtful circumstances. A woman once invited a friend to dinner and then to an evangelistic service afterward. When the evangelist failed to get responses to his normal invitation at the end of his sermon, he resorted to crowd pressure to move the unconverted. His tactic was to ask everyone in the sanctuary to stand. They did. After a time of exhortation he quickly commanded all who were "born-again Christians" to sit down. This tactic left all strangers untutored in theological jargon standing alone, exposed to the observing eyes of all the initiated. Crowd pressure was then applied to urge the visitors to join the believers in personal commitment. Fortunately, the woman who had invited the guest refused to sit down and leave her friend standing alone. Needless to say, the visitor never returned to that church. Such tactics are unethical since they violate an individual's freedom of choice and the biblical standard of "love thy neighbor."

Confusing the Intent

Confusing the intent of an invitation may result in unethical acts. Sometimes when an invitation for salvation fails to get results, the evangelist will broaden his appeal. Thus the rather vague invitation of spiritual rededication is added to that of salvation.

One prominent pastor recently pressed this type of invitation to virtually the same audience two Sunday evenings in a row. "All who will commit yourselves to follow the Lord wherever he wants you to go, please stand," he pled. Both evenings about 75 percent of the audience arose. Such an invitation and response the first week may have been justifiable. But were they necessary, sincere, or even ethical the following week?

Sometimes baptism and church membership are included with the invitations to commit or rededicate one's life to Christ. And finally, if response to these varied invitations is not enough, the all-inclusive invitation to "come forward and pray if you have any problem" is given. Such a general and confusing appeal should reach everyone in an audience for no one is without some kind of spiritual problem.

A certain girl finally responded to the vague and general invitation of a prominent evangelist. When asked why she came forward, the hysterical girl could only cry, "I'm a Presbyterian; I don't want to be a Baptist. I'm a Presbyterian; I don't want to be a Baptist." Although that girl was probably listed as an evangelist's conversion statistic, she was anything but a willing convert. Such tactics violate human freedom and are unethical.

Emotionalism

Invitations built on extreme emotion rather than solid sermonic content may be unethical. Decisions from an audience should be sought upon the basis of faithful biblical content, rigorous logic, semantic soundness, and proper emotional appeal. To elicit response to planned invitations, speakers sometimes seem merely to inflate audience emotion through suggestion, vocal dynamics, symbol transference (identifying the speaker's cause with the cross, the church sanctuary, or the Christian flag), weeping, and other rhetorical techniques.

At one evangelistic tent meeting, the audience was raised to a high emotional pitch through the vehicle of a well-planned music program. The evangelist quickly strode to the pulpit, asked that all heads be bowed in prayer, and announced that it would be wrong to spoil the spirit of such a beautiful musical program with a sermon. He proceeded to extend an evangelistic invitation. His efforts failed because people claimed afterward that they did not know why he wanted them to come forward. The sermon, not the prevailing emotion of the moment, should have provided that direction.

On another occasion, a popular preacher nearly hypnotized an audience with his extended emotional sermon. His message had little solid content. It presented no biblical exposition, sparse evidence and reasoning, and consisted of an almost unbroken chain of emotional stories. The preacher closed his message with a dramatic, kneeling portrayal of the death of his "dear old alcoholic daddy," in his arms, without Christ. Two women were sobbing uncontrollably. The husband of one ordered her to quit crying. "I can't," she wailed, "I can't stop crying." The invitation of this preacher got "results." But were these results intelligent, responsible, lasting, and ethical? On what palpable content were such responses based?

Such examples automatically raise the question, Should ethical preachers use the emotional appeal? There can be little doubt that our culture has been suspicious of emotionalism for a long time. Classical rhetoric generally has preferred logical over emotional appeals, but by no means has it avoided the latter.[28]

Experimental studies on the effects of certain types of emotional appeals have been interesting, though somewhat contradictory and inconclusive. For example, Janis and Feshbach's famous study on fear-arousing appeals indicated that a converse effect existed between strength of fear-appeal and response.[39] The greatest conformity was to the position advocated in the minimal fear-appeal. The moderate fear appeal was less effective. And the strong threat appeal was the least effective.

In a study concerned with anxiety-arousing messages, Fredric Powell found results diametrically opposite to those of Janis and Feshbach.[30] Powell found that a strong fear appeal directed toward a loved one produced a greater opinion change toward the advocated direction than did a mild fear appeal. Other studies have explored these appeals and responses. Some of these support Janis and Feshbach's findings of a converse relationship between strength of fear appeal and response,[31] and others support Powell's findings in the opposite direction. [32]

Of special interest to ministers, however, is the relationship between source credibility and fear-arousing appeals. When messages are perceived to come from a highly credible source, high fear appeals produce more opinion change than mild fear appeals.[33]

---

28. For example see Aristotle's treatment of the emotional appeal in Lane Cooper, trans., *The Rhetoric of Aristotle* (New York: Appleton-Century-Crofts, 1932), pp. 91-131; and Edwin Black, *Rhetorical Criticism: A Study in Method* (New York: Macmillan Co., 1965), chaps. 4 and 5.

29. See Irving L. Janis and Seymour Feshbach, "Effects of Fear-Arousing Communications," *Journal of Abnormal and Social Psychology* 48 (1953): 78-92.

30. Fredric A. Powell, "The Effects of Anxiety-Arousing Messages When Related to Personal, Familial, and Impersonal Referents," *Speech Monographs* 32 (1965): 102-6.

31. See for example, J. Nunnally and H. Bobren, "Variables Governing the Willingness to Receive Communications on Mental Health," *Journal of Personality* 27 (1959): 38-46; and A. S. DeWolfe and C. N. Governale, "Fear and Attitude Change," *Journal of Abnormal and Social Psychology* 69 (1964): 119-23.

32. See for example L. Berkowitz and D. R. Cottingham, "The Interest Value and Relevance of Fear-Arousing Communications," *Journal of Abnormal and Social Psychology* 60 (1960): 37-43; and H. Leventhal and P. Niles, "A Field Experiment on Fear-Arousal with Data on the Validity of Questionnaire Measures," *Journal of Personality* 32 (1964): 459-79.

33. See M. A. Hewgill, and G. R. Miller, "Source Credibility and Response to Fear-Arousing Communications," *Speech Monographs* 32 (1965): 95-101; and G. R.

Although other emotional states are vital to the use of the emotional appeal, the fear appeal seems to be the one about which communicators are most concerned. It was to a form of fear that the apostle Paul appealed when he reminded the Corinthians, "Therefore, knowing the fear of the Lord, we persuade men" (II Cor. 5:11a).

Communication literature seems to indicate that listeners to persuasive messages are not always able to distinguish between logical and emotional material in the way the speaker intends. Even factual material may strike the listeners as being both logical and emotional. This was demonstrated in some of the communications of the American Cancer Society that showed the probability of falling victim to cancer during one's lifetime.[34] People were convinced by the facts cited. They were also motivated by the fear implied by these facts.

Communication scholars remind us that there are many listeners who are not moved by rational appeals but who will respond to emotional appeals or to combinations of logical-emotional appeals. This being true, the persuasive preacher may be unethical if he refuses to use an appeal to which some listeners will respond when other appeals fail to reach them.

There is no answer to the question, How far can you go in affecting an audience emotionally? A better question might be, How do we know the emotional appeal we are using is ethical? Professor Charles U. Larson writes concerning this problem:

> Assuming that the appeal is ethical in light of other relevant perspectives, the "emotional" device is ethical if it is undergirded by a substructure of sound evidence and reasoning to support it.[35]

For the Christian persuader the substructure of sound evidence would include sound biblical exegesis, solid facts, correct reasoning, and sound theological applications. Larson continues:

> And the emotional appeal is ethical if the audience is asked to view it not as proof for justification but as the expression of the persuader's internal emotional state. Generally, the emotional appeal is unethical when it functions as pseudoproof giving the appearance of evidence

---

Miller, "Studies on the Use of Fear Appeals: A Summary and Analysis," *Central States Speech Journal* 14 (1963), 117-24.

34. *Cancer and You.* Pamphlet 40MM, no. 2099, 9/65. The American Cancer Society, Massachusetts Division.

35. Charles U. Larson, *Persuasion: Reception and Responsibility* (Belmont, Calif.: Wadsworth Publishing Co., 1973), p. 221.

> or if it functions to short-circuit the receiver's capacity for free, informed, responsible choice.[36]

The emotional appeal, then, can be used ethically. Because research and experience have established its effectiveness, because it is a vital function of the speaker's *ethos,* because listeners do not always distinguish categorically between the rational and the emotional appeal but often respond equally to both appeals, and because many listeners will respond to emotional appeals when rational appeals fail to move them, it is both necessary and ethical to use this appeal. After all, the human personality is made up of intelligence, volition, and *emotion.* To cut out one of these human personality traits as a legitimate object of persuasive appeal is to mutilate the human personality. It is virtually to imply that God made man with part of his personality inferior, impure, and ethically questionable. Emotional appeal is ethical, acceptable, and necessary when it is part of solid content in the sermon. Used excessively by itself, it tends to insult human intelligence and may be unethical.

Sanctified Decoys

Invitations built on suggestion in connection with "sanctified decoys" verge on the unethical. Previous to an evangelistic campaign an evangelist instructed some of the leaders of a church to scatter throughout the audience in the various services. He urged them to move out of their pews, a few at a time, toward the altar as he gave the evangelistic invitation. The purpose was to suggest to the unconverted (and uninitiated) that people were responding to the evangelist's invitation and that they should join them (the bandwagon technique). The evangelist labeled these leaders "sanctified decoys." Neither the label nor the tactic is funny. It smacks of delusion and therefore is questionable as persuasive ethics. If a preacher cannot compete legitimately in the "marketplace of ideas," he should not be in the pulpit.

Misuse of the Invitation

A word ought to be said about the use of the invitation after the sermon. This practice, in one form or another, has a long history. Joshua, at the close of his farewell message, challenged the Israelites to make a decision between the Lord or whomever they

---

36. Ibid., p. 222.

might choose to serve. Simple as it might have been, his challenge was a type of invitation.

> And if you be unwilling to serve the Lord, choose this day whom you will serve, whether the gods your fathers served in the region beyond the River, or the gods of the Amorites in whose land you dwell; but as for me and my house, we will serve the Lord (Josh. 24:15).

Peter's sermon at Pentecost was brought to such a burning focus toward the end that listeners were "cut to the heart" and inquired "Brethren, what shall we do?" (Acts 2:37). The subsequent words of Peter and the apostles were a mixture of instruction and invitation, resulting in the conversion and baptism of some three thousand souls (Acts 2:38–42).

In modern times the evangelistic invitation has been popularized in evangelistic meetings by men like D. L. Moody, Billy Sunday, and Billy Graham. It is also used widely in many evangelical churches.

There is nothing unethical about extending an invitation to a congregation to respond to the challenge of the sermon as long as it is not built upon questionable tricks. Preachers, however, ought to question the indiscriminate use of the invitation.[37] Some churches demand that their pastors extend an evangelistic invitation at the close of every sermon—whether unconverted are present or not. Such a practice not only makes little sense, but it may cause the invitation to lose its significance in the calloused minds of hearers, believers or unbelievers. To make such a travesty of this tool verges on the unethical.

Ignoring Feedback

A growing concern among rhetoricians and homileticians is the need for providing feedback in the sermon, or soon after it. Dialogue in some form should be a part of many, if not all sermons.[38] Dialogue in preaching may take various forms. It may involve the preacher together with one or more participants discuss-

---

37. For contrasting views on the use of post-sermon invitations see Faris D. Whitesell, *Sixty-Five Ways to Give Evangelistic Invitations* (Grand Rapids: Zondervan Publishing House, 1945); and Iain H. Murray, *The Invitation System* (London: Banner of Truth Trust, 1967).

38. On dialogue in preaching see William D. Thompson and Gordon C. Bennett, *Dialogue Preaching the Shared Sermon* (Valley Forge, Pa.: Judson Press, 1969); Reuel L. Howe, *The Miracle of Dialogue* (New York: Seabury Press, 1963), and *Partners in Preaching: Clergy and Laity in Dialogue* (New York: Seabury Press, 1967); and Clyde Reid, *The Empty Pulpit* (New York: Harper and Row, 1967).

ing the content and purpose of the sermon in the presence of the congregation. It may involve alternating times of preaching by the preacher and feedback from the congregation during the sermon. It may involve a panel discussion of the sermon subject before it is preached so the preacher can deal with issues that vitally concern the people and eliminate matters that do not. To provide the congregation with the opportunity to talk back, to question, or to contribute to the sermon certainly enhances the ethical integrity of the pastor. Consistently depriving them of this privilege may rob the people of their human freedom and thus could be unethical.

Problems That Threaten the Standard of Loving Ourselves

Love for one's self should not be selfish, fleshly, or self-indulgent. It should be love that produces self-respect, self-confidence, and self-giving. Robert T. Oliver writes concerning the speaker's attitude toward himself.

> Calm assurance lies in the realm between arrogance and uncertainty. It is born of the speaker's knowledge that he is giving his audience the best fruits of his most thoughtful consideration, and that his proposal is consequently based upon moral thoughtfulness and not upon mere emotional intensity.[39]

To avoid violating this standard of self-love, the Christian persuader should examine certain problems that he faces simply because he is a special persuader.

Preoccupation with Results

The Christian persuader must resist the temptation of allowing a results philosophy to dominate his persuasion. In chapter 2 the philosophy of results, emphasized by the early Greek sophists, was described. Many sophistic orators became so enamored of results that they used unethical methods to attain them. Obviously preaching, like any other form of persuasion, seeks results. And seeking results is not unethical in itself. In chapter 6 we saw that the apostle Paul and his coworkers were results-oriented in their ministry to the Thessalonians. Paul and his assistants were not religious sophists by any means. They nevertheless preached for results and got them (see I Thess. 1:6–9; 2:13–14). Contemporary ministers would do well to emulate Paul and his company in such preaching. Nevertheless, when results so dominate a preacher that

39. Oliver, *Psychology of Persuasive Speech,* p. 76.

he resorts to unethical rhetorical techniques to produce them, then he not only dishonors God and degrades his audience but also compromises his self-image. Surely such tactics run the risk of being unethical.

Plagiarism

By the very nature of his preaching task, the Christian preacher runs a special risk of plagiarism. Unlike the average public speaker, the preacher must prepare and deliver anywhere from 50 to 150 sermons a year, year after year. Because, in most cases, he delivers these sermons before the same congregation every week, each sermon must be different. He can repeat them only if he preaches to a different congregation or moves to a different church. Under the tremendous and continuous weight of this responsibility, the preacher finds it exceedingly difficult to remain fresh and original. Documentation of quoted material and illustrations becomes an added burden to the already time-consuming weekly sermon preparation. It is because of this uniqueness of the minister's task that Edward Beal wrote of plagiarism.

> For the preacher, who is assumed to be the most meticulous of publicists, the genuine offense is most serious, and yet there are conditions which give him a wider range of freedom than others in the use he makes of his fellow-worker's ideas.[40]

Beal claims sermonic literature is published for preachers, there being little demand for it among laymen. Nevertheless, even though the preacher probably draws on many sermon ideas he has read in the past, he is not guilty of downright plagiarism unless he appropriates another's sermon or part of a sermon and passes it off as his own creation.[41]

At this point the observation of Webb Garrison seems on target: "Except in very rare instances, plagiarism is a matter for the conscience rather than the courts."[42] As such, plagiarism becomes not so much a legal problem as an ethical one for the Christian persuader.

Plagiarism may not seem to be much of an issue to the average churchgoer. But the practice is more widespread than one might

---

40. Edward Beal, "Honesty in Preaching," *The Congregational Quarterly* 34 (April 1956): 162.

41. Ibid., p. 163.

42. Webb Garrison, *The Preacher and His Audience* (Westwood, N.J.: Fleming H. Revell Co., 1954), p. 254.

suspect. One writer reported that an estimated "40,000 clergy" were preaching "$1 million worth of sermons purchased from a dozen firms."[43]

The preacher will seldom be sued for using another man's sermon without giving due credit. But if he is ever discovered by his congregation in such a deception, or if he publishes his sermons without giving proper credit or securing written permission for borrowed material, he may be in for serious trouble. Perhaps even more important to such a preacher is the burden of living with his conscience. His congregation may not be aware of his plagiarism, and those who unsuspectingly supply his material may never discover it, but God is aware of it and the guilty preacher knows that his plagiarism is an ethical compromise.

A preacher once used one of my published sermons as a candidating sermon. By not crediting the source of the sermon, he gave the impression it was his own. The church secretary recognized the sermon, however, and reported the plagiarism to the pulpit committee of the church. They in turn rejected him as a potential pastor.

How much better off persuaders would be if, knowing that "there is nothing new under the sun" (Eccles. 1:9b) and that preachers could profit greatly from the production of others, they would recognize that their only obligations are to credit their sources when preaching and secure permission to quote from borrowed material when publishing their messages. These simple steps would protect them from any legal suit, guilty consciences, and any damaging charges of plagiarism.

Overloading

Closely related to preoccupation with results and plagiarism is the minister's surrender to the temptation of overloading. Most preachers accept too many speaking engagements and cannot effectively prepare for every one of them. Even if a minister confined himself to the activities of his own church, without accepting outside speaking engagements, he would be hard pressed to keep up with adequate sermon preparation. Many ministers preach twice on Sunday and deliver some kind of message at a midweek service. If he spent ten to fifteen hours a week on each message, there would be little time left for other pastoral and administrative respon-

---

43. George Mitchell, "How Do Those Guys Manage to Produce a Sermon Each Week?" *The Wall Street Journal* 14 March 1972, p. 1.

sibilities. The truth of the matter, however, is that few sermons get that much preparation time devoted to them. Consequently, the quality of the sermon suffers.

Churches are partly to blame for the state of sermonizing in our day. As long as they insist that the minister prepare two or three formal messages every week in addition to all other pastoral responsibilities, they contribute to his difficulty to maintain high-level preaching. One solution to the problem is to move to one formal sermon each week, probably for the morning worship service. The evening service led by someone other than the pastor, could be given over to some type of less formal dialogue, built either upon the content of the morning sermon or some current aspect of Christian truth.

Multiple-staff use may also relieve the minister of his overloaded preaching responsibilities. Associate pastors, Christian education directors, and ministers of evangelism may be very effective both in monologue and dialogue.

At this point pastors and churches need to utilize the laymen in the communication program. We commonly see dynamic personalities, who throughout the week are effective leaders in business or education, relegated to passive roles as listeners or observers in our churches on Sundays. Our church services are like football games, where thousands of spectators desperately in need of exercise sit for hours watching twenty-two men desperately in need of rest! Why not train these laymen to preach and to participate in dialogue? Not only would such an undertaking relieve the pastor's speaking demands, but it would use gifted laymen in the vital work of the church. Those laymen who prefer not to speak in public could be trained to relieve the pastor of other administrative duties that drain his study, prayer, and sermon preparation time. Laymen readily accept the logic and responsibility arising out of that early church predicament described by Luke:

> And the twelve summoned the body of the disciples and said, "It is not right that we should give up preaching the word of God to serve tables. Therefore, brethren, pick out from among you seven men of good repute, full of the Spirit and of wisdom, whom we may appoint to this duty. But we will devote ourselves to prayer and to the ministry of the word (Acts 6:2–4).

This plan worked well in the early church. It will also work in today's church.[44]

---

44. For some profitable suggestions on lay help for preachers see Chester Pennington, *God Has a Communication Problem* (New York: Hawthorn Books, 1976).

At any rate, Christian preachers should begin to weigh the ethical implications of delivering poorly prepared sermons to congregations who deserve better. If they come for bread shall they be given a stone? The wasted man-hours alone should cause one to shudder. Taking on more preaching opportunities than preparation time allows may be unethical before the Lord, to the people, and to the preachers themselves.

SUMMARY

The above discussion of ethical problems peculiar to the preaching task reveals the overlapping nature of those problems. Even though they are categorized according to a biblical standard, in practice these problems may not always fit those categories. Thus, even though plagiarism basically compromises the minister's own soul, it also embarrasses and disillusions the congregation and dishonors God. The other ethical problems have similar effects.

Doubtless there are other persuasive techniques peculiar to preaching that need to be subjected to the searchlight of ethical judgment. If the Christian persuader will carefully consider the methods discussed in this chapter, however, he will be well on his way to a higher ethic of persuasive preaching.

Eight

The Ethical Responsibilities of the Congregation

One Christmas a former student sent me a large poster. It shows a modern suburban church congregation presumably attending a morning worship service. The preacher gesticulates behind the pulpit, emphasizing his sermon. Everybody is paying respectful attention. Everybody, that is, except one person sleeping blissfully right on the first row—directly in front of the minister. Who is that person? It is none other than the Lord Jesus Christ—out like a light! Sleeping right through the sermon. Too honest to feign interest; too bored to stay awake!

The message of this poster is painfully penetrating. It seems to say that if preachers were as honest as Jesus they would admit that many people are not listening to their sermons either. And this in spite of the fact that listening is the most used of our communicative faculties.

In 1928, Dr. Paul T. Rankin of Ohio State University found that Americans on an average spend 70 percent of each day communicating. In this day they spent 45 percent of their time listening, 30 percent speaking, 16 percent reading, and 9 percent writing.[1] More recent surveys of a practical and less technical nature have been carried out with similar results.[2]

---

1. Paul T. Rankin, "The Importance of Listening Ability," *English Journal,* college edition 17 (October 1928): 623-30.

2. The pioneer and most influential research on "listening," has been done by Dr. Ralph G. Nichols of the University of Minnesota. Of his much published material see especially Ralph G. Nichols and Thomas R. Lewis, *Listening and Speaking* (Dubuque, Iowa: Wm. C. Brown Co., 1954); and Ralph G. Nichols and Leonard A. Stevens, *Are You Listening?* (New York: McGraw-Hill Book Co., 1957). See also the studies reported by Larry L. Barker, *Listening Behavior* (Englewood Cliffs, N.J.: Prentice-Hall, 1971), pp. 3-4.

Most of us can see the practical importance of good listening—for learning, inspiration, motivation to action, or even entertainment. But what is the *ethical* obligation in listening to a preacher? "After all," someone may argue, "If I'm willing to sacrifice my Sunday football game on television to come to church, it's up to that preacher to keep my attention and interest." Or, "What moral responsibility do I have in the sermon listening process?"

From a general point of view the congregation (individuals and corporate body) does have a moral responsibility in the preaching task. Communication scholars have become increasingly insistent upon the responsibility of the listener in the communication process. Andersen, Lewis, and Murray write, "It is generally agreed that there is a positive correlation between effective speaking and good listening."[3] These authors argue that the listener as well as the speaker should understand the listening process because "listening and speaking are two sides of the same coin."[4] Monroe and Ehninger claim:

> Too often it is assumed that the speaker bears the major, if not the entire, responsibility for effective communication. But as we stressed repeatedly, speech communication is a two-way transaction *between* speaker and listener, not a one-way action of speaker *on* listener.[5]

These veteran speech professors stress the importance of the listener in the total communication process, of his need to understand what he hears, of his judgment of the probability of the speaker's conclusions and their usefulness. That Monroe and Ehninger believe the audience has a moral obligation in this listening process is clearly established when they state:

> They [listeners] must judge whether the contentions are fairly stated and adequately proved. Listeners must assess both the ethics of the speaker's purpose and proposal and the ethics of the communicative techniques he employs.[6]

Ethical obligations of listeners are more extensive and detailed than one might think. Furthermore, these ethical obligations are not always obvious. They are sometimes subtle. Some of the

---

3. Martin P. Andersen, Wesley Lewis, and James Murray, *The Speaker and His Audience* (New York: Harper and Row, 1964), p. 160.

4. Ibid.

5. Alan H. Monroe and Douglas Ehninger, *Principles and Types of Speech Communication,* 7th ed.; (Glenview, Ill.: Scott, Foresman and Co., 1974), p. 447.

6. Ibid.

listeners' ethical obligations can be classified into the following categories (allowing for overlapping): physical, intellectual, emotional, and spiritual.

PHYSICAL BARRIERS TO LISTENING

A practical place to start removing listening barriers is at the point of our bodies—our physical well-being. If listeners are uncomfortable in church, chances are they won't listen carefully to a sermon. What are some of the physical barriers to good listening?

Weariness

It stands to reason that if a person chases around all night expending his energy, indulging his appetites, and depriving himself of much needed rest, then he will not be able to listen carefully to a Sunday school lesson or sermon the next morning. Bleary-eyed auditors may be looking at their teacher or pastor, but they probably are not seeing him and certainly are not hearing what is being said. A better plan would be to get decent rest on Saturday night and arise early enough on Sunday morning to be wide awake at church time. Eliminate weariness as much as possible.

Pain

Hard seats, hunger, an aching back, or an odd sitting position can be opposition difficult to overcome. Churches might profit greatly from an investment in seat cushions. Auditors should eat enough before services to remove hunger pains but not so much as to make them drowsy. Physical afflictions may not be removable, but they can possibly be eased by sitting in the most comfortable position in the pew or on a chair. Medical attention to serious pain is not only desirable, it is imperative.

Ventilation

If ventilation is poor, people get drowsy. If too much cold air penetrates a room, people become uncomfortable. A temperature between sixty-five and seventy degrees seems most desirable, though heat alone is not the only barrier. Fresh air is necessary to keep listeners and speakers alert.

A speaker or song leader should get the congregation on its feet just before the sermon. Ushers should open windows if there is no air conditioning. Perhaps an appropriate hymn can be sung and then the people can be seated once more. Change of position, change of emphasis, and change of air will help the listening process. All of this can be done in just a few minutes. The results are incalculable.

Sound

One of the most valuable investments a church can make is a good public address system for its sanctuary. Not only would such equipment aid the listeners, it might save the voice of their pastor from serious damage. Hearing aids for the hard-of-hearing are not a badge of disgrace any more than false teeth or contact lenses.

Speakers should adequately project their voices. They should clearly enunciate vowels and sharply articulate consonants. Experimental evidence indicates that intelligibility of speech is heavily dependent on the articulation of the consonants.

Distractions

Outside singing or talking that competes with the speaker is intolerable. Sound-proofing a sanctuary may muffle the sounds of exterior traffic or aircraft. Removal of all personnel from the platform or choir loft during the delivery of the sermon will help listeners concentrate on the speaker. Lighting concentrated at the point of the speaker (though not spotlights) also directs attention toward him.

Sight

Can the speaker be easily seen? Are there posts, pulpit, women's hats, or other people blocking the listener's vision? Eye contact with the speaker is important. Listeners should move to seats that provide maximum vision and communicative contact with a speaker.

One of the most amusing yet insightful human interest incidents appearing in the Bible is the story of the young man, Eutychus (Acts 20:7–12). Eutychus sat in a window at Troas listening to Paul preach. Paul continued talking until midnight. Whether the long sermon, the many lamps in the upstairs room burning up the oxygen, or just plain weariness overcame the youth we do not know. Nevertheless, he sank into a deep sleep, fell out of the window and was picked up as dead. Fortunately, Paul was able to restore Eutychus. Undaunted, the apostle continued preaching until morning.

The analogy is clear. Physical conditions can thwart good listening. Long-winded sermons, physical weariness, or possibly stale air in a meeting room can block communication. We need to remove as many of these barriers as possible.

INTELLECTUAL BARRIERS TO LISTENING

The human mind is usually the key to good or bad listening. There are certain areas of the human intellect that can become either stumbling blocks or stepping stones to good listening.

Listen Pragmatically

Even though the sermon or Sunday school lesson at first may sound dull and uninteresting, good listeners try to learn if anything is being said that they can put to use. The key to interest is the word *use.* Often while listening to a sermon or taking notes on a Sunday school lesson, an idea will strike me as a great seed-thought for a sermon.

While president of Northern Baptist Theological Seminary in Chicago, Dr. Charles W. Koller stressed this pragmatic listening motive in connection with chapel attendance. He would remind the students, "The day you miss chapel may be the day something will be said that will completely change your life." If members of every church congregation would let that pragmatic thought imprint itself upon their minds, they would be more consistent in church attendance and avidly listen for ideas that might change their lives.

David Livingstone once slipped into a church service where the great missionary Robert Moffat was speaking. He heard Moffat say, "I have sometimes seen, in the morning sun, the smoke of a thousand villages where no missionary has ever been." These twenty words spoken by Moffat were used of God to challenge David Livingstone to go to Africa as a missionary.[7]

Such pragmatic results cannot always be expected, but life-changing words in sermons happen more frequently to the auditor who is listening for useful ideas than to those who sit in church bored and inattentive.

Listen Discerningly

Judge content, not just delivery. Don't say to yourself, "What a bore! Who could listen to such a drone? Does he have to read his

---

7. E. Myers Harrison, *Heroes of Faith on Pioneer Trails* (Chicago: Moody Press, 1945), p. 137.

sermon? His voice puts me to sleep!'' But say to yourself, ''It's what this man has to say that's important. It's not his personality or his voice that counts. What is he saying that I ought to know? To accept? Or to refute?'' Such attitudes on the part of the congregation should not be construed as an excuse for preachers to be sloppy in their delivery of sermons. Their excellent content would always be enhanced by better delivery methods. A wise jeweler would never display the Hope diamond glued to a cigar band. Yet the gospel is often presented in such fashion.

Nevertheless, listeners are wise if they judge a sermon for its content rather than its delivery. I know a great university professor who was weak in his delivery methods. His ideas, however, were unusually brilliant, fresh, and stimulating. The content of his lectures was outstanding. Students who were bored with the delivery and missed the content of his lectures were intellectually impoverished. They missed life-changing concepts and new approaches to eternal truth. Congregations should bear this example in mind when listening to sermons.

Listen Intelligently

Good listening requires intellectual preparation. Wide reading and experience challenge the mind and make it appreciative of a wide range of ideas. Specific reading and experience on a subject being discussed equip an auditor to listen both intelligently and critically. It stands to reason that a listener who is well read in the field of theology will better understand a lecture on contemporary theological problems than a listener who has done no reading in the field.

A recognition of the difference between the speed of thinking and the speed of talking is also part of the intellectual discipline of good listening. An American's average speaking rate is approximately 125 words per minute, whereas thought speed has been rated as high as 300 words per minute without significant loss of comprehension.[8] Dr. Ralph Nichols on one occasion stated that speed in thinking was in fact at least four to five times that of speaking.[9]

---

8. Nichols and Stevens, *Are You Listening?,* p. 78.

9. Ralph G. Nichols, ''Listening Instruction in the Secondary School,'' *Bulletin of the National Association of Secondary School Principals,* Department of Secondary School Administration of the National Education Association 36 (May 1952): 169.

Consequently, people listen in spurts. Their attention functions something like alternating current in electricity. Between the word and thought groups of the speaker they may agree, disagree, anticipate, or evaluate. In addition to these lightning-like activities, they allow their minds to wander to other thoughts—an appointment made for next week, a child's cold, or yesterday's golf game. Only as people thrust aside intruding thoughts and discipline themselves to sew together as many of the speaker's word and thought groups as possible will they understand him accurately. A consciousness that the speed of thought is so much greater than the speed of speech should help preparation for good listening.

Consciousness of this difference implies the need to avoid preoccupation with other matters. Dreaming, wool-gathering, thinking about personal problems, or working out one's own plans while the speaker is talking will effectively block listening. Reading the church bulletin, Sunday school leaflets, or other literature during the sermon is equally defeating.

Jesus had some pointed words to say about preoccupation. In the parable of the sower he warned against the dangers of the listener who received the seed among the thorns. Such a person allows the cares of this world and the deceitfulness of riches to choke the word, and thus he becomes unfruitful (Matt. 13:22). The gospel seed has a difficult time growing in the soil of a preoccupied mind.

Intellectual barriers have kept many out of the kingdom of heaven. People may hear the word physically but block it out mentally and thus die in unbelief. When Christ confronted the rich young ruler, the young man heard Jesus only too well. He could not, however, abandon the cares of this world and the deceitfulness of riches, and he went away sorrowing (Mark 10:17–22). It is interesting to note that Jesus did not run after the young man and try to persuade him to change his mind. Jesus simply recognized the impenetrable barrier of the youth's mental state and let him go. Intellectual barriers to good listening must be removed.

Listen Critically

Some ways of listening are better than others. Some listen without any purpose or effect and others listen with definite purpose and plans. Listening should be done critically. If one is listening to a formal speech, certain rhetorical clues will contribute to his understanding. The speech will have three general parts—an introduction, a body, and a conclusion. The speaker may start his introduction with an attention-getting illustration, quotation, or statement. Soon after that he will state the central idea of his message in the form of a basic proposition, or thesis. This basic proposition is one of the most crucial parts of the speech, and the listener should be awaiting it. The rest of the speech will be a development of this proposition, perhaps an explanation or form of argumentation.

Once the listener has discovered the basic proposition, he should study the proof or elaboration of it in the body of the speech. Each major point in the body of the speech will be a subproposition supporting the main theme. These subpropositions in turn will be established by such rhetorical processes as narration, interpretation, illustration, application, argumentation, and exhortation. The conclusion may briefly summarize the proposition and main points of proof or explanation and then bring the central idea of the speech to a climax by means of a vivid illustration, an apt quotation, or a bit of telling poetry. Although all speeches do not follow the above precise plan, this plan is the classical method hammered out over a period of some twenty-five hundred years and found to be highly effective. Listeners who familiarize themselves with this format are apt to hear most speeches with increased accuracy.

If one is listening to an informal conversation or discussion, the listening task will be much more difficult if any lasting impressions or meaning are to be retained. Informal discussions may wander aimlessly with no particular purpose or proposition in mind. Effort must be made to find the significant ideas and topics mentioned, to remember them through the listener's own restatement of them, and to try to weave them into a coherent pattern of thought with appropriate conclusions. Such a process of listening is especially important in counseling. The counselee's problem may be all but hidden in the rush of his other words, but after listening the astute counselor frequently can pick up recurring themes and repetitions that ultimately may point to the counselee's problem. Thus, when one develops proficiency as a listener, he will find it more and more simple to discover the speaker's basic idea or his central proposition, whether in a formal speech or in an informal message.

Listening must be done critically. Uncritical listeners are easy prey for demagogues. The critical auditor will listen with an open mind, learning to distinguish between important and unimportant ideas. He will train himself to distinguish between fact and inference and not allow emotionally toned words to distract him from central issues. He will be on the lookout for those logical and semantic distortions of language which are barriers to accurate communication.

Listen Sympathetically

An efficient listening method involves listening sympathetically. Though the listener may not agree with the speaker, common courtesy and a genuine interest should be demonstrated. The clarity of the speaker's message may depend upon such a response. Negative feedback in the form of an expression of disgust or violent headshaking may so upset a speaker that he may be unable to communicate his true thoughts or feelings. Sympathetic listening will at least help the speaker present his thoughts clearly and forcefully. The listener *then* has the privilege of accepting or rejecting the speaker's ideas.

Good listening requires great energy and can be a demanding experience. As a good speaker progresses toward a climax in his speech, audiences tend to become tense, concentrating on every word. Without this rapt attention, this expenditure of energy, the listener will not respond properly and the speaker may flounder, resulting in the failure of the whole communication experience. Poor mental attitudes and emotional blocks may ruin the all-important rapport between speaker and receiver.

EMOTIONAL BARRIERS TO LISTENING

Closely related to intellectual barriers to listening are emotional barriers. Several suggestions are in order.

Control Yourself

Overstimulation is almost as bad as understimulation. Pet biases, convictions, and prejudices may trigger the listener to prematurely tune out a speaker before hearing him out. Evaluations should be withheld until the speaker's point of view is clearly understood.

Control Loaded Words

Labels such as *red, pinko, communist, Marxists, Birchite, leftist, rightist, nigger, honky,* and *do-gooder* ignite powerful reactions in emotionally oriented people. In church circles, words like *liberal, modernist, fundamentalist, neoorthodox, neoevangelical, charismatic, posttribulationist,* and *amillennial* stir up bitterness and sometimes hatred, even among professing Christians.

One preacher, while speaking in a conservative church, quoted the liberal theologian, Dr. Harry Emerson Fosdick. Although the preacher did not support Dr. Fosdick's position, a worshiper in the congregation seemed to hear nothing else after that name was mentioned. In anger he left the church fellowship and removed his membership.

Life is full of alien ideas, and words can be used to stir base emotions. An old labor song raised workers' emotions of violence to a high pitch by admonishing:

Workers, can you stand it?
Tell me how you can!
Will you be a lousy scab
Or will you be a man?[10]

Given such emotional labeling and presented with only two extreme alternatives, one would have to be strong to resist the implied action. Sound judgment would probably not be heard.

Jesus was the victim of emotional language. Labels like "King of the Jews," "Bread of Life," and "Son of God" were heard by his enemies as fatal blasphemy. When asked what they would do with him, his emotionally inflamed enemies cried, "Crucify him" (Mark 15:13).

Discipline Your Will

Frequently people refuse to listen simply because they do not want to listen. Like belief, listening openmindedly is usually a matter of the human will. Christianity is rejected by some because it is undesirable, not because it is illogical, disprovable, or unintelligible.

Be Flexible

An iron will resists ideas without allowing them to penetrate the mind. Some people reject truth even though they see it. Irving J. Lee reports the story of a man, who, though observing life facts, refused to abide by them.

> There was once a man who went around saying, "You know, I think I'm dead." His friends finally persuaded him to consult a psychiatrist. When the patient told the psychiatrist that he thought he was dead, the psychiatrist told him to clench his fists, stand before a mirror, and say, "Dead men don't bleed." He told the man to

10. As quoted by Elizabeth G. Andersch, Lorin C. Staats, and Robert N. Bostrom, *Communication in Everyday Use,* 3d ed. (New York: Holt, Rinehart and Winston, 1969), p. 216.

> repeat this motion six times a day for a month, each time saying, "Dead men don't bleed." He told the man to go home and carry out his instructions and return at the end of the month. The patient carried out the psychiatrist's instructions and at the end of the month he returned. The psychiatrist told him once again to go through the motions. The reason he had him tighten his fists was so the veins would come to the surface of the man's wrist. The man tightened his fists, and just as he said, "Dead men don't bleed," the psychiatrist jabbed a scalpel into the man's wrist. The blood gushed out and the man hollered, "By God, dead men do bleed!"[11]

Such inflexibility—at least to some degree—is not uncommon among listeners.

Work at Listening

Listening is hard work! A listener should avoid fatigue, slouched posture, overeating, daydreaming, woolgathering, and faking attention before and during a sermon or lesson. Eye contact with the speaker should be established and maintained. The listener can help further by sitting erect and nodding agreement wherever possible, but without overdoing it. A listener's friendly, interested facial expression promotes good communication. Such reactions are the speaker's only palpable feedback.

Elijah, running from Jezebel (I Kings 19), escaped to Mount Horeb. There he moaned to God:

> I have been very jealous for the Lord God of hosts: for the children of Israel have forsaken thy covenant, thrown down thine altars, and slain thy prophets with the sword; and I, even I only, am left; and they seek my life, to take it away. And he said, Go forth, and stand upon the mount before the Lord. And, behold, the Lord passed by, and a great and strong wind rent the mountains, and brake in pieces the rocks before the Lord; but the Lord was not in the wind: and after the wind an earthquake; but the Lord was not in the earthquake: And after the earthquake a fire, but the Lord was not in the fire: and after the fire a still small voice. And it was so, when Elijah heard it, that he wrapped his face in his mantle, and went out . . ." (vv. 10–13, KJV).

Unfortunately, the story indicates that Elijah went out still moaning. Apparently he had not heard God's still small voice; he merely repeated his dirge about being alone in a hostile world. He had not worked at listening to God. The Lord had to add to his previous communication the promise, "Yet I have left me seven

11. Irving J. Lee, *Language Habits in Human Affairs* (New York: Harper and Brothers, 1941), pp. 135-36, quoting from a speech delivered by Irving Fink, Northwestern University, reprinted in the *Daily Northwestern,* 18 February 1941, p. 5.

thousand in Israel, all the knees which have not bowed unto Baal, and every mouth which hath not kissed him" (v. 18, KJV).

As listeners, we need to remove the emotional, volitional, and other barriers to listening. We need to be flexible and to work hard at listening, both to the voice of God and the voice of our fellowman.

CONCLUSION

Is listening really that important? Yes. Paul tells us, "Faith cometh by hearing, and hearing by the word of God" (Rom. 10:17, KJV). The Israelites were constantly warned to "hear the words of the Lord," (i.e., Josh. 3:9, et pass.). Although the actual term "listen" is used infrequently (i.e. Isa. 49:1), the command to "hear," or to "hearken" to the Lord or to his servants is used many times (i.e. Josh. 3:9; Ps. 50:7; 81:8; Isa. 55:3; Amos 3:1; 4:1; 5:1; 8:4; Matt. 13:9; John 12:47; Rev. 2:7, et pass.).

Little doubt exists that the Lord expects his people to listen to his messages, through the Word and through his communicators. To disobey his commands to listen is to compromise our ethics.

Speaking and listening are mutual responsibilities and therefore have mutual ethical obligations. Professor Seth Fessenden and his cowriters remind us, "Your active cooperation as a listener not only insures better understanding on your part; it even has a stimulating effect on the speaker himself, as he senses your response."[12] Congregations should not just attend church. They should come to listen as their moral responsibility in the process of the communication of the gospel.

---

12. Seth A. Fessenden et al., *Speech for the Creative Teacher* (Dubuque, Iowa: Wm. C. Brown Co., 1968), p. 138.

Nine

Accepting Ethical Responsibility

Assuming an understanding of biblical standards for ethics of persuasion, it remains for the Christian persuader to accept his responsibility of preaching as ethically as he possibly can. Such a conclusion may raise a few plaguing questions that the preacher desires to settle before he wholeheartedly accepts this responsibility, questions that he may honestly and justifiably ask.

HOW DO I KNOW MY VIEWS ARE RIGHT?

A complete, absolute, and final answer to this question is impossible. The extreme relativist holds that no man has all the truth, and one man's ideas are as valid as another's. The extreme absolutist, by contrast, says "The Bible states it, I believe it, that settles it." Somewhere between these two extremes the Christian persuader must find solid ground on which to base his convictions and upon which he accepts his responsibility. Several suggestions may prove helpful.

First, the Christian persuader can take great satisfaction in the knowledge that Christianity has always been willing to take its chances in the "marketplace of ideas." From the earliest times of the Israelites, through the period when Jesus preached, through the beleaguered years of church history, to the present day of mass media, the Judeo-Christian religion has asked no immunity from the scrutiny of scholars nor has it received special favors. The Bible and Christian theology have been attacked, maligned, discredited, rejected, and derided but never eliminated. Pouring abuse on Christianity is like pouring gasoline on a fire—it merely causes it to spread.

A vast body of apologetic literature, philosophy of religion, and Christian evidences has grown up over the years. This defense of

Christianity has been offered by some of the most brilliant minds of human history. Today Christianity willingly takes its place in the marketplace of ideas, ready to challenge any intellect, great or small. A Christian preacher is not vain, ignorant, or naive in believing profoundly that the gospel he persuades men to accept is right. He takes seriously the words of Christ, "I am the way, and the truth, and the life; no one comes to the Father, but by me" (John 14:6). The Christian preacher does not espouse blind faith. He reads, studies, and wrestles with ideas before he stands in the pulpit and preaches the Word.

Second, the Christian persuader, viewing the gospel, must make a decision. He must answer the question posed by Donald K. Smith, "What is the order of reality I wish to share with them [the people]?"[1]

Rhetoricians differ in their answers to this question. Some wish to reflect the order of reality seen in rigorous, rational thought and empirical science. Others wish to reflect the great values of our democratic society. Still others insist on reflecting the order of reality represented by the dignity of man and humanitarian and social ideals.

The Christian persuader sees value in all these orders. He integrates them into his biblical-theological order of reality. He takes his stand, understands his limitations, and holds unsolved problems in abeyance until he gets information to help solve them. Then as he stands to persuade men, his message reflects this order of reality. He stakes his life on the veracity of the gospel.

IS THE AVERAGE MAN CAPABLE OF DETERMINING HIS OWN FUTURE?

Most rhetoricians believe the answer is yes, but some have nagging doubts. Some argue that any theory of persuasion must assume that man has the ability to understand the American democratic process, to think through issues, and make decisions about them.[2] Others, though in general agreement, point to man's

---

1. Donald K. Smith, *Man Speaking: A Rhetoric of Public Speech* (New York: Dodd, Mead, and Co., 1969), pp. 246 ff.

2. For a representative of this view see Karl R. Wallace, "An Ethical Basis of Communication," *The Speech Teacher* 4 (January 1955): 1-9.

degree of irrationality.[3] His needs, desires, and anxieties influence his choices and sometimes contribute to his irrationality.[4]

Nevertheless, those who hold to man's limited rationality argue that if people are to be provided with significant choices, their capacity for intelligent judgment will have to be assumed.[5]

The Christian persuader rejects the view that the pastor of a church is an autocrat and that the congregation has no mind of its own. The pastor, by measuring his persuasion against the biblical standard of loving one's neighbor and desiring to edify the congregation so they can grow in freedom and love, rather seeks to honor the people's judgment. He knows that no man knows everything and that the people in the congregation must trust various authorities—teachers, writers, economists—for their welfare. Likewise, these same people have trust in the pastor—his life, his training, his integrity, his teaching, and his preaching—to guide them in making decisions. The Christian pastor who is familiar with theology and human experiences understands the debilitating power of sin, and thus he believes that the messages he prepares and delivers will be used by the Holy Spirit to change people's lives.

In answer to the question, then, Is the average man capable of determining his own future? the Christian persuader must say yes, with qualifications. He joins John in extending the last invitation of the Bible to all who will listen,

> The Spirit and the Bride say, "Come." And
> let him who hears say, "Come." And let him
> who is thirsty come, let him who desires
> take the water of life without price (Rev. 22:17).

SHOULD ONE MAN TRY TO PERSUADE ANOTHER?

Like the first one, this question arises from relativistic philosophy and syncretistic religion. After all, if there are no absolutes whatsoever, no eternal truths at all, then one man's views have as much validity as another man's. If there is no such thing as one divine revelation of truth, if religions are man-made, and if all

---

3. For a representative of this view see Thomas R. Nilsen, "Free Speech, Persuasion, and the Democratic Process," *Quarterly Journal of Speech* 44 (October 1958): 235-43.

4. Ibid.

5. See Thomas R. Nilsen, *Ethics of Speech Communication,* 2d ed. (Indianapolis: Bobbs-Merrill Co., 1974), chap. 3, "On Significant Choice."

religions lead to the same destination, then why should they not dissolve their differences and merge their similarities into one great syncretistic effort? The extent of these views, both in secular circles and in ecclesiastical institutions, is almost unbelievable. And the notions of relativism and syncretism seem irresistible and tolerant in a permissive society. There are those, however, who feel that relativism and syncretism are too neat and too simplified and do not answer plaguing questions that arise.

Persuasion of one man by another is not the unique problem of the Christian preacher, it is the problem of humanity throughout history. Even before the first system of rhetoric was formulated by Corax of Sicily in the fifth century B.C., men have engaged in persuasion. If the ethical principles of that day justified a man in arguing for his property rights, the same principles hold true today. The morals of these two widely separate societies have not changed that much.

But the justification of persuasion extends far beyond a man defending his property rights. Wherever a man must choose between significant alternatives, between high and low motives, between good and bad causes, between war and peace, between marital fidelity and adultery, or between theism and atheism, and as long as he does not know everything, he is a justifiable object of persuasion in the world's marketplace of ideas.

One view of relativism is that "all morals are relative." This view is buttressed by an empirical review of supposedly changing moral convictions among the various tribes and nations of the world over a period of time. Those who hold this view then conclude that moral standards are relative to the cultures wherein they grow. Persuasion, in such a view, may be suspect.

The weakness in this view is pointed out by Edward John Carnell who writes:

> Since a person will reveal no more of his true convictions than he cares to, a scientific review of moral habits can only serve, at best, as an index to what others *profess* to believe. The true moral convictions of an individual may be beneath the veneer of social pretense, and science is powerless to penetrate this stratum.[6]

In today's society, permissiveness is published as the prevailing moral climate. Relativists claim loudly that this generation has forsaken the sexual mores of former "puritanical generations." But

---

6. Edward John Carnell, *Christian Commitment: An Apologetic* (New York: Macmillan Co., 1957), p. 52.

have they? Probably there are many youths in the present society who, to be accepted by society, may outwardly support the sexual revolution but inwardly loathe the very moral laxness in which they are participating. Hypocrisy is preferred to open confession of moral belief. If this is true on any large scale, then these people are justified targets for persuasion in the open marketplace of ideas.

Syncretism, in its quest for a universal religion, is willing to take values from many "faiths" but by its very nature must deny that God has made a decisive self-disclosure in history. As a result, man is left to rely on his own insights, speculations, and gropings for the ultimate meaning in life.

Christianity cannot compromise with sheer humanistic and relativistic views and remain intact. The central truth of Christianity was summarized by the apostle Paul when he wrote:

> God was in Christ reconciling the world to himself, not counting their trespasses against them, and entrusting to us the message of reconciliation (II Cor. 5:19).

Religious syncretism cannot accept that central Christian claim and still be syncretistic. Christianity cannot sacrifice that claim and still remain Christian. One man may reject this claim and go his own way, and another can accept it and proclaim it. But neither can compromise on it. As Louis Cassels points out, regarding Christ,

> Either it is the most important truth ever proclaimed—or it is a damnable falsehood which has led hundreds of millions of people astray. In neither case can it be fitted into a neat synthesis with other religions.[7]

The Christian persuader does not proclaim this message with a superior sneer, but rather in the spirit described by D. T. Niles of Ceylon defining evangelism, "It is one beggar telling another beggar where to get food."[8] Thus, in answer to the question, Should one man persuade another? the Christian preacher must answer yes. He takes seriously the words of his Lord, "Go therefore and make disciples of all nations . . ." (Matt. 28:19).

DOES THE MINISTER HAVE AN ETHICAL RESPONSIBILITY TO PREACH AT HIS BEST?

The Christian preacher has this one final question to answer, in spite of the criticisms leveled at persuasion. Having been con-

7. Louis Cassels, *What's the Difference? A Comparison of the Faiths Men Live By* (Garden City, N.Y.: Doubleday and Co., 1965), p. 216.

8. Daniel T. Niles, *That They May Have Life* (New York: Harper and Brothers, 1951), p. 96.

fronted with many ethical problems connected with persuasion, the reader may well ask whether the Christian preacher ought to develop rhetorical and homiletical skill. Although these tools may improve his preaching significantly, maybe the Christian persuader ought not to use them.

Drawing such conclusions would seem to be not only unwarranted but potentially harmful. The best possible persuasion, as long as it is ethical, is needed in every area of life. The Christian preacher should develop every aspect of his life. As a young man, "Jesus increased in wisdom and in stature, and in favor with God and man" (Luke 2:52). His growth was intellectual, physical, spiritual, and social. This is how the Christian preacher must develop if he is to improve his communication.

Communicators have felt the burden for ethical and skillful development for a long time. Quintilian (A.D. 35-93), Roman teacher of rhetoric, felt that the ideal orator should be not only a good man but one who could speak well.[9] Both of these qualities could be developed, according to Quintilian. In modern times, Professor Donald K. Smith focuses on this matter in an even more pointed way.

> And we shall also observe that speaking skill is prerequisite to certain ethical purposes. Thus, the inept speaker may conduct an immoral action because of his lack of skill rather than his unworthy purposes. In this sense, the man who would fulfill himself as a moral agent must seek skill in speaking.[10]

If Professor Smith is right, then the sin of inept preaching is widespread and harmful. Far from avoiding persuasive skills because of their ethical vulnerability, the preacher needs to develop them and use them in an ethical and skillful way.

Professor Erwin P. Bettinghaus pleads for better understanding and use of persuasion methods through research saying, "I prefer to know what I am likely to be doing to people rather than to do the same things out of ignorance."[11] For example, a thorough understanding of the effects of strong emotional appeals helps the speaker keep them under control. This principle is applicable to almost every aspect of persuasion and homiletics.

---

9. H. E. Butler, trans., *The Institutio Oratoria of Quintilian* (Cambridge, Mass.: Harvard University Press, 1953), 1.9 ff.

10. Smith, *Man Speaking,* p. 227.

11. Erwin P. Bettinghaus, *Persuasive Communication* (New York: Holt, Rinehart and Winston, 1968), p. 283.

Rhetorical and homiletical understanding also increases the preacher's potential of preparing sermons of consistently good quality. Dr. Charles W. Koller, for many years a superb teacher of preachers, observes:

> Occasionally a preacher, with or without training, will hit upon an excellent outline; but unless he understands just what he did, and how he did it, he will not be able to make such outlines come again two or three times every week.[12]

An obvious disparity, however, remains between a speaker's ethical potential and his ethical attainment. Ideally the preacher must keep working toward the goal of ethical perfection in persuasion, but he seldom, if ever, reaches that perfect ideal. The question then becomes, Should I always do the best I can? This question should apply not only to moral decisions on what to say but also to practical decisions on how to say it.

Given the alternatives of telling more or less of the truth, of appealing to the highest or the lowest motives, of offering significant or insignificant choices, surely doing the "optimific" thing, the best we possibly can, is our obligation.[13] At the same time, choosing between poor and good rhetoric, better and best homiletics, sufficient or superior persuasion should be no chore. If a preacher wishes to stretch his mind, sharpen his persuasion, improve his voice, in a word, "develop," he should consistently do his best in any sermon. He may pay a severe penalty if he does not. Dr. Koller continues:

> When a preacher goes to the pulpit with less than his best, he begins to deteriorate. This may account for the loss of momentum occasionally to be seen in the ministry of a man who was outstanding at the age of thirty and mediocre at fifty.[14]

Experience has shown that the opposite of the above practice is also true. When a man goes to the pulpit with his best, he begins to grow, and this may account for the truly effective Christian persuaders in some of our pulpits today.

If the Christian preacher will take the *long view* instead of the *short view* of his ministry, his goals and methods will take on

---

12. Charles W. Koller, *Expository Preaching Without Notes* (Grand Rapids: Baker Book House, 1962), p. 10.

13. See Nilsen, *Ethics of Speech,* chap. 5, "On the Optimific Word," for a good discussion of doing one's best.

14. Charles W. Koller, *Expository Preaching,* p. 106.

tremendous ethical perspective. Many young preachers get discouraged because they do not see immediate and dramatic results from their preaching. This may be because they unconsciously have set short range goals that, when not attained, lead them to drift into unethical persuasive methods for quick production. Either they do not know or have forgotten that in winning people to the kingdom there is a time of sowing and a time of reaping. Experience shows that preaching is cumulative. It takes more than one sermon to change people's lives. Isaiah could have been describing the preaching task when he wrote: "For it is precept upon precept, precept upon precept, line upon line, line upon line, here a little, there a little" (28:10).

If a preacher wants to do what will please God and best edify the people, he will not try to get quick and huge results from his congregation and then leave them. He will plan to build them up over a long period of time, perhaps sacrificing personal satisfaction for the moment in hopes of producing lasting fruit. Doing the best he can by planning for long range goals will tend to help the Christian preacher maintain an ethical balance.

One increasingly influential concept has been growing out of this book—integrity! With integrity the Christian preacher finds his preaching taking on an ethical "tone." Without it, efforts at being ethical seem "brassy," like a "noisy gong or a clanging cymbal" (I Cor. 13:1). Whether agape love and Christian integrity can be identified as the same thing is difficult to prove. But surely they grow from the same stalk.

In a research course, a former professor of mine constantly hammered home to us the fundamental concept, "The most vital factor in any research project is the integrity of the researcher." Correspondingly, the integrity of the preacher is the most vital factor in the ethics of persuasive preaching.

"Therefore, knowing the fear of the Lord, we persuade man."
(II Cor. 5:11a)

Letter of Inquiry

CONSERVATIVE BAPTIST
THEOLOGICAL SEMINARY

RAYMOND W. McLAUGHLIN
PROFESSOR OF HOMILETICS AND SPEECH

Dear

I would deeply appreciate your help in a research project. I am writing a book on "The Ethics of Persuasive Preaching." I am concerned about meeting the really rough and tough, everyday, practical, ethical problems preachers face as they prepare and preach each sermon.

Accordingly, I have enclosed a questionnaire which lists a number of categories of potential ethical problems I think preachers might face. You could help me greatly if you would complete the questionnaire as instructed, and return it to me in the enclosed, self-addressed envelope.

I do not ask that you sign the questionnaire unless you want a copy of the results. If you want the results, I ask that you include your legibly printed or typed name and address on the questionnaire. All statements or results will be kept anonymous.

Because of practical necessity I must set a deadline on returns as of November 15. Responses received after this day may not be included in the tabulation.

I thank you in advance for cooperation in this matter and pray with you for a greater preaching ministry in the power of the Holy Spirit.

Sincerely yours,

Raymond W. McLaughlin
Professor of Homiletics and Speech

RWM:ed

BOX 10,000 UNIVERSITY PARK STATION, DENVER, COLORADO 80210 TELEPHONE 303-761-2482

ETHICS OF PERSUASIVE PREACHING

Questionnaire

Would you please look over the following potential ethical problems you or your fellow preachers face in preparing and delivering your sermons. Then indicate the frequency with which you face these problems by circling one of the letters at the left of the problem. N = Never; S = Sometimes; F = Frequently. For example:

1. Interpreting the Bible:

N (S) F (1) Reading into the text.

Please repeat this process for all of the following specific problems.

1. Interpreting the Bible (Hermeneutical Problems):

N S F (1) Reading into the text.
N S F (2) Violating the context.
N S F (3) Spiritualizing the text.
N S F (4) Making the text fit the sermon idea rather than vice versa.
N S F (5) Giving only one of several interpretations.

2. Distorting the truth:

N S F (1) Exaggeration.
N S F (2) Toning down or softening the truth.
N S F (3) "White" lies.
N S F (4) Stacking evidence in your favor.
N S F (5) Omitting damaging truth.
N S F (6) Deceiving audience about intent of message.

3. Personal Preparation:

N S F (1) Procrastination, or avoiding preparation.
N S F (2) Depending on God to put words in your mouth.
N S F (3) Depending on yourself alone.
N S F (4) Failing to prepare to preach at your best.
N S F (5) Using other men's sermons without credit.
N S F (6) Using others' material without giving credit.

4. Personal ethical practices:

N S F (1) Preaching for personal glory, power, prestige, money (circle which ones).
N S F (2) Preaching what you don't believe.
N S F (3) Preaching what you fail to practice.
N S F (4) Acting as an authority in field where you aren't an authority.
N S F (5) Bluffing through when not prepared.
N S F (6) Name dropping to impress listeners.

5. Using unethical rhetorical methods:

N S F (1) Use of smear tactics, harmful labeling.
N S F (2) Propaganda devices (i.e., name-calling, glittering generalities, transfer devices, testimonial devices, plain-folks device, card-stacking, bandwagon device) used unethically.
N S F (3) Excessive emotional appeal without solid sermonic content.

(over)

N S F (4) Excessive suggestion without solid sermonic content.
N S F (5) Unethical appeal to tradition.
N S F (6) Unethical appeal to authority.
N S F (7) Unethical appeal to majority opinion.
N S F (8) Unethical appeal to prejudices.
N S F (9) Unethical appeal to the crowd.

6. Using logical fallacies:

N S F (1) Overgeneralization.
N S F (2) False analogies.
N S F (3) Unsound statistics.
N S F (4) Invalid cause and effect reasoning.
N S F (5) Begging the question.
N S F (6) Use of specious reasoning.
N S F (7) Believing that the end justifies any means of attaining it.

7. Audience Adaptation:

N S F (1) Preaching what people want rather than what they need.
N S F (2) Avoiding unpleasant, controversial, or troublesome subjects.
N S F (3) Using entertaining rather than needful content.
N S F (4) Avoiding audience feedback.

8. Post-sermon invitation:

N S F (1) Use of psychological pressures.
N S F (2) Use of crowd pressures.
N S F (3) Use of decoys (believers moving forward suggesting invitation response).
N S F (4) Singling people out.
N S F (5) Misleading people about response sought.
N S F (6) Confusing invitation purposes.
N S F (7) Promising oversimplified solutions to complex human problems.
N S F (8) Wearing people down with extended invitations.
N S F (9) Proselytizing instead of evangelizing.

The previous problems are suggestive, not exhaustive. If you have other, or more plaguing "gut issues" of ethics a contemporary preacher faces, would you list them briefly below. Add a sheet if necessary.

Print or type your name and address only if you want a report of results. Then return this completed questionnaire in accompanying envelope by November 15, 1974 to:

Dr. Raymond W. McLaughlin
Conservative Baptist Seminary
Box 10,000 University Park Station
Denver, Colorado 80210

THANKS FOR YOUR HELP

CONSERVATIVE BAPTIST
THEOLOGICAL SEMINARY

RAYMOND W. McLAUGHLIN
PROFESSOR OF HOMILETICS AND SPEECH

December 5, 1974
OUR 25th YEAR

Dear Friend:

Enclosed is the tabulation of results on the Ethics of Persuasion questionnaire you helped me with recently. Several general observations concerning the results should be kept in mind.

1. A number of qualifications appeared on the returned questionnaires. For example: "not intentionally," or "at times I find myself doing this," etc. This is understandable because men do not want to be dogmatically categorized.

2. These qualifications correlated with several objections to the three-choice categories of "Never," "Sometimes," and "Frequently," used to determine the frequency of occurrence of the ethical problems mentioned.

3. Other qualifications had to do with the situations in which ethical problems were confronted. For example, omitting damaging truth--"only when greater damage would result," etc.

4. Some question was raised regarding the two-choice "you" or "your fellow preachers" vantage point of answering the questions. This was an effort to protect the anonymity of the respondents. Such a procedure should be avoided in the future.

5. Several ethical problems not included in my list were added by respondents. These appear at the end of the tabulation.

A word of explanation is due. The purpose of the survey was not to procure iron-clad statistics to publish as absolute ethical conditions in the ministry. Exact precision was not expected. My desire is to discover those areas where evangelical pastors tend to have the most ethical difficulties. I believe the tabulation suggests those tendencies.

I was well pleased at the response to the questionnaire and thank each of you busy pastors for your cooperation.

Sincerely,

Raymond W. McLaughlin
Professor of Homiletics
and Speech

RWM:ed

BOX 10,000 UNIVERSITY PARK STATION, DENVER, COLORADO 80210 TELEPHONE 303-761-2482

ETHICS OF PERSUASIVE PREACHING
Tabulation of Questionnaire

Below is the list of problems you and others circled together with the frequency of response tabulated at the right of each. No editorial comment is included. Readers are cautioned against drawing dogmatic generalizations from these statistics. Add-on problems are listed at the end of the questionnaire. N = Never; S = Sometimes; F = Frequently. Total number of responses = 66 out of 103 sent out.

	N	S	F
1. INTERPRETING THE BIBLE (Hermeneutical Problems)			
(1) Reading into the text.	20	47	4
(2) Violating the context.	41	21	4
(3) Spiritualizing the text.	19	37	9
(4) Making the text fit the sermon idea rather than vice versa.	24	31	10
(5) Giving only one of several interpretations.	6	39	21
2. DISTORTING THE TRUTH			
(1) Exaggeration.	25	37	4
(2) Toning down or softening the truth.	25	37	4
(3) "White" lies.	53	11	1
(4) Stacking evidence in your favor.	23	34	7
(5) Omitting damaging truth.	31	33	1
(6) Deceiving audience about intent of message.	55	9	1
3. PERSONAL PREPARATION			
(1) Procrastination, or avoiding preparation.	18	40	9
(2) Depending on God to put words in your mouth.	33	25	8
(3) Depending on yourself alone.	23	35	9
(4) Failing to prepare to preach at your best.	9	44	13
(5) Using other men's sermons without credit.	41	23	3
(6) Using others' material without giving credit.	22	40	5
4. PERSONAL ETHICAL PRACTICES			
(1) Preaching for personal glory (18), power (4), prestige (12), money (4), (circle which ones)	29	34	3
(2) Preaching what you don't believe.	62	2	0
(3) Preaching what you fail to practice.	9	50	6
(4) Acting as an authority in field where you aren't an authority.	32	32	2
(5) Bluffing through when not prepared.	36	29	1
(6) Name dropping to impress listeners.	45	20	1
5. USING UNETHICAL RHETORICAL METHODS			
(1) Use of smear tactics, harmful labeling.	58	8	0
(2) Propaganda devices (i.e., name-calling, glittering generalities, transfer devices, testimonial devices, plain-folks device, card-stacking, bandwagon device) used unethically.	49	16	0
(3) Excessive emotional appeal without solid sermonic content.	48	16	2
(4) Excessive suggestion without solid sermonic content.	41	23	2
(5) Unethical appeal to tradition.	56	10	1
(6) Unethical appeal to authority.	51	14	1
(7) Unethical appeal to majority opinion.	46	19	1
(8) Unethical appeal to prejudices.	54	12	1
(9) Unethical appeal to the crowd.	52	13	1

(over)

	N	S	F
6. USING LOGICAL FALLACIES			
(1) Overgeneralization.	17	44	4
(2) False analogies.	43	23	0
(3) Unsound statistics.	49	16	1
(4) Invalid cause and effect reasoning.	41	25	0
(5) Begging the question.	39	25	1
(6) Use of specious reasoning.	42	22	0
(7) Believing that the end justifies any means of attaining it.	60	6	0
7. AUDIENCE ADAPTATION			
(1) Preaching what people want rather than what they need.	33	30	3
(2) Avoiding unpleasant, controversial, or troublesome subjects.	22	39	5
(3) Using entertaining rather than needful content.	34	30	2
(4) Avoiding audience feedback.	24	36	5
8. POST-SERMON INVITATION			
(1) Use of psychological pressures.	46	16	2
(2) Use of crowd pressures.	55	16	0
(3) Use of decoys (believers moving forward suggesting invitation response).	58	9	1
(4) Singling people out.	58	4	0
(5) Misleading people about response sought.	59	5	0
(6) Confusing invitation purposes.	46	17	0
(7) Promising oversimplified solutions to complex human problems.	41	22	2
(8) Wearing people down with extended invitations.	60	4	1
(9) Proselytizing instead of evangelizing.	55	9	0

Several problems were added at the close of the questionnaire. Some related to questions already asked and were therefore not included. The following seemed distinctive enough to include in writers' own words:

1. "Preaching at people instead of preaching to meet personal needs."
2. "Choosing a topic with a particular person in mind."
3. "The vanity of cleverness by use of jokes (not a sense of humor), 'brilliant' interpretations, excessive fantasy, imagination, etc."
4. "False impressions of academic scholarship by quoting from book reviews as if speaker had read all these books. Stressing the root of Greek or Hebrew words of text to audience with average grade school education."
5. "Preaching 'over-lengthy' sermons of a personal preference, e.g. prophecy, book studies."
6. "Using a text-verse from which speaker simply takes his departure."
7. "Same type of sermon week-in, week-out."
8. "Striving for an emotional 'blessing,' or 'spiritual orgasm,' rather than serving and worshipping God. A form of idolatry--worshipping the creation rather than creator."
9. "Shattering a person's confidence in self and relationship with God, legalism, etc., falling short, rather than pointing to love of God and His grace. This can be a maneuver to bind people to pastor (the flawless "example") and church rather than to the Lord with freedom and independence."

Some of the above added problems may seem debatable as "ethical," but they are difficulties that weigh on some pastors' minds and handling them may involve ethical decisions. Doubtless there are others.

Please accept my hearty thanks for your generous cooperation.

Sincerely,

Raymond W. McLaughlin

Bibliography

BOOKS

Abbey, Merrill R. *The Word Interprets Us.* Nashville: Abingdon Press, 1967.

Abbot-Smith, G. *A Manual Greek Lexicon of the New Testament.* 3d ed. Edinburgh: T. & T. Clark, 1937.

Alinsky, Saul D. *Reveille for Radicals.* New York: Vintage Books, 1969.

________. *Rules for Radicals.* New York: Random House, 1971.

Andersch, Elizabeth G.; Staats, Lorin C.; and Bostrom, Robert N. *Communication in Everyday Use.* 3d ed. New York: Holt, Rinehart and Winston, 1969.

Andersen, Kenneth E. *Persuasion: Theory and Practice.* Boston: Allyn and Bacon, 1971.

Andersen, Martin P.; Lewis, Wesley; and Murray, James. *The Speaker and His Audience.* New York: Harper and Row, 1964.

Auer, J. Jeffery. *An Introduction to Research in Speech.* New York: Harper and Brothers, 1959.

Barker, Larry L. *Listening Behavior.* Englewood Cliffs, N.J.: Prentice-Hall, 1971.

Barth, Karl. *Church Dogmatics.* 4 vols. Edinburgh: T. & T. Clark, 1961.

Bennett, John C., and others. *Storm Over Ethics.* Philadelphia: United Church Press, 1967.

Berger, Peter L. *The Noise of Solemn Assemblies.* Garden City, N.Y.: Doubleday and Co., 1961.

Berkhof, L. *Principles of Biblical Interpretation.* Grand Rapids: Baker Book House, 1950.

Berlo, David K. *The Process of Communication.* New York: Holt, Rinehart and Winston, 1960.

Berton, Pierre. *The Comfortable Pew.* Philadelphia: J. B. Lippincott Co., 1965.

Bettinghaus, Erwin P. *Persuasive Communication.* 2d ed. New York: Holt, Rinehart and Winston, 1973.

Black, Edwin. *Rhetorical Criticism: A Study in Method.* New York: Macmillan Co., 1965.

Blackwood, Andrew Watterson. *The Preparation of Sermons.* New York: Abingdon-Cokesbury Press, 1947.

Blaiklock, E. M. *The Christian in Pagan Society.* London: Tyndale Press, 1951.

Blankenship, Jane. *Public Speaking: A Rhetorical Perspective.* Englewood Cliffs, N.J.: Prentice-Hall, 1966.

Bonhoeffer, Dietrich. *Ethics.* Edited by Eberhard Bethge. New York: Macmillan Co., 1955.

Bormann, Ernest G., and Bormann, Nancy C. *Speech Communication: An Interpersonal Approach.* New York: Harper and Row, 1972.

Bosmajian, Haig, ed. *Dissent: Symbolic Behavior and Rhetorical Strategies.* Boston: Allyn and Bacon, 1972.

Brembeck, Winston Lamont, and Howell, William Smiley. *Persuasion: A Means of Social Control.* New York: Prentice-Hall, 1952.

________. *Persuasion: A Means of Social Influence.* 2d ed. Englewood Cliffs, N.J.: Prentice-Hall, 1976.

Broadus, John A. *On the Preparation and Delivery of Sermons.* Revised by Jesse Burton Weatherspoon. New York: Harper and Brothers, 1944.

Buber, Martin. *Between Man and Man.* Translated by Ronald Gregor Smith. New York: Macmillan Co., 1965.

________. *I and Thou.* 2d ed. Translated and edited by Ronald Gregor Smith. New York: Charles Scribner's Sons: 1958.

________. *The Knowledge of Man.* Translated by Maurice S. Friedman and Ronald Gregor Smith. London: George Allen and Unwin, 1965.

________. *Pointing the Way.* Translated by Maurice S. Friedman. New York: Harper and Row, 1960.

Bultmann, Rudolph. *Jesus and the Word.* New York: Charles Scribner's Sons, 1958.

Bustanoby, André. *You Can Change Your Personality: Make It a Spiritual Asset.* Grand Rapids: Zondervan Publishing House, 1976.

Butler, G. Paul., ed. *Best Sermons.* Vol. 9. Protestant ed. Princeton, N.J.: D. Van Nostrand Co., 1964.

Butler, H. E., trans. *The Institutio Oratoria of Quintilian.* Cambridge, Mass.: Harvard University Press, 1953.

Caemmerer, Richard R. *Preaching for the Church.* St. Louis: Concordia Publishing House, 1959.

Campbell, Ernest T. *Christian Manifesto.* New York: Harper and Row, 1970.

Cancer and You. Pamphlet 40MM, no. 2099, 9/65, The American Cancer Society, Massachusetts Division.

Carnell, Edward John. *Christian Commitment: An Apologetic.* New York: Macmillan Co., 1957.

Cassels, Louis. *What's the Difference? A Comparison of the Faiths Men Live By.* Garden City, N.Y.: Doubleday and Co., 1965.

Chase, Stuart. *The Tyranny of Words.* New York: Harcourt, Brace and Co., 1938.

Cooper, Lane., trans. *The Rhetoric of Aristotle.* New York: Appleton-Century-Crofts, 1932.

Cox, Harvey., ed. *The Situation Ethics Debate.* Philadelphia: Westminster Press, 1968.

Dargan, Edwin Charles. *A History of Preaching.* 2 vols. Reprint. Grand Rapids: Baker Book House, 1968, 1970.

Davis, Henry Grady. *Design for Preaching.* Philadelphia: Muhlenberg Press, 1958.

DeVito, Joseph A. *The Psychology of Speech and Language: An Introduction to Psycholinguistics.* New York: Random House, 1970.

Doob, Leonard. *Public Opinion and Propaganda.* New York: Henry Holt, 1948.

Dunham, Barrows. *Man Against Myth.* Boston: Little, Brown and Co., 1947.

Dunnam, Maxie D.; Herbertson, Gary J.; and Shostrom, Everett L. *The Manipulator and the Church.* Nashville: Abingdon Press, 1968.

Erickson, Millard J. *Relativism in Contemporary Christian Ethics.* Grand Rapids: Baker Book House, 1974.

Fessenden, Seth A., and others. *Speech for the Creative Teacher.* Dubuque, Iowa: Wm. C. Brown Co., 1968.

Fletcher, Joseph. *Moral Responsibility: Situation Ethics at Work.* Philadelphia: Westminster Press, 1967.

________. *Situation Ethics: The New Morality.* Philadelphia: Westminster Press, 1966.

Fosdick, Harry Emerson. *The Living of These Days: An Autobiography.* New York: Harper and Row, 1956.

Fotheringham, Wallace C. *Perspectives on Persuasion.* Boston: Allyn and Bacon, 1966.

Friedman, Maurice. *Martin Buber: The Life of Dialogue.* New York: Harper Torchbooks, 1960.

Gaines, Steven S. *Marjoe: The Life of Marjoe Gortner.* New York: Harper and Row, 1973.

Garrison, Webb B. *The Preacher and His Audience.* Westwood, N.J.: Fleming H. Revell Co., 1954.

Geisler, Norman L. *Ethics: Alternatives and Issues.* Grand Rapids: Zondervan Publishing House, 1971.

Gorman, Margaret. *General Semantics and Contemporary Thomism.* Lincoln, Nebr.: University of Nebraska Press, 1962.

Griffin, Em. *The Mind Changers: The Art of Christian Persuasion.* Wheaton, Ill.: Tyndale House Publishers, 1976.

Harrison, E. Myers. *Heroes of Faith on Pioneer Trails.* Chicago: Moody Press, 1945.

Haselden, Kyle. *Morality and the Mass Media.* Nashville: Broadman Press, 1968.

________. *The Urgency of Preaching.* New York: Harper and Row, 1963.

Hawthorne, Nathaniel. *The Scarlet Letter.* New York: Random House, 1937.

Hayakawa, S. I. *Language in Thought and Action.* New York: Harcourt, Brace and Co., 1949.

Henry, Carl F. H. *Christian Personal Ethics.* Grand Rapids: Wm. B. Eerdmans Publishing Co., 1957.

Hitler, Adolf. *Mein Kampf.* Translated by Ralph Manheim. Boston: Houghton Mifflin, 1953.

Horne, Charles Silvester. *The Romance of Preaching.* New York: Fleming H. Revell Co., 1914.

Hovland, Carl I.; Janis, Irving L.; and Kelley, Harold H. *Communication and Persuasion: Psychological Studies of Opinion Change.* New Haven, Conn.: Yale University Press, 1953.

Hovland, Carl I., and others. *The Order of Presentation in Persuasion.* New Haven, Conn.: Yale University Press, 1957.

Howe, Reuel L. *The Miracle of Dialogue.* New York: Seabury Press, 1963.

________. *Partners in Preaching: Clergy and Laity in Dialogue.* New York: Seabury Press, 1967.

Huff, Darrell. *How to Lie with Statistics.* New York: W. W. Norton and Co., 1954.

Janis, Irving L., and others. *Personality and Persuasibility.* New Haven, Conn.: Yale University Press, 1966.

Johannesen, Richard L. *Ethics in Human Communication.* Columbus, Ohio: Charles E. Merrill Publishing Co., 1975.

________, comp. *Ethics and Persuasion: Selected Readings.* New York: Random House, 1967.

Johnson, Wendell. *People in Quandaries.* New York: Harper and Brothers, 1946.

Jones, Edgar DeWitt. *The Royalty of the Pulpit.* New York: Harper and Brothers, 1951.

Jowett, Benjamin, trans. *The Dialogues of Plato.* 4th ed. Oxford, England: Clarendon Press, 1953.

Ker, John. *Lectures on the History of Preaching.* New York: Hodder and Stoughton; George H. Doran Company, n.d.

Kirkpatrick, Alexander F. *The Doctrine of the Prophets.* London: Macmillan and Co., 1907.

Kittel, Gerhard, ed. *Theological Dictionary of the New Testament,* 9 vols. Translated and edited by Geoffry W. Bromiley. Grand Rapids: Wm. B. Eerdmans Publishing Co., 1968.

Knox, John. *The Integrity of Preaching.* New York: Abingdon Press, 1957.

Koller, Charles W. *Expository Preaching Without Notes.* Grand Rapids: Baker Book House, 1962.

Korzybski, Alfred. *Science and Sanity: An Introduction to Non-Aristotelian Systems and General Semantics.* 2d ed. Lancaster, Pa.: International Non-Aristotelian Library Publishing Co., 1941.

Larson, Charles U. *Persuasion: Reception and Responsibility.* Belmont, Calif.: Wadsworth Publishing Co., 1973.

Latourette, Kenneth Scott. *A History of Christianity.* New York: Harper and Row, 1953.

Lee, Irving J. *Language Habits and Human Affairs.* New York: Harper and Brothers, 1941.

Lehmann, Paul. *Ethics in a Christian Context.* New York: Harper and Row, 1963.

Lewis, C. S. *Christian Behavior.* London: Centenary Press, 1943.

Lewis, Gordon R. *Decide for Yourself: A Theological Workbook.* Downers Grove, Ill.: Inter-Varsity Presss, 1970.

Lewis, Ralph L. *Speech for Persuasive Preaching.* Wilmore, Ky.: Speech Department, Asbury Theological Seminary, 1968.

Lewis, Sinclair. *Elmer Gantry.* New York: Harcourt, Brace and Co., 1927.

Liske, Thomas V. *Effective Preaching.* New York: Macmillan Co., 1951.

Luccock, Halford E. *In the Minister's Workshop.* New York: Abingdon-Cokesbury Press, 1944.

Lutzer, Erwin W. *The Morality Gap: An Evangelical Response to Situation Ethics.* Chicago: Moody Press, 1972.

McCroskey, James C. *An Introduction to Rhetorical Communication.* 2d ed. Englewood Cliffs, N.J.: Prentice-Hall, 1972.

McKeon, Richard, ed. *The Basic Works of Aristotle.* New York: Random House, 1941.

McLaughlin, Raymond W. *Communication for the Church.* Grand Rapids: Zondervan Publishing House, 1968.

________. "The Place of the Holy Spirit in Preaching." Unpublished Th.D. dissertation. Chicago: Northern Baptist Theological Seminary, 1950.

Marsh, Patrick O. *Persuasive Speaking: Theory, Models, Practice.* New York: Harper and Row, 1967.

Martin, Howard H., and Colburn, C. William. *Communication and Consensus: An Introduction to Rhetorical Discourse.* New York: Harcourt Brace Jovanovich, 1972.

Matson, Floyd, and Montague, Ashley, eds. *The Human Dialogue.* New York: Free Press, 1967.

Mickelsen, A. Berkeley. *Interpreting the Bible.* Grand Rapids: Wm. B. Eerdmans Publishing Co., 1963.

Minnick, Wayne C. *The Art of Persuasion.* Boston: Houghton Mifflin Co., 1957.

________. *The Art of Persuasion.* 2d ed. Boston: Houghton Mifflin Co., 1968.

Monroe, Alan H. *Principles and Types of Speech,* 5th ed. Chicago: Scott, Foresman and Co., 1962.

Monroe, Alan H., and Ehninger, Douglas. *Principles and Types of Speech Communication.* 7th ed. Glenview, Ill.: Scott, Foresman and Co., 1974.

Morris, James. *The Preachers.* New York: St. Martin's Press, 1973.

Mounce, Robert H. *The Essential Nature of New Testament Preaching.* Grand Rapids: Wm. B. Eerdmans Publishing Co., 1960.

Murray, Iain H. *The Invitation System.* London: Banner of Truth Trust, 1967.

Nichols, Ralph G., and Lewis, Thomas R. *Listening and Speaking.* Dubuque, Iowa: Wm. C. Brown Co., 1954.

Nichols, Ralph G., and Stevens, Leonard A. *Are You Listening?* New York: McGraw-Hill Book Co., 1957.

Niebuhr, H. Richard. *The Responsible Self.* New York: Harper and Row, 1963.

Niebuhr, Reinhold. *The Nature and Destiny of Man: A Christian Interpretation.* New York: Charles Scribner's Sons, 1949.

Niles, Daniel T. *That They May Have Life.* New York: Harper and Brothers, 1951.

Nilsen, Thomas R. *Ethics of Speech Communication.* Indianapolis: Bobbs-Merrill Co., 1966.

________. *Ethics of Speech Communication.* 2d ed. Indianapolis: Bobbs-Merrill Co., 1974.

Nygren, Anders. *Agape and Eros.* Translated by Philip S. Watson. London: S.P.C.K., 1953.

Oden, Thomas C. *Radical Obedience: The Ethics of Rudolph Bultmann.* Philadelphia: Westminster Press, 1964.

Oliver, Robert T. *Culture and Communication.* Springfield, Ill.: Charles C. Thomas, 1962.

———. *The Psychology of Persuasive Speech.* New York: Longman, 1942.

———. *The Psychology of Persuasive Speech.* 2d ed. New York: Longman, 1957.

Packard, Vance. *The Hidden Persuaders.* New York: David McKay Co., 1957.

Packer, J. I. *Evangelism and the Sovereignty of God.* London: Inter-Varsity Fellowship, 1961.

Pareto, Vilfredo. *The Mind and Society.* Edited by Arthur Livingston and translated by Borgiomo and Livingston. New York: Harcourt Brace and Co., 1935.

Parson, Donn W., and Linkugel, Wil, eds. *The Ethics of Controversy: Politics and Protest.* Lawrence, Kans.: House of Usher, 1968.

Pattison, T. Harwood. *The History of Christian Preaching.* Philadelphia: American Baptist Publication Society, 1903.

Pennington, Chester. *God Has a Communication Problem.* New York: Hawthorn Books, 1976.

Perelman, Chaim and Obrechts-Tyteca, L. *The New Rhetoric: A Treatise on Argumentation.* Notre Dame, Ind.: University of Notre Dame Press, 1971.

Pierson, Arthur T. *The Divine Art of Preaching.* New York: Baker and Taylor Co., 1892.

Powell, John. *Why Am I Afraid to Tell You Who I Am?* Chicago: Argus Communications, 1969.

Ramm, Bernard. *Protestant Biblical Interpretation.* 3d rev. ed. Grand Rapids: Baker Book House, 1970.

Ramm, Bernard, and others. *Hermeneutics.* Grand Rapids: Baker Book House, 1971.

Ramsey, Paul, *Basic Christian Ethics.* New York: Charles Scribner's Sons, 1950.

———. *Deeds and Rules in Christian Ethics.* New York: Charles Scribner's Sons, 1967.

Reid, Clyde. *The Empty Pulpit.* New York: Harper and Row, 1967.

Robertson, A. T. *The Glory of the Ministry: Paul's Exultation in Preaching.* Grand Rapids: Baker Book House, 1967.

Robertson, Jr., D. W., trans. *Saint Augustine: On Christian Doctrine.* Book 4. New York: Liberal Arts Press, 1958.

Robinson, John A. T. *Honest to God.* Philadelphia: Westminster Press, 1963.

Rogers, Carl. *Client-Centered Therapy.* Boston: Houghton Mifflin, 1951.

________. *On Becoming a Person.* Boston: Houghton Mifflin, 1961.

Rosnow, Ralph L., and Robinson, Edward J., eds. *Experiments in Persuasion.* New York: Academic Press, 1967.

Ross, Raymond S. *Persuasion: Communication and Interpersonal Relations.* Englewood Cliffs, N.J.: Prentice-Hall, 1974.

Schaeffer, Francis A. *The God Who Is There.* Downers Grove, Ill.: Inter-Varsity Press, 1968.

Schramm, Wilbur. *Responsibility in Mass Communication.* New York: Harper and Brothers, 1957.

Shostrom, Everett L. *Man the Manipulator: The Inner Journey from Manipulation to Actualization.* Nashville: Abingdon Press, 1967.

Simons, Herbert W. *Persuasion: Understanding, Practice and Analysis.* Reading, Mass.: Addison-Wesley Publishing Co., 1976.

Simpson, E. K. *The Pastoral Epistles.* Grand Rapids: Wm. B. Eerdmans Publishing Co., 1954.

Smith, Donald K. *Man Speaking: A Rhetoric of Public Speech.* New York: Dodd, Mead, and Co., 1969.

Smith, George Adam. *The Book of the Twelve Prophets.* 2 vols. New York: Harper and Brothers, 1929.

Stevenson, Charles L. *Ethics and Language.* New Haven, Conn.: Yale University Press, 1944.

Stewart, James S. *Heralds of God.* New York: Charles Scribner's Sons, 1946.

Sweazey, George E. *Effective Evangelism: The Greatest Work in the World.* New York: Harper and Brothers, 1953.

Terry, Milton S. *Biblical Hermeneutics.* 2 vols. New York: Phillips and Hunt, 1883.

Thielicke, Helmut. *The Trouble with the Church.* Translated and edited by John W. Doberstein. New York: Harper and Row, 1965.

Thompson, William D., and Bennett, Gordon C. *Dialogue Preaching: The Shared Sermon.* Valley Forge, Pa.: Judson Press, 1969.

Thonssen, Lester. *Selected Readings in Rhetoric and Public Speaking.* New York: H. W. Wilson Co., 1942.

Thonssen, Lester and Baird, A. Craig. *Speech Criticism.* New York: Ronald Press, 1948.

Tillich, Paul. *Love, Power, and Justice.* New York: Oxford University Press, 1954.

Wagner, C. Peter. *Frontiers of Missionary Strategy.* Chicago: Moody Press, 1971.

Walker, Williston. *A History of the Christian Church.* Rev. ed. New York: Charles Scribner's Sons, 1959.

Walter, Otis M., and Scott, Robert L. *Thinking and Speaking: A Guide to Intelligent Oral Communication.* 2d ed. New York: Macmillan Co., 1968.

Watson, J. S. *Cicero on Oratory and Orators.* Philadelphia: David McKay, 1897.

Weaver, Richard M. *Language Is Sermonic: Richard M. Weaver on the Nature of Rhetoric.* Edited by Richard L. Johannesen, Rennard Strickland, and Ralph T. Eubanks. Baton Rouge: Louisiana State University Press, 1970.

________. *The Ethics of Rhetoric.* Chicago: Henry Regnery Co., 1953.

Wenburg, John R., and Wilmot, William W. *The Personal Communication Process.* New York: John Wiley and Sons, 1973.

Werkmeister, W. H. *An Introduction to Critical Thinking.* Rev. ed. Lincoln, Nebr.: Johnson Publishing Co., 1957.

Whitesell, Faris D. *Sixty-Five Ways to Give Evangelistic Invitations.* Grand Rapids: Zondervan Publishing House, 1945.

Winans, James Albert. *Public Speaking.* New York: Century Co., 1917.

Wiseman, Gordon, and Barker, Larry. *Speech-Interpersonal Communication.* San Francisco, Calif.: Chandler Publishing Co., 1967.

Yates, Kyle M. *Preaching from the Prophets.* New York: Harper and Brothers, 1942.

Young, Edward J. *My Servants the Prophets.* Grand Rapids: Wm. B. Eerdmans Publishing Co., 1952.

PERIODICALS

Anderson, Raymond, E. "Kierkegaard's Theory of Communication," *Speech Monographs* 30 (March 1963): 1-14.

Ayers, Robert H. "The Church and Truth-Telling," *The Iliff Review* 19 (Winter 1962): 15-21.

Beal, Edward. "Honesty in Preaching," *The Congregational Quarterly* 34 (April 1956): 162-7.

Berkowitz, L., and Cottingham, D. R. "The Interest Value and Relevance of Fear-Arousing Communications," *Journal of Abnormal and Social Psychology* 60 (January 1960): 37-43.

" 'Black Manifesto' Declares War on Churches," *Christianity Today,* 23 May 1969, p. 789.

Boillat, Maurice. "Evangelism and Proselytism," *Christian Heritage* 27 (January 1966): 13 ff.

Bosmajian, Haig. "Nazi Persuasion and the Crowd Mentality," *Western Speech* 29 (Spring 1965): 68-78.

Burgess, Parke G. "Crisis Rhetoric: Coercion Vs. Force," *Quarterly Journal of Speech* 59 (February 1973): 61-73.

Butler, Jack H. "Russian Rhetoric: A Discipline Manipulated by Communism," *Quarterly Journal of Speech* 50 (October 1964): 229-39.

Dance, Frank E. X. "Communication Theory and Contemporary Preaching," *Preaching* 3 (September-October 1968): 20-32.

________. "Communication Theory: Hope for the Sagging Pulpit," *Preaching Today* 11 (March-April 1971): 12-15.

DeWolfe, A. S., and Governale, C. N. "Fear and Attitude Change," *Journal of Abnormal and Social Psychology* 69 (1964): 119-23.

Diggs, B. J. "Persuasion and Ethics," *Quarterly Journal of Speech* 50 (December 1964): 359.

Fosdick, Harry Emerson. "What Is the Matter with Preaching?" *Harper's Magazine* 157 (July 1928): 133-41.

Funk, Alfred A. "Logical and Emotional Proofs: A Counterview," *The Speech Teacher* 17 (September 1968): 210-16.

Haiman, Franklyn S. "Democratic Ethics and the Hidden Persuaders," *Quarterly Journal of Speech* 44 (December 1958): 385-92.

________. "The Rhetoric of the Streets: Some Legal and Ethical Considerations," *Quarterly Journal of Speech* 53 (April 1967): 99-114.

Hewgill, M. A., and Miller, G. R. "Source Credibility and Response to Fear-Arousing Communications," *Speech Monographs* 32 (March 1965): 95-101.

"Hollow Holiness," *Time,* 14 August 1972, p. 45.

Hunt, Everett Lee. "Rhetoric as a Humane Study," *Quarterly Journal of Speech* 41 (April 1955): 114-17.

"Itemizing the Reparations Bill," *Christianity Today,* 6 June 1969, p. 839.

Janis, Irving L., and Feshbach, Seymour. "Effects of Fear-Arousing Communications." *Journal of Abnormal and Social Psychology* 48 (1953): 78-92.

Johnson, W. Walter. "The Ethics of Preaching," *Interpretation* 20 (October 1966): 412-31.

Keller, Paul W., and Brown, Charles T. "An Interpersonal Ethic of Communication," *The Journal of Communication* 18 (March 1968): 73-81.

Kruger, Arthur N. "The Ethics of Persuasion: A Re-examination," *The Speech Teacher* 16 (November 1967): 295-305.

Levanthal, H., and Niles, P. "A Field Experiment on Fear-Arousal with Data on the Validity of Questionnaire Measures," *Journal of Personality* 32 (September 1964): 459-79.

Litfin, A. Duane. "The Perils of Persuasive Preaching," *Christianity Today,* 4 February 1977, pp. 14-17.

McLaughlin, Raymond W. "The Ethics of Persuasive Preaching," *Journal of the Evangelical Theological Society* 15 (Spring 1972): 93-106.

———. "Well, Are You Listening?" *The Pastor's Manual,* Summer, 1976, pp. 9-14.

Miller, Clyde Raymond, "Propaganda Analysis," Institute for Propaganda Analysis, 1.2 (November 1937): 1-3. Reprinted in *The National Educational Journal* 29 (October 1940): 201-2.

Miller, G. R., "Studies on the Use of Fear Appeals: A Summary and Analysis," *Central States Speech Journal* 14 (May 1963): 117-24.

Mitchell, George. "How Do Those Guys Manage to Produce a Sermon Each Week?" *The Wall Street Journal,* 14 March 1972, p. 1.

"The 'Morality' of Terrorism," *Newsweek,* 25 February 1974, p. 21.

"The New War on Terrorism," *Newsweek,* 31 October 1977, pp. 52-53.

Nichols, Ralph G. "Listening Instruction in the Secondary School," *Bulletin of the National Association of Secondary School Principals,* Department of Secondary School Administration of the National Education Association 36 (May 1952): 169.

Nilsen, Thomas R. "Free Speech, Persuasion, and the Democratic Process," *Quarterly Journal of Speech* 44 (October 1958): 235-43.

Nunnally, J., and Bobren, H. "Variables Governing the Willingness to Receive Communications on Mental Health," *Journal of Personality* 27 (March 1959): 38-46.

Parker, Douglas H. "Rhetoric, Ethics and Manipulation," *Philosophy and Rhetoric* 5 (Spring 1972): 69-87.

Peterson, John. "Can We Cope with Rising Terror?" *The National Observer,* 23 February 1974, p. 24.

Powell, Fredric A. "The Effects of Anxiety-Arousing Messages When Related to Personal, Familial, and Impersonal Referents," *Speech Monographs* 32 (March 1965): 102-6.

Rankin, Paul T. "The Importance of Listening Ability," *English Journal,* College edition 17 (October 1928): 623-30.

Robinson, Haddon W. Review of *Communication for the Church* by Raymond W. McLaughlin in *Bibliotheca Sacra* 126 (January-March, 1969): 88-89.

Rogge, Edward. "Evaluating the Ethics of a Speaker in a Democracy," *Quarterly Journal of Speech* 45 (December 1959): 419-25.

Rothwell, J. Dan. "Verbal Obscenity: Time for Second Thoughts," *Western Speech* 35 (Fall 1971): 231-42.

Saucy, Robert L. "Doing Theology for the Church." *Journal of the Evangelical Theological Society* 16 (Winter 1973): 1-10.

Schomer, Howard. "The Manifesto and the Magnificat," *The Christian Century,* 25 June 1969, pp. 866-67.

"Schweitzer's Words: Light in the Jungle," *The New York Times Magazine,* 9 January, 1955, p. 73.

Scott, Robert L. and Smith, Donald K. "The Rhetoric of Confrontation," *Quarterly Journal of Speech* 55 (February 1969): 1-8.

Simons, Herbert W. "Persuasion in Social Conflicts: A Critique of Prevailing Conceptions and a Framework for Future Research," *Speech Monographs* 39 (November 1972): 227-47.

Sperry, Willard L. "The Minister as a Man of Truth," *Pastoral Psychology* 1 (October 1959): 15-19.

Stott, John R. W. "Evangelism in the Student World," *His* 21 (December 1960): 1 ff.

Stylites, Simeon [Halford Luccock]. "Klunk!" *The Christian Century,* 31 March 1954, p. 396.

"Terrorist Takeover of Cities Seen." *The Denver Post,* 13 November 1977, p. 9.

Wallace, Karl R. "An Ethical Basis of Communication," *The Speech Teacher* 4 (January 1955): 1-9.

"War Without Boundaries," *Time,* 31 October 1977, p. 41.

Wieman, Henry N. and Walter, Otis M. "Toward an Analysis of Ethics for Rhetoric," *Quarterly Journal of Speech* 43 (October 1957): 266-70.

Author Index

Subject Index